RELIGION
& ALCOHOL

PETER LANG
New York • Washington, D.C./Baltimore • Bern
Frankfurt am Main • Berlin • Brussels • Vienna • Oxford

RELIGION & ALCOHOL

SOBERING THOUGHTS

EDITED BY

C.K. ROBERTSON

PETER LANG
New York • Washington, D.C./Baltimore • Bern
Frankfurt am Main • Berlin • Brussels • Vienna • Oxford

Library of Congress Cataloging-in-Publication Data

Religion and alcohol: sobering thoughts / edited by C. K. Robertson.
p. cm.
Includes bibliographical references and index.
1. Alcoholism—Religious aspects. 2. Drinking of alcoholic beverages—
Religious aspects. 3. Drinking of alcoholic beverages—History.
I. Robertson, C. K. (Charles Kevin).
HV5175.R45 261.8'32292—dc22 2003019419
ISBN 0-8204-6793-6

Bibliographic information published by **Die Deutsche Bibliothek**.
Die Deutsche Bibliothek lists this publication in the "Deutsche
Nationalbibliografie"; detailed bibliographic data is available
on the Internet at http://dnb.ddb.de/.

Cover photo by Justin Kasulka
Cover design by Joni Holst

The paper in this book meets the guidelines for permanence and durability
of the Committee on Production Guidelines for Book Longevity
of the Council of Library Resources.

Printed in the United States of America

✧ Table of Contents

✧ Acknowledgments

In working on *Religion and Alcohol: Sobering Thoughts*, my appreciation goes first to the contributors themselves. Each of the nine other essayists in this volume are gifted individuals and scholars with whom I have found myself privileged to work.

It also goes without saying that I could not have brought together all of these marvelous essays into one coherent book if it had not been for the help of Heidi Burns, my senior editor at Peter Lang Publishing, as well as Bernadette Shade and Sophie Appel, my production coordinators.

Editing a book takes time. As with an earlier book through Peter Lang, *Religion as Entertainment*, I have in this work felt truly supported and encouraged by the people of St. Stephen's Episcopal Church in Milledgeville, Georgia, as well as by my colleagues and students at Georgia College & State University.

Finally, I remain forever grateful for the ongoing support and heartfelt encouragement I receive regularly from my wife Debbie and our three children, David, Jonathan, and Abigail.

C. K. Robertson, Editor

❖ Mixed Drinks or Mixed Messages?
An Introduction

C. K. Robertson

> What is life to one who is without wine? It has been created to make people happy.

The Wisdom of ben Sira, chapter 31, verse 27b

It is difficult, if not impossible, to imagine a world without any form of alcohol. It appears to be an all-pervasive aspect of our human culture. J.R.R. Tolkien, famed author of *The Hobbit* and *The Lord of the Rings*, met regularly with a group of authors known as the "Inklings" to share writings and opinions over pints of ale in an Oxford pub. When his fellow "Inkling" C. S. Lewis was described in the *Daily Telegraph* as "ascetic," an utterly shocked Tolkien noted that Lewis had "put away three pints in a very short session we had this morning, and said he was 'going short for Lent.'"[1] For his own part, Tolkien commemorated the end of a wartime "beer shortage" by noting that the inns were "almost habitable" again, and dreamed of a future holiday with friends spent entirely in "beer and talk."[2] Indeed, the Roman Catholic literary giant went so far as to speak of a "universal human right" to enjoy "the temperate use of wine."[3]

It is Tolkien's choice of the word "temperate" that, although predictable, is particularly interesting. This is especially so inasmuch as alcohol and temperance often do not go together. In the opening book of the Hebrew Scriptures, wine is first mentioned in the story of Noah. In Genesis 9, the legendary shipbuilder bid both the floodwaters and the animals farewell and took up a new career as owner of a vineyard. This might sound like a good idea, especially since the ancient Hebrew word for "wine," יין, finds its origin in an unused root meaning "to effervesce." As in the Wisdom of ben Sira above, wine "makes people happy." However, in Noah's case, we are told that "he drank of the wine

(ייי) and became drunk" (9:21). The inebriated and unconscious Noah "uncovered himself in his tent," thus laying naked and unconscious for all to see. This is hardly an auspicious image of the patriarch for future generations, and certainly a far cry from *The Simpsons'* Ned Flanders, the animated show's resident evangelical Christian, who boldly asserts to God, "I don't drink or dance or swear."[4]

Ned's assertion undoubtedly would receive nods of agreement from many faithful believers of various religious groups. In *The Qur'an*, followers of Islam read of prohibitions against wine and intoxicants, "abominations" (Surah 5:90) in which "there is great sin" (Surah 2:219).[5] However, not all sacred texts are as black and white in their attitude toward alcohol. Even in *The Qur'an* there exists the Parable of the Garden in which there will be "rivers of wine, a joy to those who drink" (Surah 47:15). In that most sacred text of Hinduism, the *Bhagavad-gita,* it is those who have the "demoniac mentality" who find themselves attracted to wine, along with "women, gambling, and meat-eating" (chapter 16, text 10). Refraining from intoxicants was a basic Hindu requirement on the path of *moksha*, release from the material world with its cycles of rebirth.[6] In Buddhism, the fifth of the ten *Sikkhāpadas* speaks of the need for abstinence from the use of intoxicating liquor, although it is unclear whether this means *any* use or simply *intemperate* use. It is also interesting to note that these *Sikkhāpadas* are considered rules or precepts for Buddhist monks, not commandments, per se.[7]

Throughout the Hebrew Scriptures, wine and other intoxicants are the subjects of mixed messages. On the one hand, there are hopeful prayers that God will one day bless the people with "an abundance of grain and wine" (Gen. 27:28). Flowing wine is a symbol of a yet-to-be-fulfilled state of ultimate glory. On the other hand, there are countless warnings about the dangers of intemperate drinking, particularly for those who were Aaronic priests (Lev. 10:9–11) or who had taken the solemn vows of a Nazirite (Num. 6:2–3; Jud. 13:7). Drunkenness is often linked with lewd sexual behavior, as exemplified in the story of Lot, whose daughters get him drunk in order to have incestuous relations with him, "that we may preserve the seed of our father" (19:31–32, KJV). In the Song of Songs, wine is used as a benchmark to compare the delights of true love (4:10), but Proverbs asks, "Who cries 'Woe!' who 'Alas!'

Who has quarrels, who complaints? Who has wounds without cause? Who has bleary eyes? Those whom wine keeps until the small hours" (23:29–30, Tanakh). In many ways, the ancient Hebrew approach to drinking alcohol is much like that espoused in the spurious Christian epistle of Ignatius to Hero the Deacon: "Do not altogether abstain from wine and meat, for these things are not to be viewed with abhorrence ... but all are to be used with moderation, as being the gifts of God" (*Ign. Hero* 1.3).

Indeed, long before our era of bottled water and sports (juice) drinks, in the Christendom that was Medieval Europe, wine was simply a part of daily life. Whereas there were still strong prohibitions against imbibing excessive amounts of alcohol, the fact is that much theology was done in taverns and pubs. Martin Luther, for example, spoke of his great appreciation of strong beer when depressing thoughts took hold of him.[8] Thomas Cranmer, the Anglican reformer and author of the *Book of Common Prayer,* was first "discovered" by Henry VIII's representatives in a pub, speaking to a fellow academician about the king's "privy matter" with Queen Catherine. Not all Christian traditions have followed this pattern, however, to the extent that many Protestants even avoid using wine in communion, substituting for it grape juice (or plain water, as in the Church of Jesus Christ of Latter Day Saints).[9] When questioned about the acceptance of wine (in moderation) in the New Testament, most notably in the story of Jesus's miracle of changing water into wine at a wedding feast (John 2), some believers maintain with vehemence that the transmuted substance was unfermented juice, not wine.

Prohibition on a national scale, the so-called "noble experiment," owed much to American religion, as "church members launched a temperance movement which later changed its emphasis from temperance to total abstinence."[10] The Eighteenth Amendment to the Constitution made it official in 1919, supported by many "God-fearing churchgoers," ignored by many more frustrated drinkers! The experiment lasted for fourteen years, before the repeal of prohibition in 1933, yet "when alcohol did come back, it did so under many restrictions, most of which had not previously existed."[11] Perhaps the most visible result of this merging of politics and religious fervor has been the firm conviction to this day among many Christians that alcohol is to be wholly avoided.

Of course, not all religious persons, and certainly not even all Christians, hold to this belief in abstinence. Churches in Britain and continental Europe have long been known to produce their own ales. Some monks of days past made their Lenten fasts more endurable by "padding" their beers, thus truly living for forty days on a liquid diet. Brewers can even claim a patron saint: Arnulf (Arnold) of Metz, who died in 640.[12] The perennial stereotype of a sodden Roman Catholic cleric has been reinforced all too often in film and other media. The perceived hypocrisy among some churchgoers provides an impetus for much inappropriate, though not necessarily inaccurate, humor. Question: "What is the difference between a Methodist and a Baptist?" Answer: "A Methodist will say hello to you in the liquor store." As a priest in the Episcopal Church (an offshoot of the Church of England), I am all too aware that my denomination is viewed by other Christian groups as especially lenient when it comes to alcohol. So goes the old joke, "Whenever there are four Episcopalians in a room, you're sure to find a fifth!" However, it is interesting to find *Alcoholics Anonymous* chapters in many of my own "whiskeypalian" churches.

Indeed, this last point is evidence once more of the mixed messages that many modern religious groups send to their communities. On any given evening, my own parish might well sponsor a wine and cheese reception in one part of the church facilities while in another section three dozen recovering alcoholics come together in an AA meeting to support and encourage one another in their fragile states of sobriety. Lest this be considered a fact of life found only in "liberal" mainline church bodies, I know several evangelical believers involved in "non-denominational" groups who have little problem indulging in a beer or two when in safe company but who strongly speak out against businesses seeking to renew liquor licenses. One fellow Christian likened the situation to cursing, "I don't think that God minds if I cuss a bit or enjoy a drink when I am with someone who knows me well, but I do not ever want to confuse a weaker believer." This invocation of Paul's warning to the Corinthian believers in Corinth—"It is good not to eat meat or drink wine or do anything that makes your brother or sister stumble" (14:21)— is quite common among modern believers, particularly in the case of alcohol consumption. In focusing almost exclusively on the issue of

Christian witness before "weaker brethren," the larger question of the healthiness of drinking alcohol on any level is usually left unaddressed. Indeed, owing either to the "all or nothing" attitude toward drinking or to a public versus private dichotomy in the name of Christian witness, it may appear that any serious attempt to consider thoughtfully the often complex issues of religion and alcohol is doomed from the start. It is assumed here, however, that what is needed is a more holistic approach to the subject, one represented in the broad diversity of essays contained in this volume

Before offering a brief preview of the chapters that follow, a final introductory point should be made concerning the relevance today of a study of religion and alcohol. In the precursor to this book, *Religion as Entertainment* (New York: Peter Lang, 2002), S. Clark Heindel presents an essay on the Dionysian spirituality of rock 'n roll. Even as "Dionysus was said to roam the world hosting nocturnal celebrations of the forbidden urges," Heindel argues that today's young people "weave across crowded dance floors, hips moving suggestively, mouths smiling, and neurons humming to the music."[13] Whereas Heindel appropriately focuses on sex and rock music in his essay, he still alludes to the second member of the Dionysian triumvirate: intoxicants ("sex, drugs, and rock 'n roll"). It is important to note that Dionysus is a deity associated with "the vine, the grape, and the making and drinking of wine."[14] Indeed, in Euripides's tragedy *The Bacchae,* the concerned and conservative Penthius of Thebes speaks out against Dionysian revelry taking place in the city, specifically linking gross sexual immoralities performed by worshippers with the consumption of large bowls of wine. Coming to the diety's defense, Tiresias, the local priest of the traditional religion, asserts to Penthius that the wine that Dionysus brings to mortals is a gift and a blessing, inasmuch as it "releases suffering mortals from their pain, when they take their fill of the juice of the vine, [and] gives them sleep and makes them forget their daily troubles."[15] Dionysus, Tiresias claims, cannot be described as *im*moral, simply *non*moral, a claim that extends to the blessed nectar that he imparts to mortals. The revels of intoxication that Penthius criticizes so harshly are balanced by the pleasures that one messenger asserts can come only from alcohol: "With no more wine there could be no more love and no other pleasure for mankind."[16]

The unabashed celebration of excess in Dionysian revelry is such a radical departure from the much-professed moderation of many modern Christians, not to mention the seemingly absolute abstinence of Mormons and Moslems, that any attempt to engage such a Dionysian spirituality today might appear to result only in intellectual whiplash for the thoughtful reader. However, the fact remains that the kind of excessive drinking and pleasure-seeking that is found in the Dionysus-Penthius saga is far more familiar to many modern weekend revelers than some "religious" persons would like to admit. Almost no one today would describe herself or himself as a Dionysian in so many words. However, in England alone, where conservative estimates of church attendance list numbers ranging from 2% to 7% of the general population, more people can be expected to name a dozen different types of ale than to name the twelve apostles or the twelve tribes of Israel. Even in the United States, the so-called "churchgoing country," there is often far more lively interaction between patrons who "religiously" frequent a favorite bar on a weekend evening than in a fellowship hall on Sunday morning. Whereas church or synagogue may leave some cold, people flock to parties and taverns where "everybody knows their name." As Heindel accurately assesses today's situation, "While the traditional worship establishment sits in sedate convention on Sunday mornings, Dionysus and his pantheistic host continue to dance the night away every Saturday night."[17]

"To drink or not to drink?" Such a question is well beyond the purview of this book, which by the very diversity of its chapter contributions speaks with not one but many voices. This is neither a bartender's bible nor a teetotaler's treatise. Instead, as with *Religion as Entertainment*, this present compilation is intended for use by students, discussion groups, and discerning readers, addressing issues pertinent to history, religion, and cultural studies. The book is roughly divided into two parts, the first dealing with alcohol in the major religious traditions. More specifically, following this introduction to the subject, two chapters are devoted to issues of alcohol in the New Testament. James McGrath examines the sometimes confusing treatment of alcohol consumption in the stories about Jesus, even as B. J. Oropeza explores the complex subject of wine versus non-alcoholic juice in the Lord's Supper.

Teresa Blythe investigates modern media depictions of alcohol consumption by ordained ministers. Arthur J. Powell considers the difficulties faced by faithful Moslems in today's pluralistic world in regard to the strict prohibitions found in *The Qur'an,* while John Gamble looks into the place of alcohol in Eastern religious traditions.

The second half of the book steps back and assesses religious approaches to alcohol in several different time periods. First, Deborah Vess explores the ways in which the Medieval Age witnessed the incorporation of alcohol brewing and consumption into the monastic life. Gregory Pepetone moves forward several centuries into nineteenth-century Britain and addresses the question of a celebratory approach to alcohol in the works of Charles Dickens. Prohibition, with its aftereffects in the American South, is the focus of Gary Abbott's chapter. In my essay, the impact of *Alcoholics Anonymous* and other "twelve-step programs" is considered, both in terms of the results in individuals' lives and the religious nature of the programs themselves. Michael Rusk completes this second section of the book with an essay on the spirituality of drinking for people today. The book's conclusion attempts to bring together some of the sobering thoughts found in the various essays while simultaneously raising stimulating questions for further exploration into both the blessings and the curses that come from imbibing the nectar of the gods.

Notes

[1] From another letter to Christopher Tolkien, dated March 1, 1944. Carter, *Letters,* 68.

[2] From two letters to his son Christopher Tolkien, dated respectively September 23–25, and October 6, 1944. Again, see Carter, *Letters,* 94–95.

[3] From a 1943 draft letter to C. S. Lewis that, apparently, never was actually sent. See Humphrey Carter, editor, *The Letters of J.R.R. Tolkien* (Boston and New York: Houghton Mifflin, 2000), 60.

[4] Mark I. Pinsky, *The Gospel According to the Simpsons* (Louisville: Westminster John Knox Press, 2001), 55.

[5] In these and other passages, alcohol is usually linked with gambling, also considered an abominable practice.

[6] From Raymond Hammer, "Karma and Dharma: Hindu Ethics," *The Eerdmans' Handbook to the World's Religions* (rev. ed.; Grand Rapids: Eerdmans, 1994), 190.

[7] Richard A. Gard, ed., *Buddhism* (Norwalk, CT: Easton Press, 1961), 143–44.

[8] From the 1531 Weimar edition of Martin Luther's *Tischreden* ("Table Talk"), book 1, number 17. In an interesting analogy, Luther compared his appreciation of beer to his colleague Philip Melanchthon's fascination with astrology.

[9] From the Church Educational System's *Teachings of the Living Prophets: Student Manual Religion* (Salt Lake City: The Church of Jesus Christ of Latter-Day Saints, 1982), 20.

[10] Earl H. Brill, *The Christian Moral Vision* (New York: Seabury Press, 1979), 70.

[11] *Ibid.*

[12] David Kalvelage, "What's Brewing in Quincy?" *The Living Church* (January 12, 2003), 23.

[13] S. Clark Heindel, "It's Only Rock and Roll," in *Religion as Entertainment* (New York: Peter Lang, 2002), 279.

[14] M. P. O. Morford and R. J. Lenardon, *Classical Mythology* (New York: Longman, 1977), 187. Having said this, Robert Graves, in his 1960 foreword to his classic work *The Greek Myths* (Folio Society Edition, fourteenth printing; London: The Folio Society, 2002, 33–34), suggests that Dionysan revelry may have involved *amanita muscaria,* hallucinogenic mushrooms, more than the traditionally-believed wine, though wine and wine-making remain closely linked with Dionysus.

[15] Ibid., 193.

[16] Ibid., 200.

[17] Heindel, "It's Only Rock and Roll," 289.

Bibliography

Brill, Earl H. *The Christian Moral Vision.* New York: Seabury Press, 1979.

Carter, Humphrey, ed. *The Letters of J.R.R. Tolkien.* Boston: Houghton Mifflin, 2000.

Church Educational System. *Teachings of the Living Prophets: Student Manual Religion.* Salt Lake City: The Church of Jesus Christ of Latter-Day Saints, 1982.

Gard, Richard A., ed. *Buddhism.* Norwalk, CT: Easton Press, 1961.

Hammer, Raymond. "Karma and Dharma: Hindu Ethics." In *The Eerdmans' Handbook to the World's Religions.* Rev. ed. Grand Rapids: Eerdmans, 1994.

Heindel, S. Clark. "It's Only Rock and Roll." In *Religion as Entertainment.* New York: Peter Lang, 2002.

Kalvelage, David. "What's Brewing in Quincy?" *The Living Church.* January 12, 2003.

Morford, M. P. O. and R. J. Lenardon. *Classical Mythology.* New York: Longman, 1977.

Pinsky, Mark I. *The Gospel According to the Simpsons.* Louisville: Westminster John Knox Press, 2001.

Robertson, C. K., ed. *Religion as Entertainment.* New York: Peter Lang, 2002.

Part I

Alcohol in Religious Traditions

1 "A Glutton and a Drunkard": What Would Jesus Drink?

James McGrath

In popular piety the letters WWJD have become increasingly familiar, as an acronym for the question "What would Jesus do?" Detractors from this stream of popular piety have found other words these letters can stand for, including among them "Why Waste Jack Daniels?" It is at the intersection of these two questions that this study is being written, attempting to answer the question "What would/did Jesus drink?" It is worth pointing out from the outset that most of those who ask either of the first two questions mentioned have already made certain assumptions about the answer. Those who ask "What would Jesus do?" are convinced that they can know the answer to that question. Those who ask "Why waste Jack Daniels?" have already made up their minds that it shouldn't be wasted. In a sense, both questions are rhetorical. They define communities of thought and practice, and rarely would the answers to these questions be genuinely open to discussion and debate.

Nevertheless, it is precisely the fact that there have been radically differing viewpoints within the Christian tradition and popular piety regarding the subject of Jesus and alcohol that makes this study worth undertaking. As I began work on this chapter, it struck me as ironic that many of those who claim to be followers of Jesus are adamant about *not* doing something that most historians would agree that Jesus *did*, namely consume alcoholic wine. This chapter thus has two objectives. The first and primary aim is to assess the historical evidence, putting Jesus in his historical context and examining what the evidence really is regarding his drinking habits. We may, however, also mention a second, related goal, which is to interact with some of the arguments that are at times put forward suggesting that the historical Jesus did not consume what we today call "wine," but only unfermented grape juice. Because these two aims are not unrelated, I will not attempt to separate them, but will seek to answer the historical question of what we can know, and with what degree of certainty, from the extant sources about the question of Jesus's consumption (or nonconsumption) of alcoholic beverages. At the same time I will attempt to interact, where appropriate, with the more serious attempts to argue that Jesus never drank alcoholic wine at all. Because the literature on this subject consists of far more contributions to the genre of the "temperance tract" than scholarly studies, I shall focus particular attention on one of the better and more recent books arguing the case for total abstinence based on the Bible, namely Samuele Bacchiocchi's 1989 book, *Wine in the Bible: A Biblical Study on the Use of Alcoholic Beverages.*[1] Bacchiocchi's book is probably the most important representative of this perspective for two main reasons. On the one hand, Bacchiocchi quotes from a very large number of earlier books and studies on the subject, most of which are no longer easily available. On the other hand, one can find the arguments from Bacchiocchi's book reproduced on the countless Web pages that seek to uphold the same cause of Christians' total abstinence from all alcoholic beverages.

Context

Before we can attempt to make sense of the data from the Gospels, we require an anchor in the historical context of first-century Judaism, Galilee, and the Greco-Roman world in general. Jesus is accused at one point of being a "drunkard" (*paroinos*), but without a context, this assertion really tells us nothing, irrespective of the fact that the accusation is not necessarily true. Someone who was part of a culture wherein one was expected to abstain totally from alcoholic beverages might be called a "drunkard" or a "sinner" because he drank a glass of grape juice from a vat in which bubbles caused by fermentation had begun to appear. Without having at least some idea of what the common assumptions were about the consumption of alcoholic beverages in Jesus's time, the actions and statements attributed to him and to his opponents in the Gospels can be taken to mean almost anything.

That wine was popularly consumed in the ancient world is clear. It was customary for aristocratic meals in ancient Greece to be followed by a *symposium*, literally a "drinking together." In Plato's work by the same name, a brief discussion is to be found wherein the group acknowledges that many of them cannot cope with hard drinking, and they opt not to engage in it, mentioning as well that it is medically unadvisable to drink in excess. The assumption of those present at the *symposium*, including Socrates, seems to be that drinking is best done in moderation. Drinking undiluted wine is viewed as a custom of the barbarians in ancient Greek literature. Wine in the Greco-Roman world was normally diluted, at times by a ratio of as much as twenty parts water to one part wine, but more usually at a ratio of about three to one.[2] It ought to be noted that, in the ancient world, the only beverages to be had were water, milk, and those derived from fruit juices. It is thus not surprising that wine was extremely popular.

Those who advocate abstinence point to the fact that the words for *wine* used in the Bible (Hebrew *yayin*, Greek *oinos*) are actually broader terms and can include unfermented grape juice. They then further argue that the positive references to wine in the Bible have the unfermented variety in mind. On the one hand, it is clearly true that both the Hebrew and Greek terms for "wine" do at times have a broader meaning.[3] Both terms can be found in the extant literature to refer to a number of grape- and wine-based beverages, some fermented, some not. This linguistic point about the occasional broader usage of these terms must be considered secondary, however, to the question of what the general populace in ancient Galilee or Jerusalem would have normally thought of when they heard one of these terms for *wine*. That the Greek and Hebrew words for wine could be used in a broader sense to refer to unfermented grape juice is beside the point. References to unfermented grape juice as wine without qualification or explanation are exceedingly rare, and thus one can acknowledge that the term has a degree of linguistic flexibility, while still concluding that the normal use of both terms is in reference to alcoholic wine. To suggest that the Bible, in quite a large proportion of its mentions of "wine," actually meant "unfermented grape juice," is to take a few exceptional instances and impose them on the biblical literature in a way that is linguistically unjustifiable. Those who did abstain from fermented wine in ancient Judaism—such as, apparently, the community at Qumran—preferred the word which is normally reserved for unfermented grape must or "new wine" (*tirosh*).[4] It is not that they could not or did not use the word "wine" at times to refer to this unfermented juice; but had they used only or almost exclusively this term, then no one would have understood them to be speaking about grape *must*. The Bible, including the New Testament, may occasionally use the word for *must* to refer to wine and the word for *wine* to refer to must. However, for the most part, the distinction between the two was maintained, and thus it is linguistically indefensible to maintain that most references to "wine" in the New Testament, or indeed the rest of the Bible, in fact mean "unfermented grape juice."

Those who wish to argue that the Bible teaches abstinence sometimes assert that "wine" in the Bible means grape juice when evaluated positively and alcoholic wine when evaluated negatively.[5] This assertion is not just at best highly oversimplified, but is, in fact, completely unjustified. As mentioned above, had the positive references to wine alluded to unfermented grape juice, there would have been some indication of the fact in the immediate context in at least some or most of the occurrences. However, there are no such indications. In addition, this argument in favor of total abstinence assumes that it is impossible that the biblical authors could give assessments of the same substance (fermented wine) that were both positive and negative. The assumption, though, is unjustified. Ancient literature is full of references to *both* the enjoyable *and* the dangerous qualities of alcoholic wine. There is no contradiction involved when the same authors make both assertions.[6] Rather, it is clear evidence that not only the Bible, but likewise other ancient religious, philosophical, and medical literature, recognize that wine has pleasant effects when consumed in moderation, and negative side effects when consumed in excess.[7] Within the context of second temple Judaism, the author of Ecclesiasticus (31:25) shows that one could warn that "wine has destroyed many" and yet still advocate sobriety, meaning the moderate consumption of wine, rather than suggesting that people avoid alcoholic wine altogether.[8]

What sort of wine did people drink in the ancient world of Jesus? If they were not part of the upper echelons of society, one expects that the quality of alcoholic wine they had the opportunity to consume would have been fairly low in alcohol content, and at times bitter, produced by putting water on the skins, stalks, and seeds left over after the final pressing. Thus, it is perhaps worth keeping in mind that the *quality* of wine could differ significantly depending on one's economic and social class. When this consideration is combined with the fact that there were many customs in the ancient world involving the addition of various substances to wines at various points in the wine-making process, one realizes that the wine available in Jesus's time may well not have tasted much like the wine with which readers of this chapter may be familiar.[9] Be that as it may, wine was widely consumed, and even slaves were given access to it. Wine, whatever it may be to us, was an important source of calories for ordinary people in the ancient world, not to mention an important source of liquid refreshment in the dry season.[10]

Making wine is not as simple a process as is often thought, however. It is usually not enough to simply leave grape juice to "do its thing" and then expect to have pleasant-tasting wine at the end of the process. It is for this reason that advocates of abstinence occasionally point out that, contrary to popular belief, ancient peoples could and did keep their juices from fermenting, in spite of the heat in regions such as Galilee and Judea and the lack of modern methods of preservation. Not only that, but some have gone so far as to argue that preserving grape must was in fact a far less complicated process than making alcoholic wine. However, the truth is that people in wine-producing countries even today still find it easier to make and keep wine than to prevent grape juice from fermenting. Wine that ferments can become sour or moldy or face other problems; juice that is not adequately boiled or preserved will tend to begin fermentation. Neither process was straightforward or without pitfalls in the ancient world, nor for that matter is it for those who in our day and age grow grapes and make wine and/or juice for their own personal consumption, without the benefit of resources conveniently available in Europe and America (such as Campden tablets). The question is thus not whether one could preserve grape juice unfermented, but how frequently people chose to do this with their grape juice. One imagines that, then as now, most people chose to make most of their grape juice into wine. Presumably members of the Essenes who grew grapes would have made a different choice, and would have gone through the trouble to prevent their juice from fermenting. Many, however, would have enjoyed alcoholic wine and allowed the juice from their grapes to ferment.

More pertinent than the broader question of Greco-Roman thought and customs regarding wine and alcoholic beverages is the question of the Jewish heritage of Jesus, including the Hebrew Scriptures and the things they have to say about drinking, as well as anything we might be able to find out about wine consumption in Galilee in the Judaism of the second temple period. In the Jewish Scriptures individuals are mentioned who clearly abstained from alcohol.[11] However, their very existence and distinctiveness serves to demonstrate that most people in ancient Israel consumed alcoholic beverages. Also, there were no clear commandments demanding that they not do so. On the contrary, there is at least one unambiguous divine encouragement to drink wine and other alcoholic beverages, found in Deuteronomy 14:24–26. When Israelites find themselves too far from the central sanctuary to bring their tithe there, they are to exchange the tithe of their crops and herds for money, and then are to use the money to buy whatever foodstuffs their hearts desire, including not only wine but also *shekar*, a Hebrew word normally translated into English as "strong drink." In fact, when considered with the Babylonian *shikaru*, and in view of the fact that distillation techniques were only developed much later, the best translation of the term is probably "beer" rather than "strong drink."[12]

At any rate, Bacchiocchi goes to great lengths in his attempt to show that this cannot possibly mean what it quite clearly does mean—namely, that the Law of Moses actually encouraged people to buy alcoholic beverages, and with their tithe money no less! Instead of accepting the plain meaning of the text, he takes other texts that are ambiguous or which denounce wine as dangerous, derives from them a doctrine of complete abstinence, and then forces this text into his procrustean mold. Clearly if one is to begin anywhere in attempting to discern the teachings of the Hebrew Bible on alcoholic beverages, it should be in verses like this one, which is completely clear.

It is beyond the scope of this chapter to survey here all the passages in the Hebrew Bible that mention wine and drink. Suffice it to say that Jesus was born into a society in which wine was acknowledged as a divine blessing, but also as a potentially dangerous substance which could get one into trouble. Wine was a blessing that makes the heart glad; drunkenness was a danger to be avoided, especially by those (such as kings and rulers) who were likely to cause great damage with their power if they were to exercise their power while under the influence of alcohol. One imagines that, if religious communities in the ancient world were anything like those today, Jesus would not have gone his whole childhood without hearing warnings of the dangers of alcohol in a sermon preached in the local synagogue, nor without having an opportunity to see the sad effects of excessive drinking on some inhabitant of Nazareth who overindulged in wine on occasion.

This scenario is speculative, but it seems safe to assume that Jesus's Jewish assumptions, upbringings, and experiences were the same as those of his contemporaries unless we have clear evidence to the contrary. In short, Jesus would presumably have been brought up to appreciate wine as a blessing from God, albeit one in which it was unwise and perhaps even sinful to overindulge. Unless evidence is forthcoming that Jesus's upbringing was atypical or that his family was part of a minority group that abstained from alcoholic beverages, then it seems a safe assumption that Jesus's upbringing regarding wine and alcohol was typical of the Judaism of his time.

Alcohol and the Historical Jesus

We may now proceed from the general question of influences on and assumptions of Jesus growing up, to the more specific, more interesting, and certainly more controversial topic of the adult life and public activity of Jesus, and of his own views as a mature individual. How does one go about asking the question about Jesus and alcohol from the perspective of an historian, rather than approaching the question from a purely theological perspective? The reader, if unfamiliar with the approach of historians to ancient documents, may find what is said in the next paragraph a bit shocking, and so let me explain further what is involved in approaching our topic in the first instance from an *historical* perspective. Historical study deals with questions in the same manner as a court of law. A single witness is not, even according to biblical law (Dt. 17:6; also mentioned in John 8:17), sufficient to convict someone. History deals with cause and effect, and with probabilities, and thus in discussing the historical Jesus's view of alcoholic beverages, it may be necessary to exclude as evidence things that Jesus perhaps did in fact say. In history, as in a court of law, it is not a question of what "really happened," but of what can be proven "beyond reasonable doubt" on the basis of the available, admissible evidence. To extend the analogy further, historians cannot say that Jesus is "innocent" of having said certain things; but they are often required to return a verdict of "not guilty," meaning that the case for Jesus having said or done the thing in question has not been proven.[13] Therefore, sayings and narratives found in only one of the relatively later sources will not be examined. Rather the focus will be on the earliest sources and on sayings and events that are attested by multiple witnesses.

In light of what has just been said about historical method, it quickly becomes apparent that some of the references to wine and drinking in the Gospels may be suspect from an historian's point of view, that is, suspected of reflecting the creativity of the Gospel author rather than representing something actually said or done by Jesus himself. A key example is the famous story of the wedding of Cana found in John 2. The wedding at Cana is in a very real sense irrelevant to the study of the historical Jesus. Only John's Gospel mentions it. The Fourth Gospel is generally agreed to have been written significantly later than the Synoptics, and has its own distinctive stylistic and theological idiosyncrasies.

It is for these reasons impossible to assume that this story gives an accurate reflection of what Jesus said and did at an actual wedding in Cana. The story is told by a single witness, writing probably a good 50 years after the fact. He is a witness who regularly presents all characters in the story speaking in the same way that he himself writes. These considerations might be sufficient in and of itself for an historian to pass over the story of the wedding at Cana in John 2; the fact that the wine in the story is supposedly produced miraculously makes the text even less useful for historical purposes. The story's symbolism relates to the replacement of the water of Jewish purification with wine, and wine was already used within Judaism and Christianity to symbolize the joy of the Kingdom of God. For all of these reasons, no historian will assume that this is a factual occurrence involving the historical Jesus.[14]

A similar problem exists with the explicit warning against "drunkenness" attributed to Jesus in Luke 21:34. It clearly represents a Lukan addition to the information he inherited from Mark, and it is thus also of little or no historical value. This statement should not be interpreted to mean that historians can prove or have in fact proven that Jesus never spoke in this way about drunkenness, or indeed that he never turned water into wine. It simply means that evidence that is late and/or found in only one source is generally excluded by historians as less trustworthy, as more likely to have been embellished and elaborated over the course of time. As to what "really happened," historical study cannot ever hope to capture that—it is lost forever to the passing of time. However, historical research can and does focus attention on those pieces of information which are assessed as being most valuable, most likely to be authentic, and it is this sort of information about Jesus and alcohol that will be our focus in the remainder of this section.

The two earliest sources, apart from the letters of Paul, are Mark and "Q," a source often cited by scholars that refers to the material that both Matthew and Luke have in common but which is lacking in Mark.[15] Mark's Gospel can be quickly discussed because Mark makes no real mention of Jesus's drinking habits in any explicit manner.[16] He is presented as dining with "sinners" and tax collectors, and there is no mention of him abstaining from drinking wine or other alcoholic beverages on such occasions. However, there is no explicit reference one way or the other.

There is little an historian is led to say from this, except that Jesus's drinking practices, based on the failure of Mark to mention anything about them, probably seemed to him to be nothing out of the ordinary. In other words, had Jesus been an excessive drinker, or an abstainer, then we might have expected some mention of the fact by Mark. Failure to mention anything at all suggests (although it is admittedly an argument from silence) that there was nothing worth mentioning.

A saying found in the Q source, the selection of material shared by Matthew and Luke and believed to derive from an earlier source, will be examined next.

But to what shall I compare this generation? It is like children sitting in the
market places and calling to their playmates, "We piped to you, and you did not
dance; we wailed, and you did not mourn." For John came neither eating nor
drinking, and they say, "He has a demon." The Son of man came eating and
drinking, and they say, "Behold, a glutton and a drunkard, a friend of tax
collectors and sinners!" Yet wisdom is justified by her deeds.

                                                        Matt. 11:16–19

To what then shall I compare the men of this generation, and what are they
like? They are like children sitting in the market place and calling to one
another, "We piped to you, and you did not dance; we wailed, and you did not
weep." For John the Baptist has come eating no bread and drinking no wine;
and you say, "He has a demon." The Son of man has come eating and drinking;
and you say, "Behold, a glutton and a drunkard, a friend of tax collectors and
sinners!" Yet wisdom is justified by all her children.

                                                        Luke 7:31–35

This is one of the most often-cited texts in connection with the question
of Jesus's drinking practice (hence the allusion to it in the title of the
present chapter). The accusation of Jesus's enemies that he was "a
glutton and a drunkard" seems impossible to imagine if Jesus never
partook of alcoholic beverages. The context of the saying is generally
accepted to be a comparison between the reactions of certain people to
John the Baptist and Jesus, respectively. Of course, it is possible that
"son of man" was originally used in its more basic sense of "someone,"
and that Jesus thus was speaking about John the Baptist and saying, in
essence: "John was an ascetic, and you accused him of having a demon;
but if someone comes to you who is not an ascetic, you criticize him too!
But all Wisdom's children (both ascetics and nonascetics) prove her
right." Be that as it may, if Luke's positioning of the saying is original, it
was very early connected with the doubts expressed by John the Baptist
regarding whether Jesus is the "one who is to come." Jesus's ministry
clearly differed from John's, regardless of the exact origin and meaning
of this particular saying, but its placement in this context seems
fundamentally appropriate. John and Jesus had very obviously different
lifestyles, and this raised questions about the relationship of Jesus to his
former mentor John, both for others and apparently for John the Baptist
himself. However, what exactly is meant by the contrast between Jesus
and John over the question of "eating and drinking"?

Matthew's addition of "bread" and "wine" to the saying might make it seem more relevant to the present study, but Luke's shorter phrasing (simply "eating and drinking") is probably more original. The comparison is thus not specifically about partaking of alcoholic beverages (and bread, for that matter), but about engaging in eating and drinking as a form of social interaction. In this case, the saying is perhaps more directly addressed to criticisms of Jesus's practice rather than to critics of John. If the critics of Jesus don't like Jesus's custom of eating and drinking with "tax collectors and sinners," they should listen to John, who did neither. In fact, though, Jesus is presented as pointing out that most people refuse to listen to either of them.

It would be unwise, of course, to suggest that there is any real degree of accuracy to the depiction "a glutton and a drunkard," any more than one should assume that "having a demon" was an accurate assessment of John the Baptist. As noted in discussing the evidence from the Gospel of Mark, there is no other early reference to criticism of Jesus's eating and drinking habits per se, suggesting that his behavior in this matter was not particularly controversial in and of itself. So the language of both criticisms is probably hyperbolic. The meaning is that John practiced asceticism and/or withdrawal from society and was criticized for it. Jesus did the opposite of John and was criticized for it. The main point of the saying is thus presumably something along these lines: "No matter what sort of people address you in God's name, you find fault with them." Jesus's ethical teaching has been interpreted in countless different ways, but one thing seems clear: His lifestyle was not one of rigorous asceticism, foregoing all of life's pleasures and withdrawing from contact with people.

As John Dominic Crossan observes, even though this saying has but a single attestation (in Q), and as we observed earlier the theme of Jesus's consumption of alcohol is not explicitly mentioned in Mark, nevertheless both Mark and the Q source contrast Jesus and John on the question of asceticism.[17] Therefore, the nonasceticism of Jesus seems a firmly grounded piece of historical data. However, as Crossan also rightly points out, knowing that Jesus was not an apocalyptic ascetic like John does not tell us what he was. We can be reasonably sure that Jesus was contrasting his own practice with that of John, but anything beyond

that must be surmised, rather than being clear from the saying itself.
According to E. P. Sanders, this saying (which he presumably likewise
deems authentic) shows that Jesus, in contrast to John the Baptist, was
not a "puritan."[18] As we already noted, it is simply unthinkable that the
terms *glutton* and *drunkard* were invented by Jesus or by Christian
authors, with no one ever having made a criticism along these lines.
Thus, while there is no reason to think Jesus actually did make a habit of
getting drunk (which would presumably have required a more detailed
reply on the part of early Christian authors), it is beyond the bounds of
probability that Jesus was a teetotaler who was falsely accused. Jesus's
custom of feasting with all sorts of people should be understood to have
included all the things that would have been normal in an ancient feast,
including fermented wine.[19]

The fact that in Luke's version both Jesus and John are depicted as
Wisdom's children (according to the most common interpretation of the
Lukan version of the saying), while Christianity fairly early began to
emphasize Jesus's superiority to John and to identify him in some way
with Wisdom (as in the Matthean parallel; Colossians 1:15–20; John 1:1–
18), suggests Luke's Gospel preserves the earliest form of the saying.[20]
This is significant in at least one regard. It shows a tolerance on the part
of Jesus for expressions of piety that were different from the one he
himself advocated. Although he was not a teetotaler, he held John the
Baptist, who presumably was, in great esteem.[21] Both of them are
Wisdom's children, and both of them prove her right, each in his own
way.

To summarize, then, this saying is generally taken to mean that
although John the Baptist practiced asceticism and presumably abstained
from alcoholic beverages and from feasting in general, Jesus was known
to spend his time enjoying meals and drinking in the company of people
who were at the very least not considered "respectable." Thus, the
emphasis is probably for the most part on the fact that John did not
practice commensality with the different sorts of people that Jesus did,
rather than focusing on eating and drinking per se. The meaning of the
saying is to show that both John, who did not engage in feasting and
public social interaction with any regularity, and Jesus, who did, were
equally rejected by many of their contemporaries. Whether anyone

actually publicly called Jesus a glutton and a drunkard is difficult to determine with certainty, but it seems unlikely that Jesus and/or the authors of the Gospels would have invented such an accusation had no one ever actually made it. Conversely, had Jesus in actual fact been a glutton and a drunkard, the Gospel tradition would surely have done more to address the accusation. It thus seems clear that Jesus took part in social interactions that would have included wine and/or other alcoholic beverages, but it also seems clear that his behavior did not attract serious criticism, and could not be described as "drunken and disorderly."

The Lord's Supper

Another significant tradition regarding Jesus and wine is the institution of the Lord's Supper. The testimony to this event is so widespread and early that it seems undeniable that Jesus shared a final meal with his closest disciples.[22] However, what Jesus foresaw and intended to symbolize through that meal has been a subject of some controversy.

Although there is some ambiguity on this matter, the consensus seems to be that the Last Supper was in fact a Passover meal.[23] Some Jews in later times used unfermented grape juice for the Passover meal, believing that the prohibition of leaven/yeast covered all fermentation, including that found in wine and other fermented drinks. Was Jesus among those who held this view? Did this viewpoint, evidenced in the Rabbinic literature from later centuries, exist in Jesus's time? It is impossible to say. Within the early Church there were those who used alcoholic wine for communion and those who did not. The presentation of Jesus speaking of "fruit of the vine" rather than "wine" in Luke 22 is taken by Bacchiocchi to indicate that Jesus had similar scruples and avoided fermented wine, at least at Passover.[24] This is certainly possible, and there is evidence for differences of opinion regarding the use of fermented wine at the Lord's Supper. Nevertheless, our earliest reference to the Christian practice of the Lord's Supper is 1 Corinthians 11:17–34, where Paul refers to some having become inebriated while others did not yet have a chance to eat. Unless one is going to attempt to redefine Greek words, then it is clear that the earliest example of the Lord's Supper that we have included fermented wine. Paul criticizes the Corinthians for many things; using fermented wine is not one of them.

What did Jesus intend through commanding his followers to drink wine? Not all sources have the words "Do this in memory of me," and this certainly seems like the sort of liturgical addition that the early Church might have made. Could Jesus have foreseen that he would die, and symbolized this through the use of the cup? There is no reason to be overly skeptical regarding this matter: John the Baptist had met a violent death, and Jesus would not have required prophetic abilities in order to foresee that creating a disturbance in the Temple around the time of a major festival could, perhaps would inevitably, lead him to a similar fate. If Jesus vowed that he would not drink of "the fruit of the vine" again until the Kingdom of God comes (Mark 14:25), this presumably indicates his expectation of its imminent arrival, although it might simply indicate his expectation that he would die before having another opportunity to share a meal with his friends.[25] Be that as it may, when this saying is taken together with the prediction that the Temple would be destroyed and rebuilt in three days, suggests that Jesus expected the Kingdom of God to dawn soon.[26]

Thus, in spite of the fact that this soon became universally accepted Christian practice, it is probably inaccurate to say that the historical Jesus advocated the drinking of wine together as a way of remembering his death and celebrating the soon-to-arrive Kingdom of God. The foreshadowing of the Messianic banquet of the Kingdom may well have been part of Jesus's meals in general, and was quite probably in view in the Last Supper. However, it seems unlikely that he explicitly instructed his followers to continue the practice, because (contrary to scholarly consensus) it seems unlikely that he thought history would continue long enough into the future for it to be meaningful for them to do so.[27]

What did the cup(s) symbolize, and how did Jesus interpret or reinterpret their symbolism? At one point, Jesus is recorded to have said that he would not drink of the fruit of the vine again until he drinks it with his followers in the Kingdom of God. If the custom of drinking four cups of wine during the Passover meal already existed in this time, then the cup Jesus either refused or drank and then vowed never to drink again was either the first or second cup of the meal. The first cup probably was accompanied by a simple thanksgiving for the wine and for the special event; the second may have been accompanied (then as now) by a reminder of the ten plagues associated with the Exodus from Egypt. Jesus is recorded to have predicted signs that would precede the end (Mark 13 and parallels). Whichever cup was connected with Jesus's vow to not drink again until the Kingdom fully dawns, it would have given that Passover meal an eschatological overtone, and probably would have been understood as indicating that Jesus hoped that a second, final Exodus was near at hand, bringing the eschatological promises of God to fulfillment. If it was the second cup, and the cup was already associated with the ten Exodus plagues, then Jesus might have been understood to be vowing not to drink of "the fruit of the vine" again until God intervenes in his age to redeem his people, just as in the time of Moses.

If Paul (1 Cor. 11:25) and Luke (22:20) are correct in saying that the cup about which Jesus spoke of "the blood of the new covenant" was taken *after supper*, then this would identify it as either the third or fourth of the four cups of wine traditionally drunk at the Passover meal. This assumes once again that the customs known from later Judaism already existed in Jesus's time, and were followed consistently by Jews in Judea, Galilee, and elsewhere. These are a lot of assumptions, a lot of "ifs"! But if it was the fourth cup, the last one drunk before the Hallel psalm was sung, then it is quite possible that (then as now) this cup was associated with the expectation of the eschatological return of Elijah and the establishment of peace in Israel, free from her enemies. However, Jesus had predicted judgment rather than peace, and had apparently asserted that Elijah had already come and had been mistreated (Mark 9:11–13). Thus, it would not be surprising if Jesus had reinterpreted this cup in connection with both the establishment of the new covenant (i.e., the gathering/restoration of eschatological Israel) and a reference to his own rejection. More than that cannot be said with certainty; indeed, much of what has already been said is speculation.

However, a couple of issues have been clarified. First, because the Temple was still standing, a lamb was still part of the Passover meal. It is thus unlikely that the bread and wine in any sense would have been taken by Jesus and his disciples to represent the Passover sacrifice. Second, it is noteworthy in connection with the theme of this study that Jesus felt it appropriate to vow abstinence from "the fruit of the vine," much as the ancient Nazirites did (Numbers 6). Perhaps we might even say that Jesus made a Nazirite vow on this occasion.[28] The reason for abstinence from all grape products was not an aversion to alcohol in itself. Rather, like the growing of the hair and the avoidance of contact with corpses, it was a symbolic representation of holiness, connected with a special vow of dedication to God. Jesus presumably "swore his allegiance" to God on this occasion, subjecting himself to the restraints of a Nazirite vow until the Kingdom would dawn. In other words, Jesus seems to have had a clear understanding that now the part of his activity that used public feasting as a sign of the Kingdom was over. No more wine, no more eating and drinking with publicans and sinners, presumably also no more contact with the dead to raise them to life. A new stage had begun. A new Exodus was at hand. A Nazirite vow was a temporary measure expressing dedication to God. Jesus does not say "I will not drink of the fruit of the vine again until I have completed the days of my vow." He says he will not drink again until he does so in the Kingdom of God. It is probably this vow, rather than the symbolism of a specific Passover cup, that is most interesting and significant. Jesus did not anticipate going through the process of returning to normal life after his vow. He either expected to die, or expected the Kingdom of God to dawn on earth, or both. If this saying of Jesus is authentic, the insight it gives us into Jesus's understanding of the eschatological Kingdom of God, not to mention his attitude to ritual elements of the Law of Moses, is of great importance and value in trying to understand the historical figure of Jesus. Jesus's vow of abstinence, like his prior drinking with various types of marginalized figures, is more interesting for what it tells us about Jesus's self-understanding and mission, than for anything it might tell us about the drinking of fermented beverages.

Other References to Drinking

A few other minor references to wine and to being drunk are worth mentioning. In Q (Luke 12:45, paralleled in Matt. 24:49), Jesus is presented as warning of judgment on a servant who begins "to eat and drink and get drunk" or "to eat and drink with the drunken." I expect the former is more likely to be original, the latter perhaps being Matthew's attempt to avoid any hint that Christian leaders (who are presumably being represented by the servant in the parable) might actually "get drunk while on duty."

The authenticity of this saying is questionable because it seems to presuppose an ongoing Christian "organization" in which leaders will be appointed and with sufficient delay before the end for them to become complacent in their duties. It thus more likely reflects the situation of the early Church than the time of the historical Jesus. Even so, the saying agrees with and adds nothing to what we had already seen to be indicated by the sayings we have already surveyed: Jesus did not oppose drinking but (like most philosophers and religious authorities in the ancient world, and indeed most people with common sense both then and now) did not practice or encourage drunkenness, perhaps even explicitly warning against it. In the present passage, however, the point is only made in the context of a parable about inappropriate behavior for a servant awaiting his returning master. The principle to be taken away has to do with continuing to be alert and mindful of one's duties until one's master returns, rather than to do with drinking, per se.

Another closely related saying that is sometimes mentioned in relation to this subject is Jesus's reference to putting new wine into old wineskins:

> And Jesus said to them, "Can the wedding guests fast while the bridegroom is with them? As long as they have the bridegroom with them, they cannot fast. The days will come, when the bridegroom is taken away from them, and then they will fast in that day. No one sews a piece of unshrunk cloth on an old garment; if he does, the patch tears away from it, the new from the old, and a worse tear is made. And no one puts new wine into old wineskins; if he does, the wine will burst the skins, and the wine is lost, and so are the skins; but new wine is for fresh skins."
>
> Mark 2:19–22

Luke adds to this saying from Mark a statement that someone who has drunk old wine does not immediately desire the new (Luke 7:39). The latter is of little historical value because it is as likely to represent

Luke's own commentary on this earlier saying as it is to represent an independent saying of Jesus that made it to Luke in its original form.[29] The Markan saying is also only found in one independent source (Mark, from which both Matthew and Luke derived it), but because of its significantly earlier date, Mark's saying given above is generally considered more likely to be authentic.[30]

Bacchiocchi objects that the new wine cannot be wine which is expected to undergo fermentation because it would burst any wineskin, and not just an older one.[31] Bacchiocchi's knowledge of ancient wine-making techniques is apparently limited because Rod Phillips, an historian of wine-making and wine consumption, states that in ancient Greece some did use wineskins that were carefully filled to allow room for the gases that would be produced by fermentation; most, however, chose to use amphoras or wine jars, with small holes left to allow CO^2 to escape during the fermentation process, which were thereafter sealed.[32] Job 32:19 seems to attest to the fact that in earlier times, as also in the time of Jesus, wine was allowed to ferment in skins, which would be stretched almost to the point of bursting by the process—and occasionally beyond! Once a wineskin had been used in this manner, it would lose its elasticity, and further use of it for the same purpose would soon result in a broken wineskin and lost wine.

What did this parable mean? Presumably not that the new wine of the Gospel would inevitably burst the old wineskins of Judaism. The parable seems to encourage putting new wine in new wineskins to preserve both, and thus seems to focus on preserving both patch and garment, both wine and wineskin, rather than predicting that one or both will inevitably ruin the other. It is also unlikely to have meant that the new wine of the Gospel was to be put in new wineskins—meaning the Gentiles, or the Church. Such issues are anachronistic and were unlikely to have already been in view at this stage in the life of the historical Jesus. It is clearly a riddle, like Jesus's references to salt that loses its saltiness. The Gospel authors presumably took it to refer to the bursting of the Christian message beyond its Jewish roots. I expect that its original meaning in the context of the life and public activity of the historical Jesus still remains to be unraveled.

To summarize, we have seen how wine was essentially not an issue in and of itself for Jesus in his time. The failure to state, much less emphasize, that Jesus abstained from fermented wine points to him having partaken of it as part of his practice of dining with "sinners" and "tax collectors." He was criticized for his feasting, just as John was criticized for not doing so, and the double criticism showed that objectors were really clutching at straws. The fact that the Gospel authors and other early Christian writers do not engage more adamantly in polemic against accusations of Jesus being "a glutton and a drunkard" suggests it was an off-the-cuff remark made by some critic, and Jesus was known and respected to an extent that there was no real fear that it would be taken seriously. The significance of wine for the historical Jesus seems to have been in its symbolic use: To represent the Kingdom of God at meals; to indicate the nearness of the Kingdom and of climactic eschatological events in his vow of abstinence at the Last Supper.

The Jesus of the Gospels and Alcohol

The "Christ of faith," the Jesus presented in the Gospels, has more to say in relation to alcohol consumption than does the Jesus of history. Once again to make this distinction does not mean that Jesus has been decisively shown to have not said and done the various things attributed to him in the Gospels. It means rather that it cannot be decisively demonstrated that he actually did say and do certain things. In some cases there is only one relatively late witness to a particular saying and event; in other cases the story includes a miraculous element that is intrinsically unlikely (because miracles are by definition not everyday occurrences)—which again does not mean it could not have happened, but that one would require overwhelming evidence in order to feel confident in asserting it did in fact happen. When a friend tells you he saw an airplane, you do not normally feel the need to question him further; if the same friend tells you he saw a flying saucer, you will probably only believe him if you are certain he is not pulling your leg, if you have ruled out every other possible logical explanation, and so forth. When writing history, historians look for and expect a logical cause-and-effect explanation for events. This method is certainly the appropriate one to use in historical inquiry.

However, an historical approach is not the only one that can be taken to Jesus, and hence to the topic of Jesus and alcohol. One may also take the information from the various Gospels and ask about the teachings of Jesus as presented in the Church's foundational documents, the canonical Gospels, rather than trying to find a way through and behind them to the historical figure of Jesus. However, even when speaking of the Jesus of the Gospels rather than the historical Jesus, there are several possible ways to tackle the subject. The most appropriate would be to take each Gospel as a literary document and ask about its teaching on this topic. However, within the context of the present essay, the constraints of space only allow a few comments about the traditions we excluded as inadequately attested in relation to the historical Jesus, but which nevertheless feature prominently in Christian discussion of wine and alcoholic beverages.

Probably the most famous is the story of the wedding at Cana (John 2:1–11). Here Jesus is presented as miraculously producing an enormous quantity of wine in water vats used for Jewish purification rituals. The symbolism, according to many commentators, is that Jesus replaces Jewish purification rituals and "legalism" with the wine of the Kingdom and with joy. This interpretation is at best simplistic. The evidence of the Gospel of John is that, compared to Paul, he had a relatively positive assessment of the Law of Moses. The Law is not antithetical to grace, but the superabundant grace revealed in Jesus replaces the earlier grace of the Law, "grace replacing grace" being the best way to translate John 1:16.[33] The miracle in John 2 can almost be read as a narrative commentary on John 1:12–18 because it concludes with the statement that Jesus's disciples, seeing his miraculous production of wine, "saw his glory" and believed in him. The water of purification is not necessarily antithetical to joy. In the context of the Fourth Gospel, the meaning, if anything, is that the rituals of purification provide the foundation for the revelation of Jesus's glory. Had there been no rite of purification, there would have been no twenty gallon vats and thus no superabundance of wine. The mistake would be to complain when Jesus takes the water and decides it is better used to celebrate the arrival of the Kingdom than for purification. The arrival of the Word-become-flesh on the scene of human history is a special circumstance, and in it the divine invitation to all takes precedence over distinctions like clean and unclean, righteous and sinners, and all other distinctions of class, gender, and varying degrees of social respectability. However, these things will only become clear in light of Jesus's practice of eating and drinking with sinners, and his public teaching, which have not yet taken place. That is presumably why in John 2:4 Jesus is presented as saying his time has not yet come— it is a revelation of glory without context. His disciples believe, but for most it is a sign whose meaning will only become clear with hindsight.

Was the wine Jesus produced alcoholic wine? There are some very amusing attempts to deny this was the case. For example, Henry Morris claims that the wine was unfermented grape juice because "There was no time for the fermentation process to break down the structure of its energy-giving sugars into disintegrative alcohols."[34] Apparently God can only miraculously create unfermented drinks instantaneously, but must rely on slow-working natural processes in order to create alcoholic beverages In a similar attempt to deny Jesus made fermented wine, Bacchiocchi cites evidence from philosophers who characterize boiled or strained wines as best because their ability to cloud one's reasoning has been removed.[35] There are, however, several counterarguments.

First, the texts that Bacchiocchi cites simply do not support his conclusion. Pliny the Elder, in Book 23 of his *Natural History*, is discussing the most *useful* wines to use as treatments for various ailments. In chapter 23 he recommends undiluted fermented wine for certain problems like flatulence. The sentence Bacchiocchi quotes from chapter 24 has to do with the medicinal use of wines. In this context, Pliny notes that the most useful wine for people of all ranks who are taking wine medicinally is filtered wine, which has had at least some of the alcohol-producing fermentation stopped. This recommendation is presumably made because otherwise one who needs to consume large quantities of wine medicinally would be overcome by the effects of its alcohol content. Pliny is clearly talking about filtered (i.e., lower alcohol) wine rather than unfermented must, which he explicitly discusses in chapter 18, and the medicinal value of which he assesses somewhat differently from that of filtered wine. At any rate, it is safe to assume that the guests at the wedding in Cana were not drinking wine primarily for medicinal purposes—and so the first text Bacchiocchi quotes is irrelevant and does not prove what he claims it does. The second text he cites, from Plutarch, is a useful one to read in connection with the text from Pliny because in Plutarch's *Table Talk* 6.7 (692–93), there is a discussion of the custom of filtering wine, which clearly shows that the practice reduced the strength of the wine but by no means was intended to prevent fermentation altogether. What is recommended is a particular kind of wine, not abstinence from wine. A more relevant quote from Plutarch is found elsewhere in his *Moralia* in the section entitled "Advice About Keeping Well" (132). Here he provides some warnings about wine and advises drinking water for thirst, but nonetheless says that "wine is the most beneficial of beverages, the pleasantest of medicines, and the least cloying of appetizing things, provided that there is a happy combination of it with the occasion as well as with water."[36]

In short, Bacchiocchi's treatment of these two texts is typical of his interpretation of texts in general: He has his mind already made up, and is looking for any sentence which, taken out of context, can be made to appear to support his case. This point on its own would be enough to overturn Bacchiocchi's argument. Nevertheless, more can still be said. Second, even if Bacchiocchi's interpretation of these texts was correct, there is still simply no basis for assuming that the view of a small number of ancient philosophers was the common view of ordinary people, such as the bridegroom at this wedding. Third, there is explicit evidence from within ancient Israel that older wine was more valuable, suggesting that in the ancient world as today, the better wine was generally thought to be the older vintage.[37] At any rate, if Bacchiocchi's view of what is meant by "better" wine were correct in relation to the story in John 2, it would give the story a very strange meaning indeed! If unfermented wines are the "best," then the words of the "headwaiter" in John 2:10 would mean: "Everyone serves the better, non-alcoholic grape juice first, and when people have started to get drunk, then he brings out the poorer alcoholic wines. But you have saved the better, non-alcoholic grape juice until now!"[38] The wine Jesus produced was clearly not better by being unfermented grape juice, but by being what anyone who appreciates wines would mean by a "better vintage." Probably the wine that would be brought out later at a peasant wedding would be the low-alcohol, bitter wine made from putting water on the remaining skins and seeds, as mentioned above. What Jesus produced was a good vintage wine, better than the one that had been served at the wedding so far.

One final point about the quantity of wine produced needs to be addressed. It is often objected that Jesus would not have produced gallons of alcoholic wine for people who had already drunk quite a bit. This assumes that Jesus expected all of the wine to be drunk, which seems impossible in view of the very large quantity. As with the story of the miracle of the loaves and the fishes, God's abundant provision was clearly demonstrated not by the amount consumed but by the amount left over. In many eastern cultures even today, if there is nothing left over, the provision has not been sufficient. Moreover, because we know nothing of the number of guests and expected duration of the feast, we cannot know if Jesus made wine than might have been necessary.

Jesus is said to have provided wine in abundance, such that there would be no danger of them running out again. However, the fundamental importance of the story, according to John, has to do with the revelation of Jesus's glory. This argumentation prepares the way for the presentation of Jesus as the bridegroom in 3:29, and probably also in chapter 4. Jesus is the bridegroom, the host who provides abundantly for his guests in a way that no earthly bridegroom could. There may also be an allusion to Isaiah 55, which is in the background at other points in John's narrative, particularly John 6 and 7:37–38. At any rate, those who find Jesus's behavior in this story abhorrent and yet claim to be his followers today fail to realize that they probably would have been among the critics of his ministry had they lived then. Then again, if they had lived then, they might not have been influenced by modern ideas concerning total abstinence from alcohol, and might have been able to be among those who "saw his glory and believed in him."

The Evidence of Jesus's Earliest Followers

It is quite clear that Jesus's earliest followers did not understand him to have taught abstinence from all alcoholic beverages. The veracity of this statement can be demonstrated in a number of ways and can be proven "beyond reasonable doubt." It does not decisively determine the outlook of the historical Jesus because followers have been known to make the demands of their group either more or less rigorous after the death of their teacher/founder. Nevertheless, the general agreement of early Christianity that sobriety is a requirement while abstinence, however admirable, is not, fits well with our conclusion that this was the view of the historical Jesus.

Hegesippus (quoted in Eusebius, *Church History*, 2.23.4) notes that James, the brother of Jesus, abstained completely from wine, and from meat as well. That some early Christians adopted this position is suggested also in Romans 14:2–21. The issue in the Roman church was most probably that there were Jewish Christians who did not reside in the Jewish quarter of Rome and who thus avoided wine and meat that might have been used in idolatrous worship.[39] James's reasons for abstaining from both meat and wine are unclear. There are traditions that suggest that he took a Nazirite vow; another possibility is that he was showing concern for the scruples of Jewish Christians in the Diaspora like those in Rome, the same ones for whom Paul shows similar concern. Nevertheless, it is quite clear that James was not following a usual Christian practice; otherwise it would hardly have been noteworthy! Various groups that rejected the consumption of wine altogether were condemned as heretical by the mainstream Church.[40] Similarly, Paul himself, who expresses in Romans 14 a willingness to limit his own freedoms in order to avoid causing a brother to fall into sin, nevertheless still only advocates moderation and right use rather than abstinence. The parallelism in Romans 13:13 makes this clear. Even if Paul decided to forego marriage and sexual relations altogether, he only requires others to avoid sexual promiscuity and immorality, not sex in and of itself. Even if Paul perhaps was willing to forego drinking wine so as not to cause a brother to stumble, he calls Christians to avoid carousing and drunkenness, not consumption of alcoholic beverages in and of themselves. If Christians all practiced abstinence from sex, the warnings to avoid sexual immorality would be meaningless. If all Christians practiced abstinence from alcoholic beverages, the warnings to avoid drunkenness would be meaningless. The matter could not be clearer, but some still are willing to go to great lengths to avoid the plain meaning of these texts.[41]

One last text that may be mentioned is Acts 2, where the disciples are accused of being "drunk with *gleukos*." In view of the fact that *gleukos* is actually the word for "unfermented must" or "new wine," Bacchiocchi suggests that Acts 2:13 is actually a mocking of the early Christians' abstinence from wine. According to Bacchiocchi, an onlooker in Acts 2 says about the disciples, in effect, "Even grape juice is enough to make these tee-totalers tipsy!" Bacchiocchi is correct that the Greek word *gleukos* is normally reserved only for unfermented must. However, the New Testament authors were influenced by other languages than Greek, and they at times use words in other than their strict classical sense. It is thus quite possible that the Greek word used here may simply be a translation of the Hebrew word *tirosh* or an Aramaic equivalent. *Tirosh* is clearly alcoholic in Hosea 4:11, and so just as *yayin* normally means "wine" but sometimes means "must," likewise *tirosh* normally means "must" but occasionally means "wine."[42]

At any rate, Bacchiocchi's assumption that the onlookers, who came to Jerusalem for a feast from other parts of the world, already knew not only of the existence of the Christian movement but that they were tee-totalers is quite ridiculous. Equally incomprehensible is his assumption that the passage can be assumed to be not only historically accurate, but a verbatim transcript of what was spoken on this occasion, and that the discussion would have taken place in Greek and the term *gleukos* would have been used. If *gleukos* is simply a translation of *tirosh* (or of a corresponding term in Aramaic, or indeed of any other word of broader meaning), then Bacchiocchi's reading of the story as subtly mocking the Christians for their abstinence from alcohol loses its force. Be that as it may, an important point is raised by the story in Acts 2, namely the similarities between the manifestations of spiritual ecstasy and inebriation. The comparison made between being drunk with wine and being filled with the Spirit likewise assumes that the two phenomena are in some way comparable. The early Christians can be said to have had spiritual experiences which they describe as being not unlike inebriation. It is quite possible that Jesus, whom Marcus Borg characterizes as a "man of the Spirit," had similar experiences.[43] Perhaps the accusation of him being a "drunkard," like the accusation in Acts 2, stemmed from an occasion when (perhaps in the context of one of his customary meals) Jesus showed signs of being overwhelmed by the spiritual realities he was experiencing. Perhaps it was because of wine's association not only with feasting, not only with rejoicing, but also with mystical experience, that Jesus chose to use meals as a metaphor for the new covenant and for the dawning Kingdom of God. But the historical evidence is insufficient for us to call such suggestions anything other than speculations, however interesting they may be.

Conclusion

Perhaps it is most important to emphasize that, by asking about what and how much Jesus drank, we are asking questions that were clearly not considered of prime importance for the earliest sources we have about Jesus.[44] It seems that what made a stir was neither what nor how much Jesus ate and drank, but with whom he ate and drank. However, by examining this issue (the New Testament documents offer relatively little information) we have actually found a useful test case for the viability of "What would Jesus do?" as an ethical principle. The principle's great weakness is that it is useless at precisely those points when its need is most urgently felt by those seeking to be followers of Jesus today. Every indication is that Jesus held to something like the norms of his time regarding alcohol consumption. As far as we can tell from the available evidence, he seems to have drunk alcoholic beverages, without indulging to excess. However, his favorite drinks remain his secret. The fact, though, that Jesus's attitude to fermented beverages was "nothing special" leaves believers today with two problems. First, if Jesus simply held the views of the majority of his contemporaries, then what ought believers do today? Do they simply adopt the majority view of their contemporaries? Or should they seek to preserve Jesus's attitude, even if there is nothing specifically Christian about it? Second, how are students of the Bible today to handle the paucity of evidence regarding Jesus and alcohol? It is precisely this lack of clear evidence that allows for more than one possible interpretation. Thus, when someone today seeks guidance by asking "What would Jesus do?" it would not be inappropriate to reply "Which Jesus? Whose interpretation of Jesus?" What is most certain about Jesus is, by the nature of the way historical study works, what most strongly sets him apart from his contemporaries. Even so, Jesus was not completely different from his contemporaries in all respects, and the difficulty for would-be imitators of Jesus today is to know not just what Jesus did, but (as the saying goes) what he would do. To find this out, it would be necessary to understand why Jesus chose to disagree with some, most, or all of his contemporaries on certain issues, but not others, and how the selection was made. Therefore, it is quite challenging to imitate Jesus in today's rather different historical and cultural contexts that require a wide knowledge of not just biblical literature, but also ancient and modern cultures and the differences between them.

Although Bacchiocchi's arguments have been given consideration at various points in this essay, they really ought not to be taken very seriously by those who treat the Bible with respect, much less by those who reverence it as sacred Scripture. Bacchiocchi's final court of appeal is always "We cannot conceive...," and his answer to the question "What would Jesus do?" is consistently "Not anything that I consider wrong." This shows clearly another difficulty involved in using WWJD as a guiding ethical principle. It is difficult to read relevant ancient evidence without imposing on it the grid of today's qualms and presuppositions. Because we only have fairly sparse records about the things Jesus did, we fill in the gaps in such a way that WWJD means "What is the right thing to do?," and the answers stem as much from our cultural pool or moral values as from anything ancient sources might tell us.

Bacchiocchi argues that Jesus could not have made gallons of alcoholic wine for people at a wedding who were already at least tipsy, because that interpretation of the text would "destroy ... the moral integrity of Christ's character."[45] Clearly Bacchiocchi's view of Christian morality is not of the WWJD variety. He already knows what is right and wrong, and therefore forces the biblical evidence into his own pre-existing ethical mould, rather than trying to determine as objectively as possible what Jesus did and then seeking to imitate him. Bacchiocchi is willing to go so far as to redefine words, as well as to force parts of the

Bible whose meaning is perfectly clear (e.g., Deuteronomy 14:22–26) to conform with ambiguous ones that he has managed to read as prohibiting alcoholic wine. Anyone who is concerned either with reading the Bible first and foremost in relation to its ancient context, or who considers the Bible their authority on matters of doctrine and practice, should find Bacchiocchi's reading of the relevant passages deeply disturbing. Exegesis like his might even drive you to drink! At any rate, it should be clear by this stage that the principle of WWJD is at times too subjective, at others based on too uncertain a knowledge of Jesus or of his times, at still others it fails to adequately address the question of what it means to imitate Jesus in the context of a rather different cultural and historical context.

Nevertheless, the questions of both what Jesus did and what he would do are worth asking, even when we cannot give answers that are 100% certain and unambiguous. It is reasonable to assume that Jesus and his followers had discussions of right and wrong, and of the interpretation and application of the teachings of the Scriptures. Furthermore, then as now, the greatest theological discussions took place between disciples over a couple of beers. Is that really what Jesus would do? It is hard to say for certain: Ever since Albert Schweitzer's time we have been duly warned of our tendency to make Jesus in our own image.[46] However, even if we theologians, drinking wine and beer and discussing the interpretation of the Bible, were for that very reason "sinners," Jesus might just come and join in our conversation and our fellowship, and lead us on from there.

Notes

[1] Samuele Bacchiocchi, *Wine in the Bible: A Biblical Study on the Use of Alcoholic Beverages* (Berrien Springs: Biblical Perspectives, 1989). Because Bacchiocchi is one of the advocates of total abstinence who seeks to use historical and scholarly arguments in the service of his cause and does so in quite some detail, his arguments and the evidence he cites will be closely examined.

[2] Cf. Rod Phillips, *A Short History of Wine* (New York: HarperCollins, 2000), 44. Phillips also notes that because the alcohol content of the wine was often relatively

high (perhaps as much as 16%), diluting it in this fashion resulted in a drink that had an alcohol content in the range of 5–10 %.

[3] See, for example, Aristotle, *Metereologica*, 384.a.4–5 and 388.b.9–13, and Athenaeus, *Banquet*, 2.24; 6.89, both cited in Bacchiocchi, *Wine*, 60–61. These examples, taken from a couple of centuries before and after the New Testament period, can legitimately be used as indicative of a consistent broader usage of the Greek word, although this nevertheless does not prove anything other than that the word *oinos* was used for unfermented wine exceptionally rarely. This circumstance is no more surprising than that those who drink only decaffeinated coffee will at times simply speak of "coffee."

[4] See Geza Vermes, *The Dead Sea Scrolls In English*, 4th ed. (New York: Penguin, 1995), 7.

[5] See, for example, Bacchiocchi, *Wine*, 101.

[6] Cf. Phillips, *Short History*, 23–24.

[7] Cf. Philo, *De Plantatione* 140–63; Leviticus Rabbah 12:1. For Plato, see *Euthyphro* 4d; *Symposium* 176d; *Laws* 637–66b, 672a; *Republic* 475a.

[8] Bacchiocchi's attempt (*Wine*, 198–202) to show that the word "sober" in the New Testament means *abstinent* must be deemed a failure. Translating the word as he suggests simply does not fit many of the New Testament occurrences, never mind the many more extrabiblical instances of the word group. Because those who abstain from alcohol are by definition sober, it is not surprising that the word *abstinent* fits many instances as well as *sober* does. However, this evidence is inconclusive; what really counts is the many instances where "sober" fits perfectly well and "abstinent" not at all. Those interested are invited to try substituting both words in the examples Bacchiocchi himself gives, and to judge for themselves, which is the more appropriate translation.

[9] Phillips, *Short History*, 43.

[10] Cf. Carey Ellen Walsh, *Fruit of the Vine: Viticulture in Ancient Israel*. Harvard Semitic Monograph 60 (Winona Lake: Eisenbrauns, 2000), 221.

[11] The (high) priest (Leviticus 10:8–11), those who have taken a Nazirite vow (Numbers 6:4), and the Rechabites (Jeremiah 35). The assumption that the prohibition or rejection of wine in these instances was for *moral* reasons is often assumed but by no means as obvious as is often thought. For example, the Rechabites avoided wine as part of their preservation of their earlier nomadic lifestyle; the priests had to avoid many things that were considered ritually unclean, but these did not normally have anything to do with morality, which was a separate issue. See further Walsh, *Fruit*, 5–7, 222–23.

[12] Walsh, *Fruit*, 201–2, prefers to identify it as date palm wine. Although distillation was not unknown in the ancient Greco-Roman world, it only began to be widely used much later to produce distilled alcoholic beverages. See further Griffith Edwards, *Alcohol: The World's Favorite Drug* (New York: St. Martin's, 2000), 4–5, and also Phillips, *Short History*, 124.

[13] For a helpful discussion of the meaning of "the historical Jesus" and the usefulness of applying historical method to these problems, see John P. Meier, *A Marginal Jew*, vol. 1 (New York: Doubleday, 1991), 1–6, 21–31.

[14] For a discussion see Robert T. Fortna, "The Gospel of John and the Historical Jesus," in *Profiles of Jesus*, ed. Roy W. Hoover (Santa Rosa: Polebridge, 2002), 229 and passim. Bruce Chilton, in his book *Rabbi Jesus: An Intimate Biography* (New York: Image Books/Doubleday, 2002), is a peculiar exception.

[15] For those unfamiliar with "Q," this is short for the German *Quelle* meaning "source." Matthew and Luke have significant differences from one another (note, for example, the disparate genealogies in Matt. 1 and Luke 4). This discrepancy suggests that neither Matthew used Luke nor vice versa. The most frequent scholarly explanation for the common material is that both Matthew and Luke used the same earlier source, no longer extant, which scholars have nicknamed "Q."

[16] The one place Mark mentions Jesus's use of a cup and referring to "the fruit of the vine" is at the Last Supper (Mark 13:23–25).

[17] John Dominic Crossan, *The Historical Jesus* (San Francisco: Harper Collins, 1991), 260. See also Joachim Jeremias, *New Testament Theology*, Vol. 1 (London: SCM, 1971), 49.

[18] E. P. Sanders, *The Historical Figure of Jesus* (New York: Penguin, 1993), 203.

[19] Bacchiocchi rightly recognizes that the emphasis in this saying is on the different types of mission and social interaction of Jesus and John; his attempt to argue that the contrast focused on John's abstinence from grape juice over Jesus's willingness to drink unfermented grape juice is nonetheless unconvincing.

[20] Cf. David Catchpole, *The Quest for Q* (Edinburgh: T & T Clark, 1993), 48, on this subject.

[21] From an historian's perspective, the depiction of John as a Nazirite or teetotaler from birth in Luke 1:15 is of little or no historical value, since Luke has modeled his birth narratives on those in the Jewish Scriptures, and thus may have taken inspiration from Jdg. 13:7. Luke's presentation of John in this way does suggest, however, that Luke as well as Matthew may have considered wine consumption a point of contrast between Jesus and John.

[22] Cf. E. P. Sanders, *Jesus and Judaism* (London: SCM, 1985), 307, 324.

[23] Mark calls it a Passover (Mark 14:12–14) and also significantly mentions the singing of a hymn after the meal (Mark 14:26).

[24] Bacchiocchi, *Wine*, 158–68. Bacchiocchi unfortunately equates an apparently minority position in the later Rabbinic literature with the teaching of the Law on this matter, and without justification assumes it to have been the generally accepted practice in the time of Jesus. Bacchiocchi also argues that Jesus would not have drunk fermented wine because leaven/fermentation symbolizes corruption and sin in the Bible. He fails to see that, had this symbolism determined practice in everyday life, then we would have expected Jesus to abstain from bread made with yeast as well.

[25] It presumably also indicates that Jesus's eschatology was that typical of ancient Judaism, envisaging a restored Earth on which God's Kingdom is inaugurated, but in which eating and the drinking of wine continue to take place, rather than the ethereal vision of heaven which has become the mainstream of the Christian tradition under the influence of Greek philosophical thought.

[26] The saying about the Temple is found in Mark 14:58 and John 2:19. The criterion of embarrassment weighs strongly in favor of the saying's authenticity. In other words,

the fact that the early Christians were embarrassed by the saying and sought to either reinterpret its meaning or deny that Jesus said it, suggests that this was something Jesus was widely known to have said.

[27] On this "apocalyptic" understanding of Jesus see especially Sanders, *Historical Figure*, 169–88; Bart D. Ehrman, *Jesus: Apocalyptic Prophet of the New Millennium* (Oxford: Oxford University Press, 1999).

[28] This would explain nicely why Jesus said "fruit of the vine" rather than simply "wine": those who dedicated themselves to God through a Nazirite vow had to abstain from all grape products, and not only fermented wine.

[29] The saying, as most commentators rightly note, does not express a preference on the part of Jesus for "old wine" rather than new; it is the person who drinks old wine in the parable who expresses this viewpoint. The point of the saying is presumably that those who have become accustomed to the old have a hard time accepting something new. If the saying were authentic, all it might add to the present study is the observation that Jesus was not biased in favor of fermented wine. He was perfectly capable of using it as a negative as well as a positive image, representing at times the joy of the Kingdom of God, at other times the failure of those who are accustomed to the way things are to be open to the "new thing" that God is doing, a theme also met on several occasions in the Israelite prophetic literature. At any rate, the saying also implicitly indicates what one would have anticipated to be the case: that older wine, then as now, was normally preferred by those who drank wine. The criticism of the parable is not aimed at this preference, but uses this preference to indicate the unfortunate similarity of this quite natural preference with the attitude of people to the "new wine" of the Kingdom of God.

[30] Cf. W. D. Davies and Dale C. Allison, *The Gospel According to St. Matthew*, Vol. 2 (Edinburgh: T & T Clark, 1991), 114–16, who also note the difficulty in determining precisely what the parable means. Crossan, *Historical Jesus*, 439, judges both the Markan and Lukan sayings to be authentic because they are also attested in the Gospel of Thomas, Logion 47. It has not been clearly established that Thomas represents a source independent of the canonical Gospels. For those interested, there is a complaint about drunkenness in Logion 28, and also a positive use of the image of intoxication in Logion 13.

[31] Bacchiocchi, *Wine*, 146–47.

[32] Phillips, *Short History*, 38.

[33] See the article by Ruth Edwards on this subject "ΧΑΡΙΝ ΑΝΤΙ ΧΑΡΙΤΟΣ (Jn 1:16). Grace and Law in the Johannine Prologue" *JSNT* 32 (1998): 3–15.

[34] Henry M. Morris, *The Bible Has the Answer* (Nutley, NJ: Harris, 1971), 163, quoted in Bacchiocchi, *Wine*, 140.

[35] Bacchiocchi, *Wine*, 141, apparently deriving the quotations and arguments from Barnes.

[36] Plutarch, *Moralia*, trans. Frank Cole Babbitt, Loeb Classical Library 2 (New York: G. P. Putnam's Sons, 1928), 265.

[37] Walsh, *The Fruit of the Vine*, p.58.

[38] The verb *methuô* normally means "to get drunk, inebriated, intoxicated." Bacchiocchi's attempt to deny this is circular, arguing from biblical occurrences (and ones where

the meaning "to get drunk" fits quite well. The texts he cites are the Septuagint of Genesis 43:34; Song of Songs 5:1; and Genesis 9:21) without adducing external evidence (see Bacchiocchi, *Wine,* 142–43, 184–86). The context also indicates that the custom is to wait until those drinking have lost somewhat their ability to discern what they are drinking. Unfermented grape juice does not normally have this effect. If Bacchiocchi's arguments are correct, there would be no terminology in Greek or Hebrew that corresponds to English words such as *wine* and *drunk,* only words with multiple meanings that leave us guessing from the context.

[39] See further Francis Watson, "The Two Roman Congregations: Romans 14:1–15:13," in *The Romans Debate,* ed. Karl P. Donfried (New York: Hendrickson, 1991), 204.

[40] See Charles de Koninck, *Abstention and Sobriety* (Quebec: Les Presses Universitaires Laval, 1953), 14.

[41] Also noteworthy is that the author of 1 Timothy 5:23 makes a point of advising a tee-totaler to add wine to his diet in small quantities for the sake of his health. If the author had meant "unfermented must" one would have expected him to use the word *gleukos,* which normally has this meaning. There is no reason to think that Timothy previously abstained from all grape products and that what Paul was advocating that he add to his diet was "wine" in the broadest sense of the word.

[42] See Walsh, *Fruit,* 194–97, on the term *tirosh.*

[43] See, for example, Marcus Borg, *Jesus: A New Vision* (New York: Harper & Row, 1987), 25–75.

[44] See D. F. Watson, "Wine," in *Dictionary of Jesus and the Gospels,* ed. Joel B. Green, Scot McKnight, and I. Howard Marshall (Downers Grove: InterVarsity Press, 1992), 872, who rightly notes that Jesus's view of wine was that common in his time.

[45] Bacchiocchi, *Wine,* 142–44.

[46] See Albert Schweitzer, *The Quest of the Historical Jesus* (Reprint, Baltimore: Johns Hopkins University Press, 1998.

Bibliography

Bacchiocchi, Samuele. *Wine in the Bible: A Biblical Study on the Use of Alcoholic Beverages.* Berrien Springs: Biblical Perspectives, 1989.

Borg, Marcus. *Jesus: A New Vision.* New York: Harper & Row, 1987.

Catchpole, David. *The Quest for Q.* Edinburgh: T & T Clark, 1993.

Chilton, Bruce. *Rabbi Jesus: An Intimate Biography.* New York: Image Books/ Doubleday, 2002.

Crossan, John Dominic. *The Historical Jesus.* San Francisco: Harper Collins, 1991.

Davies, W. D., and Dale C. Allison. *The Gospel According to St. Matthew.* Vol. 2. Edinburgh: T & T Clark, 1991.

de Koninck, Charles. *Abstention and Sobriety.* Quebec: Les Presses Universitaires Laval, 1953.

Edwards, Griffith. *Alcohol: The World's Favorite Drug.* New York: St. Martin's, 2000.

Edwards, Ruth. "ΧΑΡΙΝ ΑΝΤΙ ΧΑΡΙΤΟΣ (Jn 1:16). Grace and Law in the Johannine Prologue." *JSNT* 32 (1998): 3–15.

Ehrman, Bart D. *Jesus: Apocalyptic Prophet of the New Millennium.* Oxford: Oxford University Press, 1999.

Fortna, Robert T. "The Gospel of John and the Historical Jesus." In *Profiles of Jesus.* Edited by Roy W. Hoover. Santa Rosa: Polebridge, 2002.

Hoover, Roy W., ed. *Profiles of Jesus.* Santa Rosa: Polebridge, 2002.

Jeremias, Joachim. *New Testament Theology.* Vol. 1. London: SCM, 1971.

Meier, John P. *A Marginal Jew.* Vol. 1. New York: Doubleday, 1991.

Morris, Henry M. *The Bible Has the Answer.* Nutley, NJ: Harris, 1971.

Phillips, Rod. *A Short History of Wine.* New York: HarperCollins, 2000.

Plutarch, *Moralia.* Translated by Frank Cole Babbitt. Loeb Classical Library 2. New York: G. P. Putnam's Sons, 1928.

Sanders, E. P. *The Historical Figure of Jesus.* New York: Penguin, 1993.

———. *Jesus and Judaism.* London: SCM, 1985.

Schweitzer, Albert. *The Quest of the Historical Jesus.* Reprint, Baltimore: Johns Hopkins University Press, 1998.

Vermes, Geza. *The Dead Sea Scrolls In English,* 4th edition. New York: Penguin, 1995.

Walsh, Cary Ellen. *Fruit of the Vine: Viticulture in Ancient Israel.* Harvard Semitic Monograph 60; Winona Lake: Eisenbrauns, 2000.

Watson, D. F. "Wine." In *Dictionary of Jesus and the Gospels.* Edited by Joel B. Green, Scot McKnight, and I. Howard Marshall. Downers Grove: InterVarsity Press, 1992.

Watson, Francis. "The Two Roman Congregations: Romans 14:1–15:13." In *The Romans Debate.* Edited by Karl P. Donfried. New York: Hendrickson, 1991.

2 Wine and the Lord's Supper in the Gospels, Paul, and Today

B. J. Oropeza

I first drank from a shared cup in a Eucharist service as a student at the University of Durham. It was during a harsh northern England winter when almost everybody I knew had the flu or were just getting over it. The people at church sneezed, wheezed, and coughed as they sipped and passed the wine. They all touched the same loaf of bread with hands that carried more germs than their mouths. This liturgical ritual played foreign to someone who had been weaned on little plastic cups sporting shots of grape juice and a side order of cracker snippets—a perfectly individualized communion. To be honest I did not want to partake! My mind wondered if perhaps drinking from one cup was the real reason why people were getting sick at the Corinthian church after they participated in the Lord's Supper (1 Cor. 11:29–30). I appreciated the stress on unity, eating and drinking from one cup and one loaf, but the true meaning of the Eucharist got lost somewhere in my worries. My turn. I whispered a prayer as I partook, not of thanksgiving, but for protection against the germs.

This incident captures a little bit of the controversy surrounding the Lord's Supper. Jesus no doubt intended his disciples to band together and honor him by virtue of their shared meal. We may call it the Lord's Supper (1 Cor. 11:20), Holy Communion (1 Cor. 10:16), Eucharist ("thanksgiving" Luke 22:19), the breaking of bread (Acts 2:42–46), the Lord's table (1 Cor. 10:21), or mass (Latin "missa" indicating dismissal at the end of a religious service). Whichever name we use, reenacting the Last Supper remains the hallmark of Christian liturgy 2000 years later, even though few agree on how it should be observed. Do we serve one big cup or multiple miniatures? Do we serve red wine, white wine, grape juice, soda, or water (as did the ascetic Christian Aquarians)? How frequently should it be served? Daily, weekly, monthly, on special occasions, or never? Is communion reserved for church members alone, for visitors who share the beliefs of the host church, or for everyone?[1]

Then we have theological differences: How does the bread and wine represent Jesus? Does it actually become him in substance after the priest consecrates it (Thomas Aquinas, transubstantiation)? Is his body and blood really present in the bread and wine, i.e. consubstantiation (Martin Luther)? Is it a spiritual presence (John Calvin), a symbolic presence (Ulrich Zwingli), or no presence at all (George Fox)?

These issues are being raised not to resolve them all but to unveil the chasms. Many church statements affirm the Lord's Supper is indeed "the highest expression of the unity of the church."[2] If so, why are there so many divisions related to it? Here lies the paradox: What was originally intended as a unifying act has become a major source of division among Christians over the centuries. Hopefully my task in this study will enlighten readers to understand the Lord's Supper more in line with how the earliest Christians may have understood it. I will then address the present situation. Perhaps this will help mend some rifts while at the same time raise new questions.

The Lord's Supper in Early Christian Tradition

Controversy about the Lord's Supper is nothing new; it has existed since the first century as attested by the problem in the Corinthian congregation (1 Cor. 11:17–34). In those days it seems the bread and wine played a part in a full dinner, love feast or agape meal, as they were known; sort of an ancient potluck called *eranos*.[3] Inconsiderate congregation members threatened the fellowship and unity in the church, and social differentiation created problems related to the celebration of the Eucharist. The Corinthians apparently worshipped in the homes of the wealthier members who ate better meals than the poorer members. A famine in the region may have also contributed to the dichotomy between rich and poor.[4] The larger homes in Corinth contained a room set aside for dining called a *triclinium*. Once the room reached its capacity, other guests would have to eat in the *atrium* or outer court.[5] More prominent members of a banquet were offered the best dinner seats and food selection. Hence, in this congregation the poorer members were being neglected of choice foods consumed by the wealthy. The Corinthians divided into two groups: the "well-to-do" (those who have houses in 1 Cor. 11:22a, 34) and the "have-nots" (1 Cor. 11:22b).[6] Some members went away hungry while others were getting drunk on wine (1 Cor. 11:21). Although Paul does not use the word *wine* in 1 Corinthians 11, no one seriously contests that he means wine when referring to drinking from the cup. The Corinthians certainly did not get drunk on water or grape juice! In this setting the love feast resembled a pagan banquet and drinking party rather than the Lord's Supper.[7] The nature of the agape meal no longer centered on love and unity but on status, faction, and debauchery.

The tradition Paul uses in 1 Cor. 11:23–26 to undergird his position sounds very similar to instruction Jesus gives his disciples in the Gospels:

> For I received from the Lord what also I delivered to you: that the Lord Jesus in the night in which he was betrayed took bread, and when he had given thanks he broke it and said, "This is my body which is for you. This do in remembrance of me." Likewise also the cup after dinner, saying, "This cup is the new covenant in my blood. This do as often as you drink in remembrance of me." For as often as you eat this bread and drink (from) the cup, you proclaim the Lord's death until he comes.

Paul's solution was not to end all Christian love feasts (although this did happen later on in church history)[8]; instead, he handles the situation by reiterating to the Corinthians the meaning of the Lord's Supper. He exhorts the Corinthians to remember the Lord's Supper (1 Cor. 11:24–25), the act of partaking in the bread and wine commemorates Christ's unselfish sacrifice on the cross ("...this is my body which is for you" 11:24). In his letter Paul wants the Corinthians to imitate the model of Christ's sacrificial humility by having an unselfish attitude and love for one another (1 Cor. 1:18–2:2; 8:1, 11; 10:31–11:1; 13:1–14:1; 15:1–3; 16:14, 22). He suggests the members eat at home before coming together (1 Cor. 11:33–34).

Moreover Paul fosters unity by appealing members to self-examination (1 Cor. 11:27–32). The Corinthians should be mindful not to take the bread and cup in an unworthy manner, such as acting with divisive behavior, greed, and drunkenness. They must discern the body and not become liable against the body and blood of Christ. These notions captivate the idea that Christ's body represents the church as a corporate solidarity (cf. 1 Cor. 6:14; 12:12–27) and that hurting the church body results in hurting Jesus. C. K. Barrett rightly affirms, "to eat and drink *unworthily* ... is to contradict both the purpose of Christ's self-offering, and the spirit in which it was made, and thus to place oneself among those who were responsible for his crucifixion, and not among those who by faith receive the fruit of it."[9] In any case the believers are called to discern the sacredness of the event—it is neither an ordinary gathering nor an ordinary consumption of bread and wine.

Most likely Paul did not receive this tradition as a direct revelation from the Lord.[10] He is recollecting a Lord's Supper oral or written source handed to him by other Christians. True he received the information "from the Lord" (1 Cor. 11:23), but he uses similar language when referring to instructions received from earlier traditions that have authoritative force because they originate with Jesus (1 Cor. 7:10–12 cf. Mark 10:11–12; Matt. 5:31–32; Luke 16:18/1 Cor. 15:1–4 cf. Isa. 53:5; Hos. 6:2; Jon. 2:1; Matt. 16:21; Luke 24:34; John 21:15; Mark 16:14). This is how he normally writes in relation to receiving or delivering a tradition (1 Thes. 4:1; 2 Thes. 3:6; Phil. 4:9; Col. 2:6; cf. 1 Cor. 11:2; 1 Thes. 2:13; 2 Thes. 2:15).[11] Paul's words about the Lord's Supper indicate a practice already set in motion by Christians before him, earlier than the mid-50s CE when he wrote 1 Corinthians.

Which tradition is Paul referring to? The Synoptic Gospels (that is, the three similar Gospels of Matthew, Mark, and Luke) record Christ's Last Supper (Matt. 26:26–29; Mark 14:22–25; Luke 22:15–20).[12] Word comparisons between 1 Corinthians and the Synoptic Gospels indicate a borrowing of traditions. The Lord's Supper in Luke and 1 Corinthians resemble each other, and Mark and Matthew are worded in a similar way.[13] Later church liturgy developments may have affected the nuance of wording we now find in the texts, but it may be wrongheaded to drive too deep a wedge between the traditions of Mark/Matthew and Luke/Paul.[14] Earliest Christian records suggest that Paul not only knew Luke (Col. 4:14; Acts 16:10–17; 20:5–21:18; 27–28),[15] but he also knew

Mark (Col. 4:10; Philem. 24; 2 Tim. 4:11; Acts 12:25; 13:5; 15:37–39), and conversed with Peter (Gal. 1:18; 2:9–14; 1 Cor. 9:5; Acts 15:7–12), one of the twelve disciples who is traditionally the Gospel of Mark's main source of information.[16] They doubtlessly would have shared recollections about the night that Jesus was betrayed. Other perspectives about the origin of the Lord's Supper seem less plausible. Even though aspects about this meal may have been influenced by Hellenistic/Greco-Roman ideas,[17] the tradition evidently points back to an original dinner Jesus shared with his Jewish disciples. In addition Jesus probably spoke Aramaic, and there is much support for Semitic language behind the Lord's Supper discourse, making it difficult to maintain a Greco-Roman or later Christian fabrication.[18]

The Last Supper in the Matrix of a Jewish Passover

The Lord's Supper has always been associated with the Last Supper of Jesus. Scholars have noticed similarities between the final meal and meals observed by the Dead Sea Scrolls sect (the Essenes),[19] the Jewish *haburah* (fellowship meal),[20] and Jewish or Greco-Roman association/memorial meals.[21] However, the Last Supper was originally celebrated in the context of a Jewish Passover (*pesach*), as we will observe below. Israel celebrated the latter meal as a result of their freedom from Egyptian slavery during the time of Moses. It originated from the Feast of Unleavened Bread (*mazzot*) that was celebrated for seven days during the month of Nisan (*Abib* or roughly March and April). The first Passover points back to the time when God's angel of death bypassed punishment on Hebrew households marked by the blood of an unblemished male lamb on their doorposts (Exodus 12).

During the time of Jesus the Passover service (*seder*) involved a meal consisting of lamb (reminding Israel about how God protected them against the angel of death), bitter herbs (reminding them of harsh slavery), unleavened bread (reminding them of deliverance from Egypt, the night they ate their bread in haste), *haroseth* (a fruit spice sauce reminding them of mixing mortar to build bricks as slaves), and other dishes (m. Pes. 10:3). The Jewish Mishnah *Pesachim* 10:1–7 indicates that four cups of wine were presented during the evening celebration.[22] At the beginning of the celebration the host or *paterfamilias* spoke a word of dedication over the first cup of wine (the *kiddus* or dedication cup). At the mixing of the second cup (the *haggadah* or instruction-lore cup), the host discussed the meaning of the Passover, and those present at the meal sang a *hallel* or hymn (probably Psalms 113–14). During the third cup, the *cup of blessing*, God was blessed for creating the fruit of the vine and bread of the earth. Afterward the celebrants sang the second part of the hymn (Psalms 115–18), and then praise was given over the fourth cup (the *hallel cup*).[23] The four cups remind the Jews of the four-fold redemption mentioned in Exodus 6:6–7: "I will bring out," "I will deliver," "I will redeem," and "I will take" (you for my people).

Regardless of our hammering out a precise date for the Passover that was celebrated during the original Last Supper (on the question of whether it occurred on Nisan 13, 14, or 15, see Figure 1 on the next two pages), the received forms of the Synoptic Gospels affirm the original event took place as a Passover meal and there is no good reason to deny their validity (Mark 14:12, 14, 16; Matt. 26:17–19; Luke 22:7–8, 11, 13, 15; cf. Exod. 12:8, 26–27; 13:8). Moreover, secondary evidence supporting Passover characteristics of this meal is substantive.[24]

First, the disciples celebrated the event in Jerusalem (Mark 14:13; John 18:1) and Jewish regulations affirmed that pilgrims spend Passover night in Jerusalem, according to early interpretations of Deut. 16:6–7: "…and you shall cook and eat [the Passover] in the place Yahweh your God shall choose." The place God had chosen was Jerusalem; accordingly we read about the Hebrews celebrating the Feast of Unleavened Bread in this city after Solomon's temple was established (cf. 2 Kings 23:21–23; 2 Chron. 30:1, 13; 35:1, 16–19).[25]

Second, the gospels record the Last Supper took place at night (Mark 14:17; Matt. 26:20; John 13:30; cf. 1 Cor. 11:23); in fact, it appears to be the only meal in the gospels that was held this late. The morning meal normally started in the later morning and the main meal came in the late afternoon (cf. Matt. 14:15; Jos. *Wars* 2.129–32).[26] It was Jewish custom for the Passover to be eaten at night but not left over in the morning (Exod. 12:8; Pes. 10:1; Jub. 49:1–12).

Alternative views about the Lord's Supper sometimes entertain their assumptions on the basis of discrepancies regarding the exact day of the meal. Was this meal on the fourteenth of Nisan (the fourteenth would begin in the evening according to Jewish reckoning), the date of the lamb sacrifices, or was it the fifteenth, the first day of the Passover/Feast of Unleavened Bread, when the Passover meal was celebrated? The festival was celebrated in the evening much the same way some families nowadays celebrate Christmas on the night of Christmas Eve (December 24 rather than December 25). If Jesus ate lamb, he probably did not eat it too late at night or in the early morning hours. The Passover meat was considered unclean after midnight (m. Pes. 10:9; cf. Exod. 34:25).

On a surface reading of texts, if John's gospel is correct (John 13; cf. 18:28; 19:14), the Last Supper seems to be celebrated the day *before* the Passover meal (the beginning of the fourteenth). R. T. France supports Jesus as crucified on Nisan 14, in part, by astronomical calculations. He maintains the probability of Nisan 14 falling on a Friday in 30 and 33 CE while no year between 27–34 CE supports Nisan 15 on a Friday (*The Gospel of Mark: A Commentary on the Greek Text*, Grand Rapids: Eerdmans, 2002:560). Differently Jeremias supports a possibility for Nisan 15 as Friday in the same year range except for 29 and 32 CE (*Eucharistic Words*, 36–41). If the Synoptic Gospels are correct (Mark 14:12; cf. Matt. 26:27; Luke 22:7), Jesus seems to celebrate the Last Supper on the Passover (the beginning of Nisan 15). The tension between these two traditions has been explained by a number of solutions, some more convincing than others.

The first possibility suggests that John's view is correct chronologically. Early Judaism (b. Sanhedrin 43a) and Christianity (Gospel of Peter 2) support the view that Jesus's death took place on the eve of Passover. Jesus's arrest was not supposed to happen during "the feast" (Mark 14:2; Matt. 26:5), and all the events of that day would be more difficult to explain if occurring on a holy day rather than an ordinary one. Cf. Raymond Brown, *The Gospel According to John XIII–XXI* (New York: Anchor Bible/Doubleday, 1970), 555–56.

A second view considers the Synoptic Gospels correct and surmises that John may be writing more from a theological than factual/historical perspective because he is concerned about interpreting Jesus as the lamb of God and Passover sacrifice through his actual crucifixion rather than his final meal (John 1:29, 35; 18:28; 19:14, 29, 36; cf. Exod. 12:10, 21–22, 46; Num. 9:12).

In a similar argument the Passover is considered a general term including the entire seven-day celebration of the Feast of Unleavened Bread. A Passover meal could generally refer to any main meal celebrated during that time (2 Chron. 30:22; cf. 2 Chron. 35:7). This is one way scholars have interpreted the religious leaders anticipating the Passover meal after Jesus was already betrayed (John 18:28). Jeremias makes an effort to explain John's passages in view of the Synoptic Gospel chronology in *Eucharistic Words*, 16–23, 75–84.

Figure 1—Alternative Views on the Dating of the Lord's Supper (continued on next page)

A third view argues that it would be difficult for all the Passover lambs to be slaughtered in one day, and so the procedure took two days (Nisan 13 and 14). Jesus may have anticipated a Passover meal before the Passover day because he knew he would be betrayed by Judas and not be able to eat the meal at the appropriate time. France notes the silence about roast lamb as part of the Last Supper, which is in keeping with the notion that the official day for slaughter had not yet come. Lambs needed to be slaughtered on the official day in the temple (*Gospel of Mark,* 562). All the events from the Lord's Supper to the crucifixion in the Synoptic Gospels and John are said to have occurred on Nisan 14. France (*Gospel of Mark,* 562) lists the events on Nisan 14 as follows: 1) just past sunset (Thursday night) the disciples make preparation for the meal; 2) at night Jesus has the meal, is betrayed by Judas, and gets arrested; 3) at dawn (Friday morning) the trial begins; 4) in the "morning/noon" the crucifixion takes place; and 5) afternoon the sacrifice of lambs takes place. After sunset (Friday night) Nisan 15 begins.

A final explanation sustains that ancient Jewish calendars defined dates differently; John may be using one calendar and Mark another. The first-century Jewish historian Josephus, for instance, refers to Nisan 14 rather than Nisan 15 as the first day of the Passover/Unleavened Bread feast (*Wars* 5.3.1). See Casey, *Aramaic Sources of Mark's Gospel,* 221–225 and Strack-Billerbeck, *Kommentar zum Neuen Testament aus Talmud und Midrasch* (Munich: C. H. Becksche, 1924) 2:812–15, for more sources, but consult Jeremias, *Eucharistic Words,* 17, for corrections on the latter. Two major views related to calendar differences are as follows: 1) The Qumran/Essene calendar has the 15th of Nisan fall on Tuesday evening/Wednesday. On this view Jesus celebrated a pre-Passover meal, was arrested Tuesday night, and then went through trials on Wednesday and Thursday before crucifixion on Friday; 2) The Pharisee/Galilean calendar interpreted the day from sunrise to sunrise while the Sadducee/Jerusalem method went from sunset to sunset. Jesus celebrated the Passover Nisan 14, Thursday evening (Galilean method), and his enemies celebrated it according to the Jerusalem scheme; Nisan 14 in the late afternoon of Friday which then turned into Nisan 15 once the sun set (cf. A. Jaubert, *The Date of the Last Supper,* Staten Island: Alba, 1965; Harold W. Hoehner, "Chronology," *Dictionary of Jesus and the Gospels.* J. B. Green, S. McKnight, I. H. Marshall, eds.; Leicester/Downers Grove: InterVarsity Press, 1992:121; Strack-Billerbeck 2.847–53; Jeremias, 16–26, 36–41. For a helpful chart of various calendar perspectives, see Marshall, *Last Supper,* Appendix, Table 4.)

Third, the bread broken at the Last Supper was no doubt unleavened,[27] and in this case, it represented the broken body of Jesus anticipating his crucifixion. Joachim Jeremias notes that the very language of "flesh" and "blood" focuses on Jesus as a sacrifice (cf. Lev. 6:24–7:7; 17:11–14; Num. 18:17–18; Deut. 12:23–27; Ezek. 39:17–19;

44:7; Heb. 13:11).[28] More than this, Deborah Carmichael, following the earlier work of David Daube,[29] discusses that in Passover meals, before reciting Jewish deliverance from Egypt, the host breaks off a small piece of unleavened bread called the *afikoman* (on this interpretation it means "the coming one," or "he that has come," derived from the Greek word *afikomenos*).[30] The host sets this broken piece aside to be divided among participants at the end of the meal. The unleavened bread depicts the entire people of the Jews and the broken piece (the *afikoman*) represents the coming redeemer or messiah. As the people celebrated redemption on Passover night, the *afikoman* symbolizes messiah uniting with the Jewish people.[31] Carmichael suggests that in light of the ancient *afikoman* ritual, when Jesus broke off a piece of bread and affirmed it as his body, he was proclaiming a self-revelation that he was the coming messiah.[32]

Fourth, the Last Supper mimics a Passover in terms of instructing participants to remember what the meal represents. Jesus affirms the poured wine as his blood and the broken bread as his body; the disciples are to practice this new interpretation of the Passover meal in his *remembrance* (Luke 22:15–20; 1 Cor. 11:24–25). He takes on the role of host or *paterfamilias* who instructs the meal takers. It is also interesting to note that in the Synoptic Gospels Jesus uses the phrase "fruit of the vine," a Jewish reference to fermented wine[33] comparable to the Passover language pronounced over drinking from the cup (cf. Isa. 32:12). Some scholars hold that Jesus instituted his words during the drinking of the fourth cup, but others normally suggest it occurred during the third cup. This interpretation makes sense in light of Paul's use of the phrase "cup of blessing" when referring to the Lord's Supper (1 Cor. 10:16–17).[34] It would be wrong to say Jesus never drank fermented wine on other occasions (e.g., Matt. 11:19; Luke 5:30), but the drink became especially relevant to celebrate festivities, and the Feast of Unleavened Bread/ Passover was one of these times.[35] The Jews reserved white, red, and black wine, but Jesus would have drunk red wine; he associated the wine's color with blood, as did other Jewish traditions (Gen. 49:11–12; Deut. 32:14; Isa. 63:3, 6; Sir. 39:26; 50:15; 1 Macc. 6:34).[36] In Jesus's case, wine represented the outpouring of his own blood on the cross.

Finally, the Last Supper ends with Jesus and the disciples singing a hymn (Mark 14:26; Matt. 26:30) leaving little doubt of this referring to the second half of the Passover *hallel*. The Hallels that are sung during Passover (Psa. 113–18) not only exemplify praises to Yahweh, but also include motifs related to praise participation from the nations/Gentiles (Psa. 113:3–4; 115:11; 117:1 contrast 118:10–12); recollection of the original exodus (Psa. 114); salvation/revival from death (Psa. 115:17–18; 116:3–13; cf. 116:15–17); and coming of a messianic deliverer (Psa. 118:14–26; cf. 118:17–18).[37] Passover was a time in which the Jews believed a future redemption awaited them through a coming messiah.[38] It not only commemorated the original event, but members of every generation were to consider themselves as coming out of Egypt (m. Pes. 10:5). The combination of all these observations confirm that Jesus celebrated a Passover meal at the Last Supper, and the significance of this event is tied into the very fabric of earliest Christian practice.

The Lord's Supper and the New Passover Exodus

A major distinction between the institution of the Passover and the Lord's Supper centers on Jesus's reinterpreting the Passover as *seder* in terms of his imminent crucifixion. The Synoptic Gospels present the motifs of a new expiation from sin and perspective of God's kingdom in relation to the cup of wine:

> And he took a cup, and when he had given thanks he gave it to them, and they all drank of it. And he said to them, 'This is my blood of the (new) covenant which is poured out for many (for the forgiveness of sins). Truly I say to you, I shall not drink again of the fruit of the vine until that day when I drink it new (with you) in the Kingdom of God.[39]
>
> Mark 14:23–25; cf. Matt. 26:27–29; Luke 22:17–18, 20

Jesus speaks of giving his life. The cup of wine represents blood poured out and given for the benefit of others. Jesus is anticipating his crucifixion and its sacrificial implications "for many." The same words are found in Mark 10:45 when Jesus affirms he will give his life as a ransom "for many." As the wine served in the four cups at Passover represent redemption for God's people, so Jesus establishes a new kind of redemption ratified by his own blood and represented by the wine. In

Exodus 24:8–11 Moses establishes Israel's law covenant with blood sprinkling, eating, and fellowship in the Divine presence. This would almost seem to foreshadow Christ's ratifying a *new covenant*[40] at the Last Supper when he ate and fellowshipped with the twelve (no doubt, representing antitypes to the twelve tribes of Israel[41]). Christ saw his upcoming death, his blood shed on the cross, as the prophetic fulfillment of a future covenant and deliverance (cf. Jer. 31:31–33). Every generation the Passover participants were instructed to consider themselves as coming out of Egypt. In a similar manner everyone who partakes of the Lord's Supper would be identified with the new deliverance.

All the same, the concepts concerning redemption in the Last Supper, as recorded in the Synoptic Gospels and Paul, point back not only to Exodus and Jeremiah but also to the writings of Isaiah. The latter prophet anticipates a suffering servant who is wounded "for" Israel's transgressions, sent by God to sprinkle the nations, "poured out" as an offering for others, and makes justification possible "for many" (Isa 52:12–53:12; esp. 53:12). Even passages in John's Gospel that may reflect ideas about the Lord's Supper unveil the same theme. Jesus mentions laying down his life for his friends, and he apparently says this at the final meal (John 15:13 cf. 13:1–2). Allusions to the Eucharist in John 6 (esp. verse 51) refer to Jesus as the bread of life who gives his flesh for the life of the world, and this all-inconclusive sacrifice resonates concepts from Isaiah 52–53. Ben Meyer makes the case that the sacrificial expiation from sin provided by Isaiah's suffering servant became part of early Christian faith formulas, and the Lord's Supper texts are evidence of this belief.[42] This type of expiation arising from the words of Jesus is perhaps one reason why the word *blood* became associated with *death* and the *forgiveness/expiation of sins* when early Christians referred to the crucifixion (cf. Rom. 3:25; 5:9; Col. 1:20; Heb. 9:14; 10:19; 1 Pet. 1:2; 2:13; 1 John 1:7; Rev. 1:5; 12:11). Jesus considered himself to be the prophetic fulfillment of the servant-messiah of Isaiah 52–53 who suffers for both the Jews and the nations/Gentiles.[43]

The servant in Isaiah 53 functions as the "inclusive representative" of God's remnant people who (in Isaiah) are judged, perishes, and revive again to new life.[44] Similar in manner the gospels confess Jesus's resurrection, and Paul considers the Corinthian believers a collective body of Christ in terms of "one bread" (1 Cor. 10:16–17; cf. 5:6–8; 12:12–13, 27). The early Christians are seen as the new remnant of God's people, comprising Jew and Gentile believers who have passed from death to new life with Jesus as their forerunner (Rom. 11 [esp. verse 5]; cf. Rom. 6:1–13; 1 Cor. 15:20–57; 2 Cor. 5:14–15).

During the Last Supper Jesus also anticipates a coming celebration in God's kingdom: "I will not drink the cup till I drink of it new in the kingdom of God" (Mark 14:25). Paul picks up this motif by asserting that in the Eucharist, the Corinthians proclaim the Lord's death "until he comes" (1 Cor. 11:26; cf. 16:22).[45] Again the Isaiah writings play a significant role here because they speak of God's suffering servant in the larger context of a new exodus. Most scholars consider Isaiah 40–55 to be a distinctive text (Deutero-Isaiah). The major theme of this unit has God delivering the remnant of Israel from their places of exile in a second exodus epoch (Isa. 40:1–11; 41:17–20; 42:14–17; 43:1–21; 48:20–21; 49:8–12; 51:9–10; 52:11–12; 55:12–13).[46] Themes related to exodus are likewise found in other sections of Isaiah (Isa. 4:2–6; 10:20–27; 11:10–16; 14:1–6; 26:20; 27:12–13; 31:5; 32:14–20; 34:16–17; 58:8; 60:2; 61:4–7; 63:8–14).

The gist of Isaiah's prophetic exodus describes how God will do a new work, creating water in the desert and leading his people with a Moses-like servant or royal messiah. Paul seems to understand that the Eucharist celebration in some sense fulfills this new exodus with Jesus as the leader of God's redeemed people (1 Cor. 10:1–4, 6, 11; cf. 15:3/Isa. 53:5; Rom. 15:8–12/Isa. 11:1–2; Rom. 15:20–21/Isa. 52:15). The Lord's Supper marks a new kind of Passover in which believers celebrate their deliverance, not from slavery to Egypt as Israel, but from slavery to sin and the fallen world (cf. 1 Cor. 5:6–13; 6:9–11; Rom. 6). In addition, while the Corinthians' deliverance already took place, they still needed to persevere through their own metaphorical wilderness journey that would eventually lead to their promised land of rest, the culmination of God's heavenly kingdom (1 Cor. 10:1–11; 13:10–12; 15:20–58; 16:22).

Other early Christian writers pick up this new exodus/wilderness journey paradigm (e.g., Heb. 3:7–4:13; 1 Pet. 1; Rev. 15), most notably the Synoptic writers: Mark, Matthew, and Luke (e.g., Mark 1; Matt. 1–5;

Acts 7).[47] This leads us to strongly suspect that the prominence of this theme in early Christian traditions takes root in the words of Jesus who gave new meaning to the Passover meal during the Last Supper. Whereas the first Passover (Exodus 12) heralded the exodus from Egyptian bondage to a wilderness expedition into the promised land, the original Lord's Supper marks the new exodus from sin. Christ's followers embark on their own journey into the full realization of God's kingdom.

For Christians the Lord's Supper not only points back to the Last Supper, but it also looks forward to a messianic banquet taking place when God's kingdom is fully realized and God's royal Messiah is fully established (Isa. 25:6–9; 53:13; 55:1–2; Matt. 5:6; 8:11; Luke 12:35–38; 13:29; Mark 7:24–30; Rev. 19:1–9; 1 En. 62:13–16; 2 En. 42:5; 2 Bar. 29:8).[48] Perhaps this is one reason why Gospel traditions depict Christ eating with his disciples after his resurrection (Luke 24; John 21). In this sense the Lord's Supper sponsors a "sneak preview" taste of the future kingdom and may be foreshadowed in the alternate translation of the Lord's Prayer: "give us today the eschatological bread that will be ours in the future" (Matt. 6:11).[49] The earliest Christian celebrations of "breaking bread" capture the joy and unity anticipated in this future banquet (Acts 2:46).[50] The Eucharist thus becomes a focal point where past deliverance, present sustenance, and future hope intersect.

The Last Supper made a significant impact on the way early Christians viewed their worship and perspective of salvation-history. They saw Jesus as both the lamb of God who takes away the sins of the world and the restorer of God's kingdom through the inauguration of a new covenant and new exodus. When drinking the wine of communion, Jewish and Gentile believers are reminded of Christ's blood that was shed to provide a new way of deliverance.

The Lord's Supper for Today

Now that it has been explored what the Lord's Supper meant to the earliest followers of Jesus, it is now being examined what it means in a postmodern western context 2000 years later.

Diluted Wine or Red Beverage Before Red Wine

"He took a cup ... 'I shall not drink again of *the fruit of the vine* until that day when I drink it new in the kingdom of God'" (Mark 14:23–25; Matt. 26:27–29; Luke 22:17–18, 20; cf. 1 Cor. 11:25). As we already noted, early Jewish and Christian evidence definitely suggests that the first communion cup contained wine, more specifically a fermented rather than nonalcoholic drink, and red wine best represented the blood of Jesus. Wine and unleavened bread were used at the original Lord's Supper, not grape juice, crackers, or communion wafers. Would Jesus choose wine to represent his blood if he had lived in our era? The question might be moot because it asks Jesus to become a twenty-first-century Generation-X westerner who perhaps was never strongly influenced by Jewish culture. If we could keep his Jewish heritage intact, he would have still adopted religious patterns related to the Passover. In such a case the answer would have to be yes—he would have used wine. Better questions to ask are: Is wine necessary for the Eucharist? Would it be the wisest choice for churches to take communion wine when situated in predominantly Muslim countries? Is wine the best Eucharist option for recent converts in a church that specializes in outreach to riffraff and druggies? Does it not seem a bit impractical in our society to offer wine to detoxifying alcoholics who wish to partake of the Lord's Supper? Are we not in essence creating a stumbling block for some people by insisting on our particular tradition?

Sometimes well-meaning ministers claim that the ancient world did not suffer from the alcoholic epidemic we face in the twenty-first century. It would be an understatement, however, to assert that the world of Jesus did not have its share of alcoholics. Greeks and Romans in particular were famous for drinking parties, saturnalia, and devotion to Dionysus/Bacchus, the god of wine. Both ancient Christians and Jews encountered many drunkards in their era (Deut. 21:20–21; Prov. 20:1; 23:29–30; 31:4–5; Isa. 5:11; 1 Macc. 16:16; Tob. 4:15; Philo *On Drunkenness* 27[5], 206[50]; Matt. 24:48–51; Acts 2:13,15; 1 Cor. 5:11; 6:9–10; 11:21; Gal. 5:19–21; Eph. 5:18). Whatever the case, the cultural leap between the ancient Mediterranean world and ours must be considered. It seems that drunken drivers on the street are more dangerous than the wino on skid row. In contrast, it is unlikely that back in the first century, chariot collisions caused by drunken Romans ended as many lives as today's intoxicated motorists.

What stands out as most different about our culture and the ancient world in relation to drinking are the beverage varieties and potency of drinks. The ancient Mediterranean world drank water, milk, wines, and other lesser-known beverages such as mead (a fermented honey, water, and herb mixture). As a result of carbonation, refrigeration, and electric blenders, our culture enjoys a plethora of beverage options and red-colored drinks other than wine: raspberry cool-aid, diet colored soda, strawberry-flavored milk, margaritas, V–8, Clamato, prune juice, and grape juice concentrate just to name a few. Is it still necessary to maintain wine as the only Eucharistic option with so many beverage choices that keep the blood symbolism intact? Certainly red-colored juices would not seem to violate the commemorative act of the Lord's Supper, and these drinks would not offend any partakers.

If we decide for wine because this is what Jesus drank, then should it not be water diluted with wine because this probably best represents what he drank? As in poorer countries today, water was not always suitable for drinking, and so wine was sometimes used as a purifying agent (1 Tim. 5:23; cf. Luke 10:34). The Jews drank wine mixed with water (2 Macc. 15:39; b. Sabbath 77a), as did Greco-Romans and early Christians. Dilution ratios varied. In Homer's *Odyssey*, it was 20 portions of water to 1 portion of wine; in Hesiod, it was 3 to 1; with Diocles it was 2 to 1; the barbarian custom was to drink wine unmixed.[51] During Passover Jewish custom notes that the four cups of wine were mixed with 3 parts water to 1 part wine (b. Pesachim 108b[.7]). Consequently the wine Jesus drank during Passover Eve probably contained only a fraction of the alcohol present in the standard wine cups today. It would have less chance of sending the former alcoholic on a downward spiral. Robert Stein affirms this:

> To consume the amount of alcohol that is in two martinis by drinking wine containing three parts water to one part wine, one would have to drink over twenty-two glasses. In other words, it is possible to become intoxicated from wine mixed with three parts of water, but one's drinking would probably affect the bladder long before it affected the mind.[52]

Unity Before Exclusion

"Take this (cup), and divide it among yourselves" (Luke 22:17b); "he took a cup... and they all drank of it (Mark 14:23b; Matt. 26:27b). The disciples all partook of the same cup.[53] The Eucharist embraces unity, fellowship, sharing, communion, and love. Contradicting these virtues is what made the Corinthian congregation's celebration so shameful. The original paradigm for Christians was to participate in the blood and body of Jesus by partaking in the Lord's Supper; namely, they identified with Christ in his atoning death as well as his lifestyle, resurrection power, and continual presence.[54] The bread represented both the physical body of Christ on one level and the church as the collective body of Christ on another level (1 Cor. 10:16–17; cf. 12:12–13, 27). All social, racial, and gender dimensions are nullified through the believer's participation as a solidarity in the body of Christ (Gal. 3:28; 1 Cor. 12:13). Otfried Hofius affirms that where the table of the Lord is, there the church members "come together" (1 Cor. 10:21, 32; 11:22, 33).[55] Hence to act in loveless and selfish behavior violates the very significance of the members making up that one body. A collective sense of belonging to Christ obligates the members to fellow members who make up the body of Christ. As disease invades a physical body, so faction and vice threaten to contaminate the church body's unity and wholeness. Along this venue, we may begin to comprehend Paul's words about the Corinthians' sufferings resulting from their selfish behavior at the Lord's table (1 Cor. 11:30).[56]

However the very consumption symbols of unity, "one cup" and "one bread," have turned into a cause for division in relation to illnesses. Participants have a legitimate concern about disease prevention when partaking of one communion cup and handling one loaf of bread. Certainly alcohol in wine can ward off germs better than a nonalcoholic beverage in this case, but it will not be able to kill all bacteria and viruses that touch the cup and bread. Whether a church uses wine or grape juice, individual cups and wafers make better sense for participants who wish to safeguard more effectively against illness. Churches that insist on the representation of unity and biblical form by all drinking from the same cup should consider that the very unity they wish to stress in symbol may be causing great distress in the sanctuary!

Of course, if we know everyone in our church is disease-free, this might relieve some tensions about drinking from the same cup and eating from the same loaf. However, this knowledge leads to another controversy. Do we wish to maintain an open or closed communion? Are we in truth persevering the unity Jesus desired by saying, "those who believe the exact same way we do may participate in the Lord's Supper"? In essence what we are really saying is: "If you don't have your theology correct about the Lord's Supper according to my denomination's (or pastor's!) standard, you are not invited to commune with Christ at my church." This haughtiness of thinking resembles more the attitude of the religious Pharisees whom Jesus rebuked than that of Jesus himself. As Christopher Mearns says: "Symbolic language and sacramental signs by their nature encompass a wide range of meaning and reference. To identify the elements in the Eucharist with any single reference or meaning so as to displace others, is to risk a distorted understanding of the sacrament. The analogies and metaphors should be kept open and multiple."[57] Notice the polyvalent way Paul interprets "bread" and "body" as both the church congregation and Christ (1 Cor. 10:16–17). Consider also how he affirms the sacrifice of Jesus in terms of a sacrificial lamb (1 Cor. 5:7–8) and the bread/cup (1 Cor. 11:24–25, 27). Here we have an early example of how Jesus is portrayed as both the Passover lamb and the Passover elements of bread and wine without any contradiction intended. In celebrating the Eucharist we may wish to replace either/or with both/and.

Note several issues not addressed regarding the Eucharist in Christian scripture:

1. Rules on what and what not to use in relation to the bread and wine: whether the bread *must* be unleavened, whether one should bake or fry barley, flour, wheat, or whole grain; whether one brews, chills, or mixes Cabernet Sauvignon, Pinot Noir, Merlot, or Port.
2. An elaborate ritual of consecration that must be followed correctly before distributing the elements.

3. Any convincing basis for claiming that only ordained ministers and priests may serve communion.
4. A list of theological prerequisites for partaking of the elements, although self-examination, impartial love for one another, and a willing heart to come to Jesus are definitely needed.

The present-day divisions and communion policies in many Christian churches often estrange newcomers and visitors. Paul's solution for unity during table fellowship is simple but rarely followed: If believers are offending someone by what they do, then stop doing it. Members' rights must give way for the sake of embracing visitors and fellow believers alike (1 Cor. 8:1–13; 9:19–23; 10:23–11:1; Rom. 14:1–4, 13–21; Phil. 2:1–4).

Reconciliation Before Condemnation

"This cup which is poured out for you is the new covenant in my blood" (Luke 22:20; Mark 14:24; Matt. 26:28; 1 Cor. 11:25b). The Lord's Supper exemplifies a celebration of reconciliation with God and humankind.[58] Drinking from the cup shows a connection between the participant and the atoning power of Christ's death. Consumption of the elements identifies an individual as a member of the redeemed community of God. The believer thus participates in the body and blood of the messianic savior. Because the Lord's death also functions as an exemplary paradigm of self-giving and sacrifice,[59] it provides a model for our own personal ethics. Even so, the Eucharist is a celebration that should not be relegated to a time of fearful dread. The original Last Supper may have been rather foreboding with Christ's betrayal and crucifixion at hand. However, we should remember that during the dinner and despite his angst, Jesus sang the *hallel*, which were songs dedicated to praising God (Mark 14:26).

The circumstances in the Corinthian congregation compelled Paul to write about divine judgment in relation to the Eucharist (1 Cor. 11:17–34; cf. 10:3–5). If this unfortunate situation had not occurred, Paul would have had no need to write about this type of chastisement. To be sure, introspection is necessary before participation. When we persist in blatant vices, fail to forgive others, or do not believe Jesus died for our sins, we might do well not to consume the Lord's Supper. We are not to partake of it in an unworthy manner (1 Cor. 11:27–34). Nevertheless, under normal circumstances this should not be our primary focus at the Lord's table. The meal centers on what Christ has done for us, not what we have done or failed to do.

Remembrance Before Physical Presence

"Do this in remembrance of me" (Luke 22:19c; 1 Cor. 11:25c). At the Last Supper when Jesus held the bread and cup and said, "this is my body," and "this is my blood," he did not intend for his disciples to understand him as both standing there in front of them and yet existing simultaneously as the bread and wine. Nothing in the text or Jewish Passover meal indicates a transformation of the elements took place. In fact the *literal* consumption of the body and blood of Jesus would have sounded repugnant to Jewish disciples who considered it sacrilegious to drink blood (cf. Lev. 3:17; 7:26–27; 17:14; Acts 15:19–20, 28–29).[60] The Jews observed the Passover "*in memory of* Israel's redemption from Egyptian slavery" (Exod. 12:14; 13:9; Deut. 16:3; Jub. 49:7–23), and remembrance is bound with proclaiming God's saving acts in praise (Psa. 9:12; 70:15–17; 77:12; 105; 113–118; 145).[61] This aspect of commemoration leads to a proclamation about redemption through Christ's accomplishment on the cross (1 Cor. 11:26). We have a retelling of the story of Jesus, a story involving a new community, delivered not from the bondage of Egypt but from the fallen world with all its sinful enterprises; a retelling not of the old Passover but the new Passover and exodus instituted by the risen savior.

Although the Last Supper's focus rests on the redemption story rather than discerning Christ's presence, this fact neither denies the reality of latter nor that grace may be imparted through consumption of the elements. A spiritual presence and grace impartation through communion appears to be supported by early Christian writings (1 Cor. 10:3–4, 16–17; John 6:53–63; Didache 10).[62] In keeping with the form of a Passover meal, the Lord may be considered as spiritually hosting or presiding over the table as the *paterfamilias* (cf. 1 Cor. 10:21).[63]

Even the early Jewish and Christian concept of remembrance does not entirely escape the possibility of grace and spiritual presence. Anthony Thiselton writes, "to remember God's mighty acts" engages the faithful in "worship, trust, and obedience, just as 'to forget' God is to turn one's back on him. ... 'Remembering' the gospel tradition (Rom. 15:15; 1 Cor. 15:3) or 'remembering' Christian leaders (Acts 20:31; Heb. 13:7) transforms attitude and action."[64] Among other things to remember Christ's death during the Eucharist requires self-involvement, worship, trust, obedience, as well as "the experience of being 'there' in identification with the crucified Christ who is also 'here' in his raised presence."[65] Similar to the preaching of the word, communion is then one *more* way of tapping into grace and the holy presence.[66] *Remembrance* of Christ's sacrificial death and resurrection in the Lord's Supper seems to reserve a place for the *presence* of Christ. The two are not mutually exclusive.

Conversely, crass literalism associated with the Lord's Supper probably needs to be avoided. Interpreting the bread and wine as the literal body and blood of Jesus sounds too much like cannibalism to outsiders, just as it did to the Romans in the early days of Christianity. Christopher Mearns rightly affirms that such language "alienates many sensitive people, and repels them from whole-hearted and regular sharing in the eucharist."[67] Likewise opting for a mystery about how the elements are transformed into the real body and blood sounds like archaic hocus-pocus to both newcomers and committed believers. Pastoral concerns might do well to override theological disputes over this issue. Paul formulates Christ as the spiritual *source* of the Lord's Supper rather than literally being transformed into the bread and drink (1 Cor. 10:3–4).

A proper balance needs to take place with the Eucharist as remembrance and then as presence. Presence without remembrance tends to mislead uninformed participants into thinking that merely eating the bread and wine will secure favors. When Jesus walked the earth, many ate and drank in his presence, but this was never enough to marshal their salvation (Luke 5:30–32; 7:34; 13:22–30; 15:1–2).[68] Even Judas Iscariot was present at the Last Supper. The Corinthians seemed influenced by earlier participation in mystery religions and mistook the sacraments as a type of "magical" confirmation of immortal status (cf. 1 Cor. 12:2).[69]

They still got sick and stood in danger of not making it to the completion of their spiritual journey despite their partaking of the Eucharist (1 Cor. 11:30; 10:3–6). The bread and wine are not magically potent; they have no intrinsic quality that makes every participant immune from all sin, sickness, poverty, bad luck, or divine punishment. If consecrated communion crumbs fall on the floor and are eaten by a mouse, she does not receive grace or protection against the exterminator! Salvation and divine blessings are benefits received by a person who places his or her faith in Christ and his sacrificial death.

Repetition Before Completion

"As often as you ... drink the cup, you proclaim the Lord's death until he comes" (1 Cor. 11:26c; Luke 22:18b; Mark 14:25; Matt. 26:29). How often should we observe the Lord's Supper? Paul settles for "as often as you drink" from the cup and eat the bread (1 Cor. 11:25–26). The phrase "as often" may indicate a weekly basis when compared with 1 Corinthians 16:2 and Acts 20:7. The latter mentions the first day of the week as a time for breaking bread. Differently, breaking bread occurs daily in the earliest days of the church (Acts 2:42–47). If the amount of times one celebrates the Eucharist were an important issue for Jesus, Paul, or the Synoptic writers, perhaps they would have instituted a more structured schedule.

The words *as often* do suggest a repetitive celebration was expected (similarly the present tense *do this* in Luke 22:19). The believers are to repeat their participation until Christ returns. In this light the Eucharist presupposes resurrection. As Jesus suffered, died, and rose again, so the believers will undergo suffering, death, and a future resurrection. The believers' recurring observance of the Lord's Supper is situated in the "messianic intermezzo"[70] of salvation-history right before the Grand Finale. The completion of the second Exodus established by the new covenant between Jesus and his followers finds its ending not in the land of Canaan but in Paradise, as Christ returns and raises the dead (1 Cor. 15:20–57). Until then, the Lord's Supper remains "food for the journey," as the early church fathers affirmed.[71]

The Lord's Supper depicts a visible sign of the Christian confession that Jesus died for our sins and rose again, and the same resurrection power is present with believers as they partake of communion. We should always recognize that the significance of the Lord's Supper centers on Jesus and his sacrificial death for fallen humanity, not our petty denominational differences. If we get this part right, we can perhaps begin to gain better perspective on how to deal with issues related to the consumption of wine or grape juice, inclusion or exclusion, real presence or symbol. In drinking the cup and partaking of the bread, the parishioner's emphasis should rest on this contemplation: "Jesus, I believe you died and shed your blood to deliver me from sin and bondage."

Notes

[1] Denominational differences are conveniently laid out in reference to participants, and Eucharist proclamations/prayers and practice in Ralph F. Smith, "Eucharistic Faith and Practice," *Interpretation* 48 (1994): 5–16.

[2] Michael Welker, *What Happens in Holy Communion* (Grand Rapids: Eerdmans, 2000), 4, 177–81.

[3] On the *eranos* meal see Peter Lampe, "The Eucharist: Identifying with Christ on the Cross," *Interpretation* 48 (1994): 38–39. Paul does not write in terms of a separation between the regular meal and the Lord's Supper. Love feasts/*agapê* meals remained a part of Christian gatherings until well into the second century CE. The separation seems to develop as a result of abusive situations similar to the division Paul addresses at Corinth. A comparison of the term *breaking bread* in Acts 2:41–46 and 20:7–12 suggests a celebration of the Lord's Supper or the agape meal or both. To break bread was to begin a meal in Jewish tradition. See Otfried Hofius, "The Lord's Supper and the Lord's Supper Tradition," in *One Loaf, One Cup*, ed. Ben F. Meyer (Macon: Peeters/Mercer University Press, 1993), 84. Jude mentions a love feast that gets blemished by the presence of false teachers (Jude 12 cf. 2 Pet. 2:13). G. Wainwright, "Lord's Supper, Love Feast," in *Dictionary of the Later New Testament and Its Developments*, ed. Ralph P. Martin, P. H. Davids (Leicester/Downers Grove: InterVarsity Press, 1997), 690–93, posits that during the postapostolic period (later first and early second centuries) the distinction is still not clear (Didache 9–10; Ignatius *Smyrna* 7:1; 8:1–2; *Phld.* 4:1; *Eph.* 20:2; Diognetus *Ep.* 5:7; cf. Pliny *Ep.* 10.96) until the time of Justin Martyr (c. 155 CE; *Apol.* I.65–67). For Patristic sources on the Eucharist, see Wainwright, "Lord's Supper"; J. N. D. Kelly, *Early Christian Doctrines* (San Francisco: Harper & Row, 1978), 193–99, 211–16, 294–95, 422–28, 440–55; G. Rouwhorst, "La celebration de l'eucharistie selon les Actes de Thomas," in *Omnes Circumadstantes: Contributions towards a History of the*

Role of the People in the Liturgy, ed. C. Caspers and M. Scheiders (Kampen: Uitgeversmaatschappij J. H. Kok 1990), 51–77.

[4] A. C. Thieslton, *The First Epistle to the Corinthians* (Grand Rapids: Eerdmans, 2000), 852–53, notes the ancient sources of Suetonius *Claudius* 18.2; Josephus *Antiquities* 3.320–21; Tacitus, *Annals* 12.43; and Dio Cassius, *History* 40.11. Acts 11:28 also claims a famine in the Roman world during the reign of Emperor Claudius (41–54 CE).

[5] Joseph Murphy-O'Conner lays out diagrams of the house in *St. Paul's Corinth: Texts and Archaeology* (Collegeville: Liturgical/ Glazier, 1983), 162, 165.

[6] Cf. Hofius, "Lord's Supper," 92; Gerd Theissen, *The Social Setting of Pauline Christianity* (Philadelphia: Fortress, 1982), 145–74. In what manner were the poor neglected? Hans-Josef Klauck prefers the idea that the wealthy ate early while slaves and common laborers still worked. By the time the "have nots" arrived for dinner, only meager leftovers remained along with the bread and wine rite. See Hans-Josef Klauck, *Herrenmahl und Hellenistischer Kult* (Münster: Aschendorff, 1982), 291–95. The time nuance here depends much on how a person translates the Greek word *prolambanô* ("to go ahead/anticipate" or "to take/devour") in 1 Corinthians 11:21 and *ekdechemai* ("wait for" or "care for") in 11:33. Hofius suggests the less popular alternative by arguing that if all persons ate what they brought, the poorer members would still go away hungry, and there is need to posit that a late arrival ("Lord's Supper," 92–93, 96).

[7] Ben Witherington suggests the drinking party (which he calls *convivium*) followed the banquet. See his *Conflict and Community in Corinth* (Grand Rapids: Eerdmans, 1995), 241. Outsiders may have interpreted these meetings as a type of *symposion*, after-dinner entertainment that included a topic of conversation. Paul mentions drinking the cup "after dinner" (1 Cor. 11:25), but when the excessive drinking started is not a major concern. Paul's sequential order reminiscences the order Jesus took the bread and wine during the Last Supper (cf. Luke 22:20).

[8] By the late fourth century we find agape meals prohibited because of their corruption. See Augustine, *Epistle 22 to Aurelius*; John Chrysostom, *Homily 27 on 1 Corinthians*; cf. Wainwright, "Lord's Supper, Love Feast," 692–93).

[9] C. K. Barrett, *The First Epistle to the Corinthians* (Peabody: Hendrickson, 1968), 273.

[10] H. Maccoby opines that Paul received this information through a vision. See H. Maccoby, "Paul and the Eucharist," *New Testament Studies* 37 (1991): 248, 262.

[11] Here the Greek words are *paralambenein* (similar to the Hebrew *qibbêl*) and *paradidonai* (resembling the Hebrew *mâsar*). The main exception in which Paul affirms a revelation directly from the Lord relates to his conversion experience and calling, which he discusses in Galatians 1:12. However, even here, if Luke has some factual merit about Paul's conversion, a believer named Ananias was summoned by the Lord to help instruct Paul about his calling (Acts 9:10–19; 22:12–16). Moreover, Joachim Jeremias shows that Paul's version of the Last Supper includes idioms alien to Paul, thus arguing against the view that the Lord's Supper tradition was something Paul originally came up with. See Joachim Jeremias, *The Eucharistic Words of Jesus* (London: SCM, 1966), 101–5.

[12] Some other records/allusions to the Lord's Supper in the New Testament besides the main texts include Mark 6:35–44 *and Synoptic parallels*; Mark 8:1–9, 14–21; Luke 13:26; 24:28–35; John 2:1–11; 6:1–14, 22–63; 19:34; Acts 2:42, 46; 20:7–11; 27:33–38; 1 Cor. 5:7–8; 10:3–4, 16–21; 16:22; Heb. 9:14–22; 1 Pet. 1:18–19; 2 Pet. 2:13; 1 John 5:6–8; Jude 12; Rev. 2:17; 3:20; 7:16–17; 19:5–9. For other early Christian sources, see Wainwright, "Lord's Supper, Love Feast," 686–94.

[13] For a concise chart of comparisons see Robert H. Stein, "Last Supper," in *Dictionary of Jesus and the Gospels*, ed. Joel B. Green, Scot McKnight, I. Howard Marshall (Leicester/Downers Grove: InterVarsity Press, 1992), 445. Marshall expounds on various theories of origin in *Last Supper and Lord's Supper* (reprint, Carlisle: Paternoster Press, 1993), 30–56. Mark/Matthew's account is sometimes considered historical narrative genre/Passover narrative whereas Paul or Luke/Paul is viewed as the genre of cultic aetiology/eucharistic narrative. See, e.g., Rudolf Pesch, *Das Abendmahl und Jesu Todesverständnis*. (Freiburg: Herder, 1978); see the critique of this view in B. F. Meyer, "The Expiation Motif in the Eucharistic Words," in *One Loaf, One Cup* (Macon: Peeters/Mercer University Press, 1993), 22–26. The distinction between the two traditions is interesting but should not be understood as mutually exclusive. Paul's version is not entirely void of an historical framework or even Passover assumptions (cf. 1 Cor. 5:6–8; 10:16; 11:23b). Luke takes on complex characteristics, and the book itself affirms derivation from multiple sources (Luke 1:1–3). Luke's longer Lord's Supper version seems more original than the shorter version; the former has a significantly greater amount of earlier witnesses to support its reading. Cf. B. Metzger, *A Textual Commentary on the Greek New Testament*, 3rd ed. (Stuttgart: German Bible Society/United Bible Societies, 1971), 173–77.

[14] Distinctions of this sort may suggest the Passover elements come from the Jerusalem church and are exemplified in Luke 22:15–18, whereas the Mark formula is older and related to the Qumran/Dead Sea Scrolls literature. See Karl Georg Kuhn, "The Lord's Supper and the Communal Meal at Qumran," in *The Scrolls and the New Testament*, ed. K. Stendahl with James H. Charlesworth (New York: Crossroad, 1992, 90–93. Differently, the two traditions may be categorized as the Jerusalem-Acts and Pauline-Hellenistic traditions. Cf. Hans Lietzmann, *Mass and the Lord's Supper* (Leiden: Brill, 1953), 204–8.

[15] Because early tradition and a good number of scholars maintain Luke as the author of Acts, the first person plural "we" in the Book of Acts refers to Luke's own participation in Paul's missionary journeys.

[16] William R. Farmer argues persuasively about this connection in "Peter and Paul, and the Tradition concerning 'The Lord's Supper' in 1 Cor 11:23–26," in *One Loaf, One Cup*, ed. Ben F. Meyer (Macon: Peeters/Mercer University Press, 1993), 35–55.

[17] Klauck, *Herrenmahl und Hellenistischer Kult*, lists an impressive amount of religious meal examples in the Greco-Roman world and posits that the Corinthian church's main meal took place before serving the bread and cup. Roman banquets normally held the religious-ceremonial aspects of a gathering after the meal. Cf. Dennis E. Smith, "Meals and Morality in Paul and His Word," *SBL 1981 Seminar Papers* (Chico: Scholars, 1981), 319–39. If the Corinthians kept the pattern of the Passover

meal, then the breaking of bread introduced the meal and the cup closed it. Paul says the cup offered "after dinner" (1 Cor. 11:25). Klauck rightly affirms that similarities between the Lord's Supper and pagan meals do not prove origins; yet a complete bifurcation between Hellenistic and Jewish perspectives is unwarranted.

[18] Rudolf Pesch, Joachim Jeremias, and Maurice Casey all discuss Semitisms in the Lord's Supper by comparing Aramaic equivalents with the Greek language of gospels. See Pesch, *Das Abendmahl und Jesu Todesverständnis*; Jeremias, *The Eucharistic Words of Jesus*, 173–86; Maurice Casey, *Aramaic Sources of Mark's Gospel* (Cambridge: Cambridge University Press, 1998), 219–52.

[19] Kuhn suggests that in Qumran meals, the Aaronic Messianic priest was the first to bless the meal and *tirosh* (wine), then the Davidic Messiah. The meal and drink belonged to the anticipated messiahs. See Kuhn's "The Lord's Supper and the Communal Meal at Qumran," 70–71.

[20] Lietzmann, *Mass and the Lord's Supper*, 160–71, 185. See Jeremias, *Eucharistic Words*, 26–36; Marshall, *Last Supper and Lord's Supper*, 20 for criticisms of non-Passover views.

[21] For Jewish memorial meals see Jeremiah 16:7 and cf. W. Von Meding, "1 Korinther 11,26: Vom geschichtlichen Grund des Abendmahls," *Evangelische Theologie* 6 (1975): 544–52; for Greco-Roman examples, see Klauck, *Herrenmahl*, 76–88. See J. D. G. Dunn, *The Theology of Paul the Apostle* (Grand Rapids: Eerdmans, 1998), 604, for criticisms of this type of meal.

[22] Mishnah Pesachim 10:7 forbids drinking wine between the third and fourth cup because "wine taken after food may cause insobriety and will thus prevent a sober conclusion of the *Hallel.*" See P. Blackman, *Mishnayoth*. Vol. 2. *Order Moed* 2nd ed. (Gateshead: Judaica Press, 1990), 220–21. As early as Jubilees 49:6 (c. 100 BCE) wine is associated with the Passover. References such as Deut. 26:5–11; Exod. 12; Jub. 49:6; Philo *De Spec. Leg.* 2.158; Jos. *Ant.* 2.316; assist in interpreting Passover *haggadah.* Specifications about the feast vary depending on tradition, but a footnote on Mishnah Pesachim 10 suggests a pre-70 CE origin (Blackman, *Mishnayoth,* 2: 218), lending credibility that these *seder* instructions may be similar to the ones Jesus and his disciples followed in the first century. We do not know to what extent Jesus would have followed them in the original Last Supper, but evidence in the Gospels seems to resemble the procedures. For the *seder* model in the Mishnah, see Blackman's Hebrew text and English translation in *Mishnayoth,* 217–22. For more examples, see Norman Theiss, "The Passover Feast of the New Covenant," *Interpretation* 48 (1994): 18–23; Jeremias, *Eucharistic Words,* 84–86; Thieslton, *1 Corinthians,* 758.

[23] Barry L. Bandstra, "Wine," in *International Standard Bible Encyclopedia*, ed. Geoffrey Bromiley (Grand Rapids: Eerdmans, 1988) 4:1068–72. mentions that it also became a tradition for the last cup to be set aside for Elijah's return ("Wine," 1071).

[24] For studies on Passover and Lord's Supper associations, see Gustav Dalmon, *Jesus-Jeshua* (reprint, New York: KTAV, 1971), 106–84; Jeremias, *Eucharistic Words,* 41–84; Marshall, *Last Supper and Lord's Supper,* 57–75.

[25] For later Jewish examples, see m. Pes. 7:9; Makk. 3:3.

[26] See Jeremias, *Eucharistic Words,* 44–46, for more Jewish sources.

[27] New Testament Greek uses *artos* for the Lord's Supper. Although the Septuagint uses *azuma* for unleavened bread, it also uses *artos* when referring to the unleavened bread. For sources, see Jeremias, *Eucharistic Words,* 62–66.

[28] Jeremias, *Eucharistic Words,* 221–22.

[29] Deborah Bleicher Carmichael, "David Daube on the Eucharist and the Passover Seder," *Journal for the Study of the New Testament* 42 (1991): 45–67; David Daube, *He That Cometh* (London: Diocesan Council, 1966).

[30] Carmichael, "David Daube on the Eucharist," 53–54. It is suggested that a family member strapped the *afikoman* to his shoulder, visited neighbors, and heralded the coming messiah. The later meaning and functions of the *afikoman* became distorted over time. The piece of bread is later considered an after-meal dessert. For various meanings, see Carmichael, 52–54. Carmichael also mentions *Peri Pascha,* a document written by Melito, second-century bishop of Sardis. This document preserves the Christian Quartodeciman tradition in which the early saints would await the coming messiah at the Passover feast. They considered Jesus as the Messiah in terms of *afikomenos,* similar to wording of *afikoman.* See Carmichael, 59–60.

[31] This meaning tends to support the unified concept of God's people and their messiah as expressed in "one loaf" and "one bread" in 1 Corinthians 10:16–17. However, as Carmichael admits, the *afikoman* ritual as stated "may not have been widely practiced"; indeed, the Passover was not celebrated in a standard way, and yet the early ritual does not reflect the later idea that *afikoman* refers merely to a game children play at Passover ("David Daube on the Eucharist," 49–50, 56).

[32] Carmichael, however, may be taking this theme too far by substituting the idea of self-revelation for self-surrender as the original intention of the Lord's Supper in relation to the broken bread. To buttress her claim, she plays down the importance of the wine, another symbol of sacrificial death ("David Daube on the Eucharist," 55, 63–67). It is unclear why the early church could not have entertained both ideas because the Eucharist takes on a multifaceted meaning.

[33] The normal Hebrew word for wine was *yayin* and the Aramaic *ch^amar.* New wine is read as *tîrôs* and is often used in the Dead Sea Scrolls literature. Other Hebrew words include *chemer, sobe',* and *'âsîs.* In Greek *oinos* is usually used for wine but *neos* and *gleukos* are also used at times. All words indicate a fermented grape (alcoholic) drink. The Hebrew *sêkâr* and Greek *sikera* refer to strong drink, a beverage fermented from barley. On the varieties of wine and fermented drinks in the ancient Hebrew, Jewish, and Christian world, see John Pairman Brown, "The Mediterranean Vocabulary of the Vine," *Vetus Testamentum* 19 (1969): 146–70; S. M. Paul, "Classifications of Wine in Mesopotamian and Rabbinic Sources," *Israel Exploration Journal* 25 (1975): 42–44; Odelia E. Alroy, "Kosher Wine," *Judaism* 39 (1990): 452–60; Duane F. Watson, "Wine," in *Dictionary of Jesus and the Gospels,* ed. J. B. Green, S. McKnight, I. H. Marshall (Leicester/Downers Grove: InterVarsity Press, 1992), 870–73; H. Seesemann, *oinos* in *Theological Dictionary of the New Testament,* ed. Gerhard Friedrich and trans. G. W. Bromiley (Grand Rapids: Eerdmans, 1967), 5:162–66; Bandstra, "Wine," 4:1068–1072.

[34] For a perspective supporting the fourth cup, consult D. Cohn-Sherbok, "A Jewish note on τὸ ποτήριον τῆ^ϝ εὐλογία^ϝ," *New Testament Studies* 27 (1981): 704–9; for the third cup, see P. Sigal, "Another Note to 1 Cor. 10:16," *New Testament Studies* 29 (1983): 134–39. Joseph and Aseneth mention a "cup of blessing" and "cup of immortality" in relation to a cultic meal (Jos. As. 8:5, 9). Nothing much should be made from the phrase "fruit of the vine" uttered during the third cup. I. Howard Marshall contends that these words were mentioned over other cups also. See I. Howard Marshall, *The Gospel of Luke: A Commentary on the Greek Text* (Grand Rapids: Eerdmans, 1978), 797. It is possible that Luke's mentioning of the cup twice (Luke 22:17–18, 20) might indicate two different cups.

[35] On wine in the Passover meal, see Jubilees 49:6–9; b. Pesachim. 109a; m. Pesachim. 10:1; Berakot. 8:8; Sukka 2:5. If John 2:1–11 alludes to the Eucharist, this would be another example, but it is probably best to affirm it only as evidence that wine was important for festivities. On wine and special occasions, see B. Bandstra, "Wine," in *International Standard Bible Encyclopedia,* ed. G. Bromiley (Grand Rapids: Eerdmans, 1988), 4:1070.

[36] On the color red in relation to Passover wine, see j. Pes. 10:37c 27; cf. Prov. 23:31; b. Sanh. 70a.

[37] For early Jewish sources in relation to the interpretation of the *Hallel* Psalms, see Jeremias, *Eucharistic Words,* 256–61.

[38] For more Jewish references, see Exodus Rab. 15:1 [on 12:2]; 18:11–12 [on 12:42]; Jeremias, 59, 206–7; Daube, *He That Cometh.*

[39] Luke adds the idea of sacrifice with the bread: "this is my body which is given for you" (Luke 22:19; cf. 1 Cor. 11:24).

[40] Luke and Paul's version of the Lord's Supper add the word "new" before "covenant." Even so, both the Synoptic Gospels and Paul mention a "covenant" related to the Lord's Supper, and there seems to be no good reason for arguing against Jesus attempting to establish a new sacrificial tradition that evening.

[41] We should not infer from this, however, that only Jesus and the twelve ate the Last Supper. Maurice Casey in his *Aramaic Sources of Mark's Gospel* (Cambridge: Cambridge University Press, 1998), 226–28, argues convincingly that more followers of Jesus may have been present.

[42] B. F. Meyer, "The Expiation Motif in the Eucharistic Words: A Key to the History of Jesus?" 18–19, presents five New Testament aspects related to the expiation motif found in Isaiah 53. First, the word combination of "poured out" with "many" connects the Eucharist text of Mark 14:24 (cf. Matt. 26:28; Luke 22:20; John 6:51) with Isaiah 53:11–12; second, the confession formula that Christ died "for our sins" in 1 Corinthians 15:3–5 reflects Isaiah 53:5; third, the formula "gave himself for" + genitive in Galatians 2:20; Ephesians 5:2, 25 echo Isaiah 53:5, 12 (Targum) or 53:6 (LXX), while the formulas in Gal. 1:4; 1 Tim. 2:6; Titus 2:14; Mark 10:45; and Matt. 20:28 resonate Isaiah 53:10; fourth, phrases related to "suffering for" + genitive (Rom. 5:6–8; 2 Cor. 5:14–15; 1 Pet. 2:21; 3:18) relate to several Isaiah 53 passages; and fifth, Romans 8:3 and 2 Corinthians 5:21 refer to Isaiah 53:10 (LXX). Meyers notes that expiation faith formulas are "pre-Pauline," even though Paul extrapolates on their meaning (e.g., Rom. 3:21–26; 4:22–25; 5:6–11; 8:32). Other

New Testament authors pick up this theme (John 10:11, 15; Heb. 7:27; Pet. 3:18; 1 John 3:16).

[43] Here the "many" must be understood in the Aramaic sense of all-inclusive (cf. Matt. 8:11; John 6:51; 1 Tim. 2:6). See Meyers ("The Expiation Motif," 25–26) and Jeremias (*Eucharistic Words,* 179–82) for argument.

[44] Cf. R. E. O. White, *The Biblical Doctrine of Initiation* (London: Hodder & Stoughton, 1960), 222–23. White opines for the corporate personality of this Servant, with the collective community influencing Paul's perception of believers mystically "in Christ."

[45] "Proclaiming" in this sense probably refers to verbal recollections of the Passover narrative and the words of Jesus spoken at the Last Supper. See Barrett, *The First Epistle to the Corinthians,* 270. The Aramaic *maranatha* phrase ("our Lord come" 1 Cor. 16:22; cf. Rev. 22:20) later became a proclamation associated with the Eucharist (cf. Did. 10:6).

[46] For elaboration the Isaiah texts and sources, see B. J. Oropeza, "Echoes of Isaiah in the Rhetoric of Paul: New Exodus, Wisdom, and the Humility of the Cross in Utopian-Apocalyptic Expectations," in *The Intertexture of Apocalyptic Discourse in the New Testament,* ed. Duane F. Watson (Atlanta: Society of Biblical Literature, 2002), 92–97.

[47] Suffice it to say that the Synoptic writers connect the Passover exodus with the Lord's Supper and speak of the latter as inaugurating a covenant different from that of Moses. The following sources are useful for establishing the argument: Dale C. Allison, *The New Moses: A Matthean Typology* (Minneapolis: Augsburg Fortress, 1993); R. E. Watts, *Isaiah's New Exodus and Mark* (Tübingen: Mohr–Siebeck, 1997); D. W. Pao, *Acts and the Isaianic New Exodus* (Grand Rapids: Baker, 2002); Ulrich Mauser, *Christ in the Wilderness: The Wilderness Theme in the Second Gospel and Its Basis in the Biblical Tradition* (London: SCM, 1963). For passages in other early Christian traditions, see B. J. Oropeza, *Paul and Apostasy: Eschatology, Perseverance, and Falling Away in the Corinthian Congregation* (Tübingen: Mohr–Siebeck, 2000), 200–3; F. L. Fisher, "The New and Greater Exodus: the Exodus Pattern in the New Testament, *Southwestern Journal of Theology* 20 (1977): 69–79; R. E. Nixon, *The Exodus in the New Testament* (London: Tyndale, 1963); David Daube, *The Exodus Pattern in the Bible* (London: Faber & Faber, 1963).

[48] Geoffrey Wainwright, *Eucharist and Eschatology* (Oxford: Oxford University Press, 1981), 21–25, observes five distinct early Jewish foci combining Messianic and futurist aspects in reference to eating: first, abundance of food (4 Ezra 8:52–54; 8:1; 2 Bar. 29:5); second, new manna (2 Bar. 29:8; m. Qoh 1:9); third, Passover (Jos. Wars 5.98ff; 6.290–95; cf. John 6:3–15; fourth, future feasting (1 En. 62:13–16; cf. Luke 14:15); and fifth, Qumran material (Psa. 37 4Qpsa. 37 2.10–11; 1Qsa 2:11–22).

[49] D. A. Hagner, *Matthew 1–13* (Dallas: Word Books, 1993), 149.

[50] Cf. Eduard Schweizer, *The Lord's Supper According to the New Testament* (Philadelphia: Fortress/Facet, 1967), 3.

[51] For sources, consult Robert H. Stein, "Wine-Drinking in New Testament Times," *Christianity Today* 19, June 20, 1975, 9–10, and John Brown, "Mediterranean Vocabulary," 154–55. Perhaps the earliest Christian text supporting water and wine mixture, 1 Timothy 5:23 aside, comes from Justin Martyr, c. 155 CE (*Apologia* 1. 67.5). Although the Greek normally has *oinos* for wine, it often refers to mixed wine; unmixed wine was named *akratesteron* wine.

[52] Stein, "Wine Drinking," 11.

[53] Cf. Marshall, *Last Supper and Lord's Supper*, 63.

[54] Thieslton, *First Epistle to the Corinthians*, 761–67 elongates this idea.

[55] Cf. Hofius, "Lord's Supper," 113.

[56] Dale B. Martin's *The Corinthian Body* (New Haven: Yale University Press, 1995) provides helpful insight related to disease invading the body.

[57] Christopher Mearns, "Bread and Wine: Seven Propositions," *Theology* 84 (1981): 279.

[58] Michael Welker, *What Happens in Holy Communion* (Grand Rapids: Eerdmans, 2000), 67, makes similar observations.

[59] Cf. Suzanne Watts Henderson, "'If Anyone Hungers…': An Integrated Reading of 1 Cor 11.17–34," *New Testament Studies* 48 (2002): 195–207.

[60] John 6 is often interpreted as literal blood and flesh in this regard, but Mearns ("Bread and Wine," 279–80) notes that in John 6, as typical in the rest of John's Gospel, movement progresses from literal to spiritual (Compare John 6:5, 51–58 with 6:23, 35, 63, 68; cf. John 4:7 with 4:14; 4:31 with 4:34).

[61] Cf. Hofius, "The Lord's Supper and the Lord's Supper Tradition," 104–9. In the quote (from p. 104), the subquotation marks have been replaced with italics. The verdict is still out on whether Hofius is correct in affirming Paul's use of "proclaim" as best fitting Eucharistic prayers. The prayer, at least consecration aspects, may be a later development first evidenced in the second century with Justin's *Apology* 1.65.5; 66.2 (cf. Dunn, *The Theology of Paul the Apostle*, 614).

[62] It will not do to respond that the Corinthians, not Paul, were the only ones who understood the Eucharist in terms of spiritual eating in 1 Corinthians 10:3–4. Paul almost certainly considers Christ to be somehow present at the meal (as the spiritual "rock") and associates grace with this event. I argue this point more thoroughly in *Paul and Apostasy*, 106–16.

[63] Dunn identifies "the table of the Lord" (1 Cor. 10:21) in terms of Christ hosting the meal (*Theology of Paul*, 620–21 cf. 1 Cor. 11:23–25; Philo *Spec. Leg.* 1.221; Aristides *Or.* 45.27[360.10–20]).

[64] Thieslton, *The First Epistle to the Corinthians*, 879.

[65] Ibid., 880.

[66] For a similar perspective, see Marshall, *Last Supper and Lord's Supper*, 150; Schweizer, *The Lord's Supper According to the New Testament*, 37. On blessing and grace conferred through eating and drinking in ancient Jewish sources, consult Jeremias, *Eucharistic Words*, 233–34.

[67] Mearns, "Bread and Wine," 279.

[68] Cf. Wainwright, "Lord's Supper, Love Feast," 687.

[69] Cf. Oropeza, *Paul and Apostasy*, 87–90, 106–11.

[70] The term as it relates to worship is used by Jürgen Moltmann, *The Church in the Power of the Spirit A Contribution to Messianic Ecclesiology* (Minneapolis: Fortress, 1993), 272ff, and elaborated by David Nelson, "Messianic Intermezzo: Eschatology, Spirit, and Worship in the Church," in *Looking into the Future*, ed. D. W. Baker. Grand Rapids: Baker Academic, 2001), 315–24. Harald Sahlin, "The New Exodus of Salvation according to St. Paul," in *The Root of the Vine: Essays in Biblical Theology*, ed. Anton Fridrichsen et al. (London: Dacre, 1953), 93–94, uses similar language by speaking of the Eucharist as the "viaticum" for the Christians and antitype of water and manna provided by God during the original exodus (cf. 1 Cor. 10:3–4, 16–17).

[71] The phrase is cited from Patricia Wilson-Kastner, *Sacred Drama: A Spirituality of Christian Liturgy* (Minneapolis: Augsburg Fortress, 1999), 97–98.

Bibliography

Allison, Dale C. *The New Moses: A Matthean Typology.* Minneapolis: Augsburg Fortress, 1993.

Alroy, Odelia E. "Kosher Wine." *Judaism* 39 (1990): 452–60.

Bandstra, Barry L. "Wine." In *International Standard Bible Encyclopedia.* Edited by Geoffrey Bromiley. Vol. 4. Grand Rapids: Eerdmans, 1988.

Barrett, C. K. *The First Epistle to the Corinthians.* Peabody: Hendrickson, 1968.

Barth, Marcus. *Rediscovering the Lord's Supper.* Atlanta: John Knox, 1988.

Blackman, Philip. *Mishnayoth.* Vol. 2. *Order Moed.* 2nd ed. Gateshead: Judaica Press, 1990.

Brown, John Pairman. "The Mediterranean Vocabulary of the Vine." *Vetus Testamentum* 19 (1969): 146–70.

Carmichael, Deborah Bleicher. "David Daube on the Eucharist and the Passover Seder." *Journal for the Study of the New Testament* 42 (1991): 46–67.

Casey, Maurice. *Aramaic Sources of Mark's Gospel.* SNTSMS 102. Cambridge: Cambridge University Press, 1998.

Chilton, Bruce. "The Eucharist: Exploring Its Origins." *Bible Review,* Dec. 1994, 37–43.

Chrysostom, John. *Homily 27 on 1 Corinthians.*

Cohn-Sherbok, D. "A Jewish Note on τὸ ποτήριον τῆ^F εὐλογία^F." *New Testament Studies* 27 (1981): 704–9.

Dalmon, Gustaf. *Jesus-Jeshua: Studies in the Gospels.* Reprint. New York: KTAV Publishing House, 1971.

Daube, David. *The Exodus Pattern in the Bible.* London: Faber & Faber, 1963.

———. *He That Cometh.* London: Diocesan Council, 1966.

Dix, Gregory. *The Shape of the Liturgy.* Reprint. London: Dacre, 1975.

Dunn, J. D. G. *The Theology of Paul the Apostle.* Grand Rapids: Eerdmans, 1998.

Farmer, William R. "Peter and Paul, and the Tradition Concerning 'The Lord's Supper' in 1 Cor. 11:23–26." In *One Loaf, One Cup: Ecumenical Studies of 1 Cor. 11 and Other Eucharistic Texts.* The Cambridge Conference on the Eucharist August 1988. Edited by Ben F. Meyer. Macon: Peeters/Mercer University Press, 1993.

Fisher, F. L. "The New and Greater Exodus: the Exodus Pattern in the New Testament, *Southwestern Journal of Theology* 20 (1977): 69–79.

Hagner, D. A. *Matthew 1–13*. Dallas: Word Books, 1993.

Henderson, Suzanne Watts. "'If Anyone Hungers…': An Integrated Reading of 1 Cor. 11:17–34." *New Testament Studies* 48 (2002), 195–208.

Hoehner, Harold W. "Chronology." In *Dictionary of Jesus and the Gospels*. Edited by Joel B. Green, Scot McKnight, I. Howard Marshall. Leicester/Downers Grove: InterVarsity Press, 1992.

Hofius, Otfried. "The Lord's Supper and the Lord's Supper Tradition: Reflections on 1 Corinthians 11:23b–25." *One Loaf, One Cup: Ecumenical Studies of 1 Cor 11 and Other Eucharistic Texts*. The Cambridge Conference on the Eucharist August 1988. Edited by Ben F. Meyer. Macon: Peeters/Mercer University Press, 1993.

Jaubert, A. *The Date of the Last Supper*. Staten Island: Alba, 1965.

Jeremias, Joachim. *The Eucharistic Words of Jesus*. London: SCM, 1966.

Käsemann, Ernst. "The Pauline Doctrine of the Lord's Supper." *Essays on New Testament Themes*. SBT 41. London: SCM, 1964.

Kelly, J. N. D. *Early Christian Doctrines*. San Francisco: Harper & Row, 1978.

Klauck, Hans-Josef. *Herrenmahl und Hellenistischer Kult: Eine religionsgeschichtliche Untersuchung zum ersten Korintherbrief.* Münster: Aschendorff, 1982.

Knoch, Otto. "'Do This in Memory of Me!' (Luke 22:20; 1 Corinthians 11:24ff.): The Celebration of the Eucharist in the Primitive Christian Communities." In *One Loaf, One Cup: Ecumenical Studies of 1 Cor 11 and Other Eucharistic Texts*. The Cambridge Conference on the Eucharist August 1988. Edited by Ben F. Meyer. Macon: Peeters/Mercer University Press, 1993.

Kuhn, Karl Georg. "The Lord's Supper and Communal Meal at Qumran." In *The Scrolls and the New Testament*. Edited by Krister Stendahl with James H. Charlesworth. Christian Original Library. New York: Crossroad, 1992.

Lampe, Peter. "The Eucharis: Identifying with Christ on the Cross." *Interpretation* 48 (1994): 136–49.

Leon-Dufour, Xavier. *Sharing the Eucharistic Bread*. New York: Paulist Press, 1987.

Lietzmann, Hans. *Mass and the Lord's Supper: A Study in the History of the Liturgy*. Leiden: Brill, 1953.

Maccoby, Hyam. "Paul and the Eucharist." *New Testament Studies* 37 (1991): 247–67.

Marshall, I. Howard. *Last Supper and Lord's Supper*. Reprint. Carlisle: Paternoster Press, 1993.

―――. "Lord's Supper." In *Dictionary of Paul and His Letters*. Edited by Gerald F. Hawthorn, Ralph P. Martin, Daniel G. Reid. Leicester/Downers Grove: InterVarsity Press, 1993.

―――. *The Gospel of Luke: A Commentary on the Greek Text*. Grand Rapids: Eerdmans, 1978.

Martin, Dale B. *The Corinthian Body*. New Haven: Yale University Press, 1995.

Mauser, Ulrich. *Christ in the Wilderness: The Wilderness Theme in the Second Gospel and Its Basis in the Biblical Tradition*. London: SCM, 1963.

Mearns, Christopher. "Bread and Wine: Seven Propositions." *Theology* 84 (1981): 279–81.

Metzger, B. *A Textual Commentary on the Greek New Testament.* 3rd ed. Stuttgart: German Bible Society/United Bible Societies, 1971.

Meyer, Ben F. "The Expiation Motif in the Eucharistic Words: A Key to the History of Jesus? In *One Loaf, One Cup: Ecumenical Studies of 1 Cor 11 and Other Eucharistic Texts.* The Cambridge Conference on the Eucharist August 1988. Edited by Ben F. Meyer. Macon: Peeters/Mercer University Press, 1993.

Moltmann, Jürgen. *The Church in the Power of the Spirit: A Contribution to Messianic Ecclesiology.* Minneapolis: Fortress, 1993.

Moule, C. F. D. "The Judgement Theme in the Sacraments." In *The Background of the New Testament and its Eschatology: In Honor of Charles Harold Dodd.* Edited by W. E. Davies and D. Daube. Cambridge: Cambridge University Press, 1956.

Murphy-O'Conner, Joseph. *St. Paul's Corinth: Texts and Archaeology.* Collegeville: Liturgical/Glazier, 1983.

Nelson, David. "Messianic Intermezzo: Eschatology, Spirit, and Worship in the Church." In *Looking into the Future: Evangelical Studies in Eschatology.* Edited by David W. Baker. Grand Rapids: Baker Academic, 2001.

Nixon, R. E. *The Exodus in the New Testament.* London: Tyndale, 1963.

O'Neil. J. C. "Bread and Wine." *Scottish Journal of Theology* 48 (1995): 169–84.

Oropeza, B. J. "Echoes of Isaiah in the Rhetoric of Paul: New Exodus, Wisdom, and Humility of the Cross in Utopian-Apocalyptic Expections." In *The Intertexture of Apocalyptic Discourse in the New Testament.* Edited by Duane F. Watson. SBL Symposium Series 14. Atlanta: Society of Biblical Literature, 2002.

———. *Paul and Apostasy: Eschatology, Perseverance, and Falling Away in the Corinthian Congregation.* WUNT 2/115. Tübingen: Mohr–Siebeck, 2000.

Pao, D. W. *Acts and the Isaianic New Exodus.* Grand Rapids: Baker, 2002.

Paul, S. M. "Classifications of Wine in Mesopotamian and Rabbinic Sources." *Israel Exploration Journal* 25 (1975): 42–44.

Pesch, Rudolf. *Das Abendmahl und Jesu Todesverständnis.* Freiburg: Herder, 1978.

Raymond, Irving Woodworth. *The Teaching of the Early Church on the use of Wine and Strong Drink.* Columbia University Studies in the Social Sciences 286. Reprint. New York: AMS Press, 1970.

Reumann, J. *The Supper of the Lord: The New Testament, Ecumenical Dialogues, and Faith and Order on Eucharist.* Philadelphia: Fortress, 1985.

Rordorf, W., et al. *The Eucharist of the Early Christians.* New York: Pueblo, 1978.

Rossing, Barbara. "'Are you able to drink the cup?' Grape Juice at Holy Communion." *Currents in Theology and Mission* 24 (1997): 267–72.

Rouwhorst, Gerard. "La celebration de l'eucharistie selon les Actes de Thomas." *Omnes Circumadstantes: Contributions towards a History of the Role of the People in the Liturgy.* Presented to Herman Wegman. Edited by Charles Caspers and Marc Scheiders. Kampen: Uitgeversmaatschappij J. H. Kok, 1990.

Sahlin, Harald. "The New Exodus of Salvation according to St. Paul." In *The Root of the Vine: Essays in Biblical Theology.* Edited by Anton Fridrichsen and other members of Uppsala University. London: Dacre, 1953.

Schweizer, Eduard. *The Lord's Supper According to the New Testament.* BS 18. Trans. by James M. Davis, tr. Philadelphia: Fortress Press/Facet Books, 1967.

Seesemann, Heinrich. *Oikos.* In *Theological Dictionary of the New Testament.* Vol. 5. Edited by Gerhard Friedrich and trans. by Geoffrey W. Bromiley. Grand Rapids: Eerdmans, 1967.

Sigal, P. "Another Note to 1 Cor. 10:16," *New Testament Studies* 29 (1983): 134–39.

Smith, Dennis E. "Meals and Morality in Paul and His World." *SBL 1981 Seminar Papers.* Chico: Scholars, 1981.

Smith, Ralph F. "Eucharistic Faith and Practice." *Interpretation* 48 (1994): 5–16.

Stein, Robert H. "Last Supper." In *Dictionary of Jesus and the Gospels.* Edited by Joel B. Green, Scot McKnight, and I. Howard Marshall. Leicester/Downers Grove: InterVarsity Press, 1992.

———. "Wine-Drinking in New Testament Times." *Christianity Today* 19, June 20, 1975, 9–11.

Strack, Hermann L., and Paul Billerbeck. *Kommentar zum Neuen Testament aus Talmud und Midrasch.* Vol. 2. Munich: C. H. Becksche, 1924.

Taylor, Justin. "La Fraction du pain en Luc-Actes." *The Unity of Luke-Acts.* Bibliotheca ephemeridum Theologicarum Lovaniensium 142. Uitgeverij Peeters Leuven: Leuven University Press, 1999.

Theiss, Norman. "The Passover Feast of the New Covenant." *Interpretation* 48 (1994): 17–35.

Theissen, Gerd. *The Social Setting of Pauline Christianity: Essays on Corinth.* Philadelphia: Fortress, 1982.

Thieslton, A. C. *The First Epistle to the Corinthians.* Grand Rapids: Eerdmans, 2000.

Van Cangh, Jean-Marie. "Evolution in the Tradition of the Last Supper (Mk 14,22–26 and par.)." *Antikes Judentum und Frühes Christentum. Festschrift für Hartmut Stegemann zum 65. Gebuststag. Beihefte zur Zeitschrift für die neutestamentliche Wissenschaft.* Edited by Bernd Kollmann, Wolfgang Reinbold, and Annette Steudel. Berlin: Walter de Gruyter, 1999.

Von Meding, Wichmann. "1 Korinther 11,26: Vom geschichtlichen Grund des Abendmahls." *Evangelische Theologie* 6 (1975): 544–52.

Wainwright, Geoffrey. *Eucharist and Eschatology.* Oxford: Oxford University, 1981.

———. "Lord's Supper, Love Feast." In *Dictionary of the Later New Testament and Its Developments.* Edited by Ralph P. Martin and Peter H. Davids. Leicester/Downers Grove: InterVarsity Press, 1997.

Watson, Duane F. "Wine." In *Dictionary of Jesus and the Gospels.* Edited by Joel B. Green, Scot McKnight, and I. Howard Marshall. Leicester/Downers Grove: InterVarsity Press, 1992.

Watts, R. E. *Isaiah's New Exodus and Mark.* Tübingen: Mohr–Siebeck, 1997.

Welker, Michael. *What Happens in Holy Communion.* Grand Rapids: Eerdmans, 2000.

White, R. E. O. *The Biblical Doctrine of Initiation.* London: Hodder & Stoughton, 1960.

Wilson-Kastner, Patricia. *Sacred Drama: A Spirituality of Christian Liturgy.* Minneapolis: Augsburg Fortress, 1999.

Winter, B. W. "The Lords' Supper at Corinth: An Alternative Reconstruction." *Reformed Theological Review* 37 (1978): 73–82.

Witherington, Ben. *Conflict and Community in Corinth.* Grand Rapids: Eerdmans, 1995.

Watson, Duane F. "Wine." In *Dictionary of Jesus and the Gospels*. Edited by Joel B. Green, Scot McKnight, and I. Howard Marshall. Leicester/Downers Grove: InterVarsity Press, 1992.

Watts, R. E. *Isaiah's New Exodus and Mark*. Tübingen: Mohr–Siebeck, 1997.

Welker, Michael. *What Happens in Holy Communion*. Grand Rapids: Eerdmans, 2000.

White, R. E. O. *The Biblical Doctrine of Initiation*. London: Hodder & Stoughton, 1960.

Wilson-Kastner, Patricia. *Sacred Drama: A Spirituality of Christian Liturgy*. Minneapolis: Augsburg Fortress, 1999.

Winter, B. W. "The Lords' Supper at Corinth: An Alternative Reconstruction." *Reformed Theological Review* 37 (1978): 73–82.

Witherington, Ben. *Conflict and Community in Corinth*. Grand Rapids: Eerdmans, 1995.

3 The Collar and the Bottle: Film Portrayals of Drinking Clergy

Teresa Blythe

Although most of us know that many clergypersons consume an alcoholic beverage now and then, is it not still a bit of an eyebrow-raiser whenever we see one holding a drink? Not to mention a downright shock to see one drunk? It is that titillating "oh my" reaction that filmmakers look for. The minister (usually a male) provides the filmmaker with a ready excuse to talk about God—after all, since one expects that of a "man of God"—and his drinking will convince us that he is thoroughly flawed and human, just like us. "We find ourselves in a contradictory age in which secularity and religious images co-exist."[1] Visible alcohol consumption suggests that the clergyperson indeed might be prone to the kind of emotional highs and lows that make for visual interest in films.

Thus, it is not surprising to find the drinking priest or minister as a memorable character in a number of modern major motion pictures. Think of *Mass Appeal* in 1984, *Priest* in 1994, and *Keeping the Faith* in 2000. All of these films portray leading characters—using and sometimes abusing alcohol. In none of the cases is the alcohol ever the main point of the narrative (as it was in *28 Days* or *Leaving Las Vegas*). Instead, alcohol is a statement about the character using the substance.

Using several popular films as a context for study, this chapter explores five prominent themes regarding clergy and alcohol, considering what filmmakers seem to think viewers believe about clergy and alcohol:

- Alcohol as painkiller
- Alcohol as the antidote to fear
- Alcohol as part of the culture of clergy (specifically a celibate clergy)
- Alcohol as "truth serum"
- Alcohol as barrier to transformation

Many times when clergy appear in a film, they are from the Roman Catholic tradition, possibly because there are many visual clues, such as vestments, gestures, and rituals that say "Catholic clergy." Because most of the examples here involve Catholic priests, we'll begin our discussion with the two non-Catholic portrayals.

Leap of Faith (Paramount Pictures, 1992)

If you want to give up the bottle, who you gonna talk to? Someone who's never touched a drop?
—Faith Healer Jonas Nightingale in *Leap of Faith*

Leap of Faith features fake faith healer Jonas Nightingale (played by Steve Martin) who roams from town to town making money from donations received in his healing worship services. Nightingale uses secret microphones and spies to trick the crowd into thinking he has special spiritual gifts, such as "second sight" or healing powers. Some of his "healed people" are shills that come in with crutches and walk out on their own after being touched by Nightingale.

We first see Nightingale drinking while doing a radio show in Rust Water, Kansas, where his bus has broken down. He even takes a swig from a bottle while preaching! He also drinks from a flask in front of the sheriff during a serious conversation; in the midst of a fight with his assistant after a real miracle occurs in his service; and later he gets so drunk he starts to yell at the large Jesus on a cross inside his worship tent, asking, "Why'd you make so many suckers?" It is scenes like these that make defenders of the evangelical strand of Christianity livid. Tim LaHaye, the now famous co-creator of the *Left Behind* book series, and David Noebel, head of Summit Ministries, argue that "volumes could be written on how Hollywood has devastated America's morals in the past half-century.[2] Their claim that "many films show the seamy side of America" could be applied without much difficulty to churches, faith communities, and even films such as *Leap of Faith*.[3]

For the makers of *Leap of Faith*, Nightingale's drinking appears to be designed to further confirm in our mind that he is a fraud and he is not concerned with people smart enough to figure out that he is a fraud. Hence, the drinking in front of the sheriff—who knows he is a fake. Nightingale also drinks when he is angry and after he is confronted with what appears to be a true healing.

There is a direct relationship between drinking and religion here. When Nightingale realizes that God can and will work even sometimes through a fraud, he suddenly realizes he is no longer in charge. For a con man who made his living manipulating situations in order to make money, this is enough of a realization that he turns to alcohol as the antidote to his fear.

The Apostle (October Films, 1997)

The Lord don't want me drinkin'.
—Fugitive-turned-revivalist preacher Sonny in *The Apostle*

Many critics consider *The Apostle* to be one of the most powerful films ever made about a "man of God"—a man who is complex, gifted, and deeply flawed. "Sonny," a Texas Holiness preacher (played by Robert Duvall who also wrote the script for the film), is a sincere and talented preacher in a broken marriage. Not portrayed as a heavy drinker, the one pivotal scene in this film in which Sonny is seen taking a drink is so brief that if you blink you might miss it. Sonny takes a sip from a flask upon arriving at a softball game where his estranged wife and son are socializing with the youth minister, a man with whom Sonny's wife has been having an affair. The combination of the alcohol and Sonny's unmanageable anger end in tragedy as Sonny beats the youth minister with a baseball bat. The young man goes into a coma and eventually dies. Knowing he is guilty of attempted murder, Sonny hits the road, fakes his own death, changes his name, renovates a small country church in Louisiana, and returns to preaching. He is not seen drinking again.

For Sonny, drinking appears to be a weakness that feeds his greater flaw—violent acts of anger. There is no suggestion here that Sonny drinks because of his lifestyle. In fact, Sonny drinks in spite of his calling, for, in the Holiness tradition, any use of alcohol is frowned upon.

In this film, we are led to believe that the alcohol use was just one in a string of sins leading up to the murder. Alcohol is one of Sonny's barriers to a truly holy and transformed life. As mentioned before, portrayals of Catholic priests who drink are easier to find.

Going My Way (Paramount Pictures, 1944)

~Good stuff!
~Oh, yes!
—Frs. O'Malley and Fitzgibbon with a goodbye drink in *Going My Way*

Winner of a number of Academy Awards the year it was released, *Going My Way* includes two important drinking scenes. Father O'Malley is sent to the financially strapped St. Dominic's parish to revive the congregation and quietly take the reins from the older Father Fitzgibbon, an Irishman who has given much of his life to that one parish. Fitzgibbon figures out that he is being "retired" and, as one might predict, the generation gap causes tension between the two priests. O'Malley— played by Bing Crosby as the most likable guy on earth—looks for ways to improve the relationship under the adverse conditions.

This improvement occurs while sharing a bottle. O'Malley encourages Fitzgibbon to "take a little something" to warm up after spending a lonely evening sulking out in the rain. The elder priest directs O'Malley to the place where he hides his "little something"—in the bookcase behind a book entitled *The Life of General Grant*. It is kept in the special wooden music box that his mother gave him. She sends him a bottle of Irish whiskey every Christmas, and he tries to make it last all year. Looking at the box and listening to it play his favorite Irish lullaby, Fitzgibbon begins to reminisce about his elderly mother and how he kept putting off a trip to Ireland to see her because of financial problems at the parish. O'Malley tells the older priest that his mother died many years ago. They drink to "mothers gone and far away."

This scene indicates that the priests drink for several reasons: First, it is stated, with a wink, that the alcohol is for medicinal purposes— supposedly to ward off the elderly priest catching a cold from being out in the rain. Then they drink to remember, to cement their relationship, and to kill the pain of being separated from their beloved mothers. There is also a sense that drinking is smiled upon in the Irish culture, so it is only natural that two Irish priests would share a nightcap.

A second scene in *Going My Way* is similar to the first—it is a bonding experience. As Father O'Malley is leaving the parish to do similar work in a new parish, Father Fitzgibbons opens his wooden music box to pour a celebratory goodbye drink for the two of them. The drinking scenes in *Going My Way* are bookends marking the beginning and end of the relationship between the priests. However, where they were slightly mournful in the first scene, the two men were blessing one another in the final scene.

Because *Going My Way* was, in 1944, feel-good escapism from World War II, it is no surprise that the drinking has a harmless and uplifting feel to it. In James A. Fischer's literary study, *Priests*, he notes that the media "use priests and monks and nuns because they are instantly identifiable with certain values the public either thinks it embraces or wishes it could."[4] Certainly in this film, priests are used to show the value of religious life in a community. Only a few years later, John Ford's 1947 film *The Fugitive* adapted Graham Greene's novel *The Power and the Glory*, a book that had portrayed "how a very *un*heroic alcoholic priest became a saint and martyr." It is noteworthy that "the film omitted all these negative features, presenting an uncomplicated Catholic superman."[5] Even so, *Going My Way* does not show viewers how human or flawed these priests are. Rather, it depicts them using alcohol as a way to open up to one another, disclosing parts of their life that have been painful. We will see this theme of "alcohol as truth-serum" used again in the film *Priest* 50 years later.

M*A*S*H* (Twentieth Century Fox, 1970)

Cold, filthy, lonely, scared, bored, tired, frightened and very drowsy.
—Hawkeye and Trapper's reasons for drinking too much in *M*A*S*H**

Robert Altman's classic film about a medical unit in the Korean War, *M*A*S*H** is interesting to evaluate because everyone in it *but* the

Catholic priest drinks at almost every off-duty opportunity. There is one scene at the end of the film in which the priest (played by Rene Auberjonois) pops open a celebratory bottle of champagne after the men of the 4077th unit win a football game, but he is not shown drinking. In the few scenes involving Father Mulcahy, the viewer gets the idea that he is so devoted to saying the right words, doing the right rituals, and being faithful to the role of "religious professional" that he would not dare think of drinking. He is, as Philip Jenkins puts it in *The New Anti-Catholicism: The Last Acceptable Prejudice,* "at worst an amiable fool," quintessentially out of touch with the men and women he serves.[6]

Fans of the television show that was spun off from the film, however, will recall an episode entitled "Alcoholics Unanimous," first aired November 12, 1974, in which Father Mulcahy (played by William Christopher) ironically takes a drink before giving a mandated sermon on the evils of drinking. He embarrasses himself by losing his place in the sermon and mush-mouthing his way through a reflection on Leviticus 10: "Drink no wine or strong drink ... when you enter the tent of meeting, that you may not die." Because the commanding officer was concerned about alcoholism among the troops, everyone was required to attend Father Mulcahy's sermon, and the sheer number of people listening to him preach caused the priest anxiety. So he drinks to alleviate the fear of addressing such a crowd.

Everyone else in the M*A*S*H* unit, both in the film and television series, drinks for different reasons: out of boredom, in order to be sociable, and for comfort in the face of the suffering of war. In a telling bit of dialogue in "Alcoholics Unanimous," Hawkeye (Alan Alda) admits he and the others drink to "get through their lousy, stinking 48-hour days." This is the popular portrayal of alcohol as the ultimate painkiller.

Priest (Miramax Pictures, 1994)

They used to ask us a question when we were in seminary: a man comes up to you in confession and tells you that he has poisoned the altar wine. Do you go out and say Mass? I had no problem with it; I'd go out and drink the wine. I suppose there is a little of the martyr in all of us.

—Fr. Greg Pilkington in *Priest*

Dying for your faith, figuratively rather than literally, is a theme in *Priest*—a film that packs several themes in one story. *Priest* is the story of Father Greg Pilkington (played by Linus Roache), a young, theologically conservative priest who decries the hypocrisy of his fellow priest, Father Matthew Thomas (Tom Wilkinson) for shacking up with the female housekeeper. At the same time, Pilkington secretly steals away to the all-male bar to cruise for a gay lover. So the leitmotif of drinking trails way behind treatments of celibacy, homosexuality, confessional confidentiality, child sexual abuse (by a layman against his daughter; not clergy sexual abuse), and the perils of hiding one's true nature in order to serve God as a priest. Even though it is not a major theme, alcohol is featured throughout *Priest.* Needless to say, not all Catholics appreciated the way priests were portrayed in this film. However, as Jenkins points out, at this time in history "most Catholics no longer place the clergy beyond criticism,"[7] so although *Priest* may have been shocking to some, the scenarios included in it—such as a gay priest; a priest having a heterosexual affair; and a despondent elderly priest— were certainly not unheard of to most news-savvy Catholic parishioners.

The opening scenes include a visibly drunk older priest ramming his former workplace with a large crucifix. There are many conversations among priests that include hard liquor. When Father Greg cruises, he does so in a bar. After his secret affair with a man becomes front-page news, Father Greg sits down for a drink with the elderly priest—the one who rammed the office window with the crucifix—to talk about the despair he feels over the turn of events. He has a similar drunken heart-to-heart with Father Matthew in which they discuss the difficulty of keeping the vow of celibacy. Clearly the filmmaker would have us accept that these priests drink because it is part of the culture of being a priest, and to kill pain over the conflict they feel about their vow of celibacy. In the final drinking scene, between Greg and Matthew, Greg appears to be drinking in order to face the truth that he is in love with the man with whom he is having an affair. When alcohol is used as a "truth serum" of sorts, it can be seen as having at least some religious value. If it tears down the façade and leaves us with reality, it could potentially be a spiritual aide. However, we see few instances of this use of drinking in films. This only serves to reinforce how much the on-screen treatment of clergy has changed since the mid-twentieth century, "when the Catholic Church played a major role in the shaping the standards under which Hollywood operated."[8]

The Third Miracle (Sony Pictures Classic, 1999)

~Back then you weren't drinking.
~Yeah? Back then I wasn't pretending to be a priest.
—Frs. Panak and Shore in *The Third Miracle*

Like the other films listed here, *The Third Miracle* is not about a drinking priest, although the main character, Father Frank Shore (played by Ed Harris) appears to have a drinking problem. Moreover, much like *Going My Way* and *Priest,* the drinking serves several purposes, not the least of which is to display a culture of drinking among priests.

Father Shore has several meetings with the Bishop—all of which involve sharing a drink. After a disturbing interaction, Father Shore gets drunk and ends up in his old friend's confessional booth. When asked about his drinking, Frank suggests that he is doing it in order to keep up a pretense—that his faith is strong when, in fact, he doubts the very existence of God.

While drinking, Frank gets dangerously close to an attractive young woman—the daughter of a now-deceased laywoman whose life he is investigating as part of a popular push to make this woman, Helen O'Regan, a saint. A flirtation ensues and Father Frank—while under the influence of alcohol—tells her he's afraid he's falling in love with her. Here we have another case of alcohol as "truth serum," and in this case it is challenging the vow of celibacy.

Before Frank has a chance to act on the breaking of that vow, he is called to the scene of what he comes to believe is a miracle related to the case he is working on. Feeling a new sense of call and a need to reform, Frank pours the liquor down the drain, symbolizing his refusal to give into the truth of that sexual desire or that it is possible to anesthetize the pain with alcohol. Drinking, for *The Third Miracle*, depicts falseness, and a barrier to a necessary transformation in the life of Father Shore.

Giving it up symbolizes his new life that is not perfect but is at least authentic. After Frank discards the liquor, he discontinues the budding relationship with the woman and throws himself headlong into his case for proving the sainthood of the deceased and much-loved laywoman.

Keeping the Faith (Touchstone Pictures, 2000)

I'm not drunk. I'm Irish.
> —Fr. Brian Finn as he drowns his sorrows in *Keeping the Faith*

Jenkins notes that these days there are few qualms about "the making of films or television series that might offend America's sixty million Catholics."[9] At first glance, the opening credits of *Keeping the Faith*, featuring a priest staggering out of the *Blarney Stone* bar with a bottle in a bag, falling into a heap of trash on the sidewalk, would seem to bear witness to this claim. The drunken priest is Father Brian Finn (played by Edward Norton), distraught over a woman, a childhood friend who has come back into his life only to fall in love with his best friend, Rabbi Jake Schram (Ben Stiller), instead of him. Father Finn equates drinking with the culture of being an Irish priest, a stereotype that is almost worn out from overuse. However, he also drinks to kill emotional pain such as sadness and anger. When he pours his heart out to the bartender, he pleads for penance, only to have the bartender laugh and reply, "I don't do penance. I do shots." It appears Finn's drinking is about the loneliness and frustration of having made a vow of celibacy and then reconnecting with a woman he loved as a child.

Keeping the Faith is less about religious faith than it is about human relationships. The film's tagline puts it best: "If you have to believe in something, you might as well believe in love." The fact that the love triangle involves a rabbi and a priest provides a twist to make the eternal triangle different from all the rest. However, in using alcohol as the painkiller for the dreariness of the priest's life, *Keeping the Faith* appears to perpetuate a priestly stereotype while making a comment on the structures of our faith, namely that hierarchical rules tend to confine the human person rather than free him or her.

Mass Appeal (Operation Cork Productions, 1984)

~I like being liked. It gives me a warm feeling. That and wine are the only
warmth I get. I'm not about to give up either one of them.
~You could drink less.
                                        —Fr. Farley and Deacon Dolson in *Mass Appeal*

Of all the films discussed here, this one depicts the greatest amount of
alcohol consumption. The very fact that a photograph of a glass of red
wine appears on the promotional cover of the videotape indicates that
alcohol plays an important part in the life of this likable parish priest,
Father Farley (played by Jack Lemmon). Farley drinks a lot—at social
functions; at mealtime; with his Bishop during business meetings and
while teaching Deacon Mark Dolson (Zeljko Ivanek) how to preach. On
two occasions, Farley drinks after rough sermons—a "dialogue" sermon
of his that received a challenging response, and following Dolson's
disastrously judgmental "you people" sermon. Parishioners regularly
send Farley wine as a gift, and he freely admits to "loving his crutch."
When Dolson calls Farley a drunk, the older priest responds, "I am not
your typical drunk. I am at my best when I drink."

Part of Father Farley's persona as a priest is as a "lover of wine." He
is a man who is beloved at his parish for his easy manner and acceptance
of their upper-class lifestyle. When challenged by a contentious social
activist priest-in-training, Farley has to face the façade he has built up at
his parish.

Drinking is how Father Farley anesthetizes himself so he won't
notice how far he has slipped from preaching the gospel into the comfort
of preaching the status quo. At first glance it appears that Farley's
drinking is part of the culture of being a priest in a high-income parish. A
closer look indicates that Farley is drinking to escape the loneliness ("it's
the only warmth I get...") and distance that many clergypersons feel
once they are ordained and set loose as spiritual leaders in a community
that looks up to them but doesn't want any challenging message from
them.

For Father Farley, drinking seems to create the kind of climate that
makes being a priest bearable. It relaxes him so that he is pleasant and
witty in social situations, which, in turn makes him well liked. Being

popular allows him to feel successful and revered at his parish. Being revered by parishioners garners him respect with his bishop and diocesan leaders. However, there is one problem, which Farley fails to see until Dolson points it out: in courting the status quo, Farley has lost sight of his original purpose as a priest. As a result of his drinking, which is tied up with his need to be adored, Father Farley stands in the way of a parish in need of experiencing a transforming gospel.

Father Farley's drinking also gets in the way of the transformation Dolson needs to make before becoming a priest. Farley has much to teach Dolson about hospitality, kindness, and communication, but the relationship between the two men is hampered. The hot-headed Dolson easily gets the upper hand with Farley, writing him off as "a drunk" when he ought to take his advice and counsel seriously.

More than any of the other films considered here, *Mass Appeal* shows alcohol used to bolster self-esteem in a difficult profession where drawing lines about where your needs end and another person's begin can be tricky. For Father Farley, the drinking is not just about loneliness, although he admits to being lonely. It is not just about celibacy, although that allusion also is made, and it is not just about the lifestyle. It is ultimately about what kind of gospel Father Farley is going to claim and proclaim—one of comfort and gracious living, or one that changes individuals and society.

Conclusion

Filmmakers do not pull these characters and their drinking woes out of thin air. Certainly there are clergy, from all faith traditions, who drink. Some only drink at special events and meals. Some drink to relax. Some drink because it is part of their ethnic heritage and culture. Some are killing pain and fear. However, are clergy as unhappy and alcohol-prone as these five films portray?

It is possible, because alcoholism is an equal opportunity malady. Hard data on the subject of clergy alcoholism are difficult to come by. The latest figures from the National Household Survey of Drug Use (NHSDU) on heavy use of alcohol in the workplace, conducted in 1997, do not include a specific category for clergy. However, it indicates that heavy alcohol use—defined as five or more drinks on the same occasion on each of at least five days in the previous thirty days—is frequently found among people working in service professions.[10] A 1998 survey by a University of Chicago statistics professor looking at the incidence of alcoholism in various professions showed a little over 10% of the randomly selected clergypersons described themselves as alcoholics.[11] This percentage is somewhat lower than the percentages for educators, business executives, and merchants (which made the rest of the twelve-hundred person sample). This is interesting inasmuch as a study by the National Center on Addiction and Substance Abuse (CASA) at Columbia University showed that, in general, individuals who define themselves as quite religious or spiritual—though not necessarily clergy in their vocations—*tend* to have lower rates of substance abuse. Furthermore, CASA is urging seminaries and working clergy to become more educated on substance abuse in order to offer spiritual support for parishioners with addictions.[12]

Even if it was possible to measure with greater accuracy the rate of alcoholism among clergy, it would not necessarily help explain the film images and stereotypes discussed above. As Conrad Ostwalt comments, "Religion [and clergy as its official figures] is being popularized, scattered, and secularized through extra-ecclesiastical institutions."[13] Interestingly, not one of these films labeled its drinking clergy as alcoholics—not even *Mass Appeal,* which did go so far as to have the deacon call Father Farley "a drunk." None of these clergymen attended any sort of substance abuse counseling or meetings. Affixing a label of alcoholic to one of these priests is apparently not a judgment for the producer of the film to make, but it might well be one for the viewer to make.

What a number of the films did make clear was that the priests depicted were lonely due to their vow of celibacy. Nowhere was that assumption ever challenged. However, for many priests and nuns, celibacy is not a denial of life or sexuality. Rather, that discipline is seen as a way of embracing life with all its complexities and putting one's energy into community instead of into a spouse or children. George Weigel, in *The Courage to Be Catholic,* speaks of the need for a priest to practice asceticism, "the deliberate choice of a way of life that requires disciplined self-sacrifice across the board.[14] Weigel goes on to state that "a priest is far less likely to live his vows of celibate chastity faithfully unless he is living ascetically, and by personal choice, in other aspects of his life: Dress, possessions, approach to alcohol, choice of companions and recreation."[15] If celibacy is a positive choice, why do filmmakers continue to put a negative spin on it, linking it to loneliness and abusive drinking?

Certainly part of the reason is that in the Roman Catholic tradition, a person who feels truly called as a priest or nun is currently not given the freedom to choose between celibacy and marriage. To be a Catholic priest or nun means to take a vow of celibacy. The vow itself challenges the prevailing conventional wisdom and "the American way," which says individuals ought to have the freedom to choose how to live their lives and employers ought not to interfere. In addition, there is a bias in our society in favor of coupling. You see very few films or television shows that celebrate celibacy.

Perhaps the larger challenge, however, is to our consumer culture in North America. We are not terribly comfortable with asceticism. People who choose vows of poverty, obedience, and celibacy seem odd and out of place to many modern persons. It can be threatening, frightening, to think of someone giving up so much. Thus, films—which in many ways are designed to maintain the status quo of consumerism—paint the life of the average priest as fairly dreary. One way to make this dreary existence more palatable to us is to give these priests a visible, relatable flaw—an addiction or an abuse problem. Alcohol remains perhaps the most common and legal mind-altering substance we have at present. Portraying a minister with a drinking "issue" may make viewers feel better about his or her asceticism. It is then possible to say with some smugness, "See, I knew that someone who gives up money, sex, and power must have a dark side!"

Although clergy drinking in films usually capture our attention, it may not be for all the right reasons. We need to ask ourselves, "Are we shocked or titillated by this portrayal because it humanizes the clergy?" If this is the case, we need to think about our attitudes toward alcohol. In what way does it "humanize" a person? Furthermore, why are we putting clergy on a pedestal in the first place?

Might it even be possible that we are shocked or titillated by this portrayal because deep down we believe the life of the average priest or minister must be fairly miserable, given all that they give up for their vocation? Perhaps this represents a projection on our part: We know there is much that we could give up in order to become more faithful people. This observation opens the door to more questions: What makes us equate freedom with access to unlimited money, sex, and power anyway? Is there not freedom in voluntary simplicity, obedience, and celibacy?

No film, especially one that is expected to recoup at least a good portion of its costs, can adequately answer those questions for us. We have to remember that if challenging the status quo is difficult for a priest or minister, it is even more difficult for a completely market-driven enterprise such as filmmaking. For a true "reality check" about the collar and the bottle, it never hurts to talk openly with a person who could answer our questions from the depth of their experience. Is the life of sacrifice and service as lonely and frustrating as films often portray it? Do these real-life ministers turn to alcohol as a painkiller, "truth serum," or antidote to fear? Or do they find the chosen asceticism an avenue to freedom? The answer might surprise us.

Notes

[1] Conrad E. Ostwalt, Jr., "Conclusion: Religion, Film, and Cultural Analysis," in *Screening the Sacred: Religion, Myth, and Ideology in Popular American Film*, ed. Joel W. Martin and Conrad E. Ostwalt, Jr. (Boulder, CO: Westview Press, 1995, 152–59), 157.

[2] Tim LaHaye and David Noebel, *Mind Siege* (Nashville: Word, 2000), 184.

[3] Ibid., 185.

[4] James A. Fischer, *Priests* (New York: Dodd, Mead, and Co., 1987).

[5] Philip Jenkins, *The New Anti-Catholicism: The Last Acceptable Prejudice* (New York: Oxford University Press, 2003), 157.

[6] Ibid., 159.

[7] Ibid., 65.

[8] Ibid., 158.

[9] Ibid., 167.

[10] *National Household Survey of Drug Use* (NHSDA) from the U.S. Department of Human Services, Substance Abuse and Mental Health Services Administration, 1997. See online at www.samhsa.gov/oas/nhsa/A-11/WrkplcPlcy2-15.htm#P1134_27321.

[11] Professor Rong Chen of the University of Chicago published the study "Incidence of Alcoholism in Various Professions" in September of 1998. Accessed at *www. uic.edu/~rongchen/i478.dir/alcohol.sps.pdf* on July 7, 2003.

[12] CASA, "So Help Me God: Substance Abuse, Religion and Spirituality," November 2001. See www.casalibrary.org/CASAPublications/Spirituality.pdf.

[13] Ostwalt, "Conclusion: Religion, Film, and Cultureal Analysis," 157.

[14] George Weigel, *The Courage to Be Catholic* (New York: Basic Books, 2002), 184.

[15] Ibid.

Bibliography

Apostle, The. Dir. Robert Duvall. Perf. Robert Duvall, Farrah Fawcett. October Films, 1997.

Fischer, James A. *Priests.* New York: Dodd, Mead, and Co., 1987.

Going My Way. Dir. Leo McCarey. Perf. Bing Crosby, Barry Fitzgerald. Paramount, 1944.

Jenkins, Philip. *The New Anti-Catholicism: The Last Acceptable Prejudice.* New York: Oxford University Press, 2003.

Jewett, Robert. *St. Paul at the Movies.* Louisville: Westminster-John Knox, 1993.

Keeping the Faith. Dir. Edward Norton. Perf. Ben Stiller, Edward Norton. Touchstone, 2000.

LaHaye, Tim and David Noebel. *Mind Siege.* Nashville: Word, 2000.

Leap of Faith. Dir. Richard Pearce. Perf. Steve Martin, Debra Winger. Paramount, 1992.

M*A*S*H. Dir. Robert Altman. Perf. Elliott Gould, Donald Sutherland. Twentieth Century Fox, 1970.

Mass Appeal. Universal. Dir. Glenn Jordan. Perf. Jack Lemmon, Zeljko Ivanek. Operation Cork Productions, 1984.

Ostwalt, Conrad, E., Jr. "Conclusion: Religion, Film, and Cultural Analysis." In Ed. Joel W. Martin and Conrad E. Ostwalt, Jr. *Screening the Sacred: Religion, Myth, and Ideology in Popular American Film.* Boulder, CO: Westview Press, 1995, 152–59.

Priest. Dir. Antonia Bird. Perf. Linus Roache, Tom Wilkinson, Robert Carlyle. Miramax, 1994.

Third Miracle, The. Dir. Agnieszka Holland. Perf. Ed Harris. Sony Pictures Classic, 1999.

Weigel, George. *The Courage to Be Catholic.* New York: Basic Books, 2002.

4 Only in Paradise: Alcohol and Islam

Arthur James Powell

> Here is a picture of the Paradise that is promised to those who fear God! In it
> are rivers of unpolluted water, and rivers of milk that does not sour, and rivers
> of wine delicious to those who drink it.
>
> *The Qur'an* 47:15[1]

"I don't like to drink," says Ghali, a Moroccan Muslim studying at a
university in the United States. "For many students here 'having fun'
means partying with alcohol and drugs. I went to some parties at first,
but it wasn't fun for me. So I'm lonely a lot."

Such is the conflict for many Muslims in America and Europe,
especially those from Muslim countries who immigrate or reside for a
time of study. This conflict is intensified by the strong prohibition
against the use of alcohol and other intoxicants in Islam, a prohibition
that emerged early in the development of this new religious faith under
the leadership of the Prophet Muhammad (570–632) in the environs of
Mecca and Medina. The need for control of the consumption of alcohol
became increasingly important in this Arabian setting where its use had
been common as a means of relieving stress and escaping from life's
tensions and difficulties.[2]

Development of Prohibition

Because drinking wine was a deeply ingrained aspect of Arab society
prior to Islam, the approach to handling the problem was a gradually
increased restriction.[3] It should be noted that although our word
"alcohol" is derived from Arabic (*al-kuhl*, an intoxicating beverage made
from fermented grains, fruits, and sugars), this is not the term that
appears in the teachings of Muhammad on the subject. Instead, the most

common expression is *khamr*, frequently translated into English as "wine" or, more broadly, as "intoxicant." Thus, the Prophet stated in regard to both alcohol and gambling, "There is in them great sin and some benefit for people, but their sin is greater than their benefit."[4] This comment left the door ajar to those who wished to continue their drinking, but it set into motion the notion that alcohol consumption did not receive the blessing of God (the Arabic word for God is *Allah*).[5] Since drunkenness contributed to social problems and interfered with the practice of religious worship Muhammad later said, "You who believe, do not approach prayer when you are intoxicated, but wait until you know what you are saying."[6] Keep in mind that the faithful were expected to pray five times throughout every day, making it virtually impossible to get drunk and to fulfill the intent of Muhammad's directive.

The citations on alcohol are preserved in the Muslim holy book, the Qur'an, revered by Muslims around the world as the dependable source of divine guidance revealed to Muhammad gradually throughout the years of his career as prophet. These revelations to Muhammad came centuries after the appearance of Jewish and Christian scriptures and contain references to biblical personages, such as Abraham, Moses, Mary, and Jesus. For Muslims, though, the authority of the Qur'an supercedes that of the Bible.[7]

Statements in the Qur'an in reference to moral subjects, including drinking intoxicants, therefore, have taken on the character of law for the faithful.[8] Eventually the Prophet made a strong appeal for total abstinence when he said, "Satan wants to sow among you hostility and hatred with wine and games of chance and to hinder you from remembering God and from prayer. So will you abstain?"[9] Tradition has it that, upon hearing this revelation from God, the citizens of Medina dumped out their supplies of wine so that the streets were like streams flowing with the now forbidden substance.[10]

The Qur'anic references to the use of alcohol laid the foundation, then, for the strong prohibition that has come to be associated with Islam over the centuries. This perspective is further reinforced by statements found in the *Hadith*, an extensive collection of sayings and actions attributed to Muhammad and substantiated by chains of dependable witnesses. Bukhari, for example, reported that alcohol (*khamr*) is the source (literally "mother") of all evils. Because of this view, the taint of alcohol was seen more broadly than the effects on the drinker alone and extended to whoever makes it, transports it, receives it, serves it, or sells it (reported by Anas).

Because of its absolutist position[11] on alcohol intake—what is intoxicating in large amounts is prohibited in small amounts—Islam has to confront the troubling issue of how to treat medicine that contains alcohol, such as a cough syrup. Although most non-Muslims will not perceive the presence of alcohol in medicine to be a problem, for Muslims it is an important matter.

The answer from the staunchest view is that a Muslim must not take any medicine containing alcohol.[12] Even a small quantity of the forbidden substance will taint the body. Some Muslims, of course, will dismiss this attitude on the matter as being overly zealous and too rigid to be practical. A moderate position recommends that whenever a physician prescribes medication containing alcohol, the patient should inquire about an alternate prescription that is alcohol-free. If this physician is a non-Muslim and supplies no alternative, then the patient should seek out a Muslim physician to explore the possibilities. The objective is clearly to find a suitable treatment that avoids alcohol, but if no feasible alternative is available and the condition of the patient is life-threatening, the patient should be allowed to take that medicine without judgment of having committed a sin.

Prohibition, of course, does not necessarily translate into universal abstinence, as we well know from the days of prohibition in America. So the question arises, "To what extent has this prohibition been effective among Muslims?" The answer to that question is complex for several reasons. One primary variable is the social context for the faithful Muslim. For some, that context is a country (such as Saudi Arabia) where 90% or more of the population is Muslim and civil laws are reflective of the religious moral traditions. For others, it is a state (such as Egypt or Syria or Iraq) with a secular government and a majority of Muslim citizens, but also many years of influence from religious traditions. Still others live in countries that have had a period of domination by western or non-Muslim influences but more recently have undergone reform to return to more orthodox ways; such is the case in Iran. Beyond that are locations such as Pakistan or Indonesia, the most populous Muslim nation today, that have converted from some other form of worship to Islam, for whom Arabic is a foreign language, and who now have a predominantly Muslim society. To complicate the picture further, many Muslims have moved from predominantly Muslim locations to places (such as Europe or America) where they are a minority and the social climate is conducive to drinking alcohol.

Studies in reference to alcohol among Muslims have shown other variables that also bear on the situation. They indicate that the type of community is important, whether it be a small, isolated village; a town; or a city. In addition, they show that the level of education, degree of religious fervor, and gender are relevant to alcohol consumption.[13]

Alcohol Consumption in Muslim Countries

It is clear that alcohol consumption is almost negligible in those social contexts where Islam has the strongest influence. Imagine, for example, Mahmoud,[14] a 26-year-old Jordanian Muslim. He has vacationed several times in Europe where he has witnessed high levels of drinking, especially among people his age. "I was shocked during my first visit to Germany. I felt that I was in an evil environment and was uncomfortable. I never saw this in Jordan." Mahmoud's reaction is typical for people in predominantly Muslim countries.

The data in the 1999 *Global Status Report on Alcohol* published by the World Health Organization (WHO) show that consumption in Iraq, Morocco, and Egypt was low (0.61, 0.58, and 0.53 liter of pure alcohol per adult 15 years of age and over in 1996) as compared, for example, with the United States (8.90 liters), the United Kingdom (9.41 liters), Germany (11.67 liters), and France (13.74 liters).[15] It may come as no surprise that the figures for Syria (0.21 liter) and Yemen (0.15 liter) are even more dramatically low by contrast.[16] Studies utilizing questionnaires administered to technical students in Egypt and medical students in Morocco showed that a significant percentage of these students had used alcohol.[17] The results were that 33% of the Egyptian students had used alcohol at least once (published in 1982), and 25% of the Moroccan students had done so, with 23% indicating that they were current users (1990). Although these studies do not reflect a cross-section of the population, they may indicate that among the student age group experimentation with alcohol goes well beyond that for other groups.

This 1999 WHO report also shows trends in alcohol consumption, comparing the years 1970–72 with 1994–96.[18] Egypt had a 74.19% increase (0.31 to 0.54 liter), Indonesia a 57.14% increase (0.07 to 0.11 liter [still almost no consumption]), and Syria a 15.79% increase (0.19 to 0.22 liter). It is interesting also that in some cases there were actually decreases in consumption; for example, Morocco posted a 20.83% decrease (0.73 to 0.58 liter), Jordan a 63.64% decrease (0.11 to 0.04 liter), and Yemen a 69.09% decrease (0.55 to 0.17 liter).

Research on the use and misuse of alcohol in Muslim settings is relatively scant, but the research that does exist indicates that in spite of the traditional judgment against alcohol use Muslims do drink and do develop alcohol problems. It is difficult, however, to obtain reliable data on drinking patterns and attitudes toward alcohol use.

While the WHO report typically makes scant reference to the influence of religion on the use of alcohol, it makes an exception in the case of Islam. Its interpretive remarks on the eastern Mediterranean region state, "The strong influence of Islam throughout much of the region leads to quite low alcohol use in most countries. Areas with substantial Christian populations, such as Lebanon, are an exception."[19] Similarly with regard to the southeast Asian region the report notes that "religion is a strong predictor of alcohol use" in Indonesia.[20] Other studies reinforce the conclusion that religion plays an important role in controlling alcohol consumption.[21] One study reveals that adolescent Muslims in Israel consider negative health consequences to be a strong motivation to abstain from drinking, a factor as important as the religious teaching on prohibition.[22]

Even within predominantly Muslim countries, there are varied attitudes toward alcohol, depending on the specific location. In the Sudan, for example, Hassaba Suliman experienced a stark difference between the village and urban environments.[23] He left his village at age ten to attend school in Khartoum, and he quickly concluded that "the laws of the village" were not in evidence within the city. Suliman's village, only about sixty miles south of the city on the bank of the Nile, was much like other villages in Northern Sudan, consisting of mud houses, a small commercial area with a mosque and administrative office. Suliman states that the villagers "very much frowned upon" those who drank the local brew and forced the brewers to set up their business three miles outside the village. When the flag went up to announce that the brew was ready, the drinkers shamefully walked to the brewery in the afternoon. In Khartoum, however, Suliman discovered a bar located right next to the main mosque! The village's restrictions and imposition of shame and embarrassment did not exist here, leading to greater availability and consumption of alcohol, even to alcoholism. By the time he published this article (1983), Suliman was Director-General of Mental Health, Ministry of Health, in the Sudan, and he stated that alcoholism was common in his country. So we may say at this point that the faithful who live in predominantly Muslim settings with substantial moral and legal traditions will consume little to no alcohol. Even in the face of all these data, alcoholism does exist in the Muslim world and, to a large extent, goes undiagnosed because people—even medical professionals— are not knowledgeable of its symptoms.[24] The question remains, however, about those who are not in such a protective environment as this and have the social freedom, if not pressure, to engage in drinking alcohol.

Muslims in Non-Muslim Settings

A British Muslim, Talha Wadee, characterizes the conflict of values he experiences as one who cherishes being a traditional (not fundamentalist) Muslim who also wants to be a participant in a society where friends meet at a local pub to socialize or where they have a drink with a meal. Many people in this situation, he observes, do not go out much and appear to be unfriendly. With regard to the university setting he confesses, "I will be honest ... university life and university culture and atmosphere is so un-Islamic and so hedonistic, as a Muslim and even maybe [even as a] Christian or a practising Jew, it is very difficult to retain your Islamic values and still be part of that university life."[25]

This account of one Muslim's personal experience provides a small glimpse into a major issue in global Islam: migration of Muslims to Europe and the United States. The clusters of cultural, ethnic, and religious beliefs and values that migrants bring with them into new settings create enormous challenges for both the migrants and the settled populations. In Eastern Europe significant numbers of Muslims have been present for a long time, but more recently all of Europe has experienced the influx of migrants who have been viewed initially as temporary workers, not as new permanent residents. There has been a tendency for the migrant Muslims to be ghettoized by the European communities or assimilated into the new society with a consequent loss of their Muslim identity; still others have been radicalized by Islamic fundamentalists. In some areas a multicultural approach is emerging. The idea of "Euro-Islam" has been put forward by Bassam Tibi as a preferred mutual adaptation for migrant Muslims and Europeans, involving both cultural pluralism and political integration.[26] The implications of Euro-Islam and multiculturalism are that Muslims become active citizens while at the same time preserving their cultural, ethnic, and religious values within an atmosphere of mutual tolerance. It is clear that the type of adaptive situation the Muslim makes in Europe will have significant impact on the matter of alcohol use.

Reliable statistical data on the alcohol consumption of Muslims in Europe and most other non-Muslim settings are nonexistent. In France, for example, the most prominent approach to including the immigrant population is assimilation, which moves toward elimination of the cultural differences from the location of origin, therefore making it more difficult to find data specifically related to Muslims. Laurence Michalak and Agha Saeed, who have given special attention to Muslims in France, have not suggested that there has been a massive rush to indulgence in alcohol consumption, but they say that most Muslims there do not drink. They even cite an example of "born-again" Muslims in France who took up Islam afresh by conviction after having been merely nominally faithful in the past.[27] One common practice among those who choose to drink, even who do so heavily, is to give up alcohol during Ramadan, the month of fasting.

Kareem's behavior will illustrate this practice.[28] He had left Tunisia when he was 16 years old so that he could find work in France. Now at age 42, he is no longer praying daily or attending Friday worship at the mosque. He began to drink wine occasionally with friends he had made, both Muslim and non-Muslim. Now he is a regular drinker, sometimes drinking heavily, and bears a weight of guilt. So he says, "I cleanse myself once a year during Ramadan, and I feel better. But afterwards I start drinking again."

The experience of Muslim migrants to the United States has been somewhat different from that of those in France. In the United States the adaptation approach has been more to a multicultural model than to an assimilation model. This difference suggests that people from Muslim cultures can, to some extent, maintain the cultural differences within the context of the majority society. The experience of Su'ad,[29] however, has been that she feels more at ease among her fellow Syrian migrants than among the general population. She finds at the bank where she works that people seem to accept her and show interest in her Muslim beliefs and practices. The temptation to drink has not been a big problem for her because, she says, "I hate the smell of beer, and whisky is disgusting!" Second-generation Muslim Americans typically maintain their ethnic and religious lineage while asserting their American nationality. In the aftermath of the September 11 terrorist attacks in 2001, non-Muslim Americans were awakened to a substantial Muslim presence in the United States and to the fact that Muslim Americans were no longer foreigners but fellow citizens who also experienced loss and grief from the attacks.

In America the constituency of the Muslim community of more than six and a half million is highly multiethnic, almost evenly divided among people of African American and European, Arab, and South Asian origins, with less than 10% of Turkish, Iranian, and other nationalities represented. Conflict between Islamic values within the context of this non-Muslim society emerges in many contexts, from business luncheons to office parties to conference cash bars to dinners with friends. Cultural celebrations, such as New Year's Eve, Independence Day, and

Christmas, not to mention athletic events (even television-viewing parties at home or at the sports bar), often provide for alcohol as part of the tradition. One Muslim writer has made this interesting observation: "It has always seemed ironic to me that New Year's Eve has a marked increase in drinking as well as a mass rush to write down a list of 'New Year's Resolutions.' As Muslims, of course, we can see the irony in this."[30] In the Muslim view, increasing sin (by getting drunk) is incompatible with resolving to live a better life in the year ahead, especially when these lists of resolutions typically do not address the alcohol question. Such celebratory events as these clearly put those who abstain to the test. While the social pressure to abstain is certainly much less in America than in a predominantly Muslim country, once again it seems that most Muslims do not drink.

Israel is a seemingly unlikely location to find data relevant to our subject, but it has been the setting for a number of studies on alcohol that include Arab Muslims as well as Jews, Christians, and Druze. A 1995 national household survey in Israel showed that approximately 20% of adult Arabs reported drinking alcohol in the previous month, of whom the men were six times more likely to drink than the women. Of these current drinkers, 39% of the Arabs considered themselves to be "heavy drinkers," consuming five or more drinks within a few hours at least once during the previous month. Although this survey does not distinguish between Muslim and Christian Arabs (it may be assumed that the number of Christians was small in comparison), it does distinguish between secular and religious respondents. As may be expected, the secular Arabs engaged in drinking more than those who were religious.[31]

Another study conducted in Israel investigated reasons for *not* drinking among adolescent students representing four religious groups— Jews (secular and religious), Muslims, Druze, and Christians.[32] The four major reasons Muslims gave for abstaining were as follows:

1. Alcohol damages health (20.44%)
2. Religion is intolerant of alcohol use (18.28%)
3. Do not like the taste/smell (12.17%)
4. Do not care for it (10.93%)

Among the participants in the study, 70% of Muslim males and nearly 90% of Muslim females were nondrinkers, whereas, by comparison, only 27% of Christian males and 48% of Christian females were abstainers. In Israel both reports of adolescent and adult habits agree that 80% of Muslims abstain from alcohol, yet despite religious taboo, 20% engage in some degree of alcohol use.

Even though surveys show that the observant Muslims in non-Muslim settings consume alcohol at a much lower level than other people in those same environments, we should nevertheless be cautious in concluding that Islam is the single causative factor. Religion is one influence among other societal and cultural factors that contribute to people's behavior, certainly in relation to drinking alcohol. One of those other factors that stands out today is the issue of health, as the study of adolescents in Israel confirms.

Even with relatively low consumption of alcohol, alcohol problems do emerge among Muslims. The question arises: How do Muslims address the matter of excessive drinking and alcoholism?

Treatment for Alcoholism

Because drinking alcohol is viewed as a sin, those who are addicted to alcohol are dealt with, in the first instance, as violators of God's law and deserving of punishment. Such punishment throughout the history of Islam has varied from scolding by the community to lashing with palm branches.[33] Due to this perspective on addiction, the more traditional Muslims have tended to consider programs like Alcoholics Anonymous and various medical treatments as inappropriate for them.[34] Instead, the devout Muslim believes that treatment must go to the root of the problem, which is disobedience to God. The addict must follow the strict path of Islam set forth in the laws and traditions as preserved in the Qur'an and Hadith; only then will the problem drinker experience the cure. Badri proposes that the process followed in achieving abstinence initially under the Prophet's leadership is a model applicable to modern society. His analysis points to Islam itself as "the real intrinsic motivation" for achieving sobriety.[35]

This traditional approach to alcohol addiction is more dynamic than it first appears. It is based on the teachings that God forgives sin and that the Muslim community must shoulder its responsibility to support those in recovery. The mosque becomes a social and religious institution of healing for those who participate in its life and activities. "The fasting month of Ramadan," notes Baasher, "and the pilgrimage to Mecca, in particular, provide optimal opportunities for breaking away from habit-forming and dependence-producing drugs."[36] Suliman, in addition to his agreement on the powerful effect of the pilgrimage (*hajj*) for reforming an alcoholic, underscores the importance of family bonds for aiding the alcoholic in recovery. The extended family in the Sudan, he says, treats the alcoholic as a sick person needing healing. He also points to a centuries-old practice in Islam of the "therapeutic village," which becomes a model for a type of group therapy for alcoholics.[37]

Research on alcohol addiction among Muslims has not been extensive due to the fact that the strong religious condemnation of alcohol has created for many people a lack of awareness that the problem exists. One study in Kuwait (that included 1001 Arab Muslims from several educational and health care institutions) showed that nearly 80% of respondents condemned drug misuse and 90% of them held what the researchers named an "enlightened attitude," meaning basically that the misuser was viewed as sick and should receive help.[38] The researchers saw a trend of favoring a more therapeutic approach to addiction among younger, educated Kuwaitis. Treatment for alcoholism, then, has typically been oriented toward traditional religious remedies, but there is a growing openness to modern therapeutic approaches.

Certainly the most successful contribution of Islam to problem drinking is its emphasis on prevention. The consistent teaching and enforcement of prohibition in Islam has resulted in very low alcohol consumption and addiction in predominantly Muslim countries. To reinforce this commitment to prevention, considerable effort has been expended in educating people about the extensive harm in terms of social evils and personal health caused by consuming alcohol,[39] although some will contend that not nearly enough has been done.[40] This effort is evident in the abundance of Web sites that discuss the subject (e.g., understanding-islam.com, islamtoday.net, zawaj.com, submission.org, islamonline.net, themodernreligion.com, islamfortoday.com, and islam-usa.com). Many of these sources tend to be moralistic and didactic in pointing out how wrong it is to consume alcohol, but some of them also provide helpful information on the medical and health aspects of the issue in order to strengthen the motivation to abstain. Moore and Weiss have made a strong point about the need to encourage preventive activities among adolescents because while some are learning to drink, they can also learn to abstain.[41] Because their research dealt with reasons that adolescents choose not to drink, they urge Muslims to use the reasons that young people themselves support for abstinence in any campaigns for preventing alcohol indulgence. The strong prohibition in Islam can be useful in positive approaches to prevention, especially among young people.

Conclusion

While the Qur'an promises that in Paradise there will be "rivers of wine delicious to those who drink it" (47:15), it does not show such a generous attitude toward its presence on earth. We have seen that the official position of Islam forbids drinking alcohol and that most Muslims adhere to that position. This prohibition has exerted a strong influence on Muslim communities since the time of Muhammad, creating a climate of condemnation on those who indulge. However, because Islam is not a monolithic structure that looks the same everywhere in the world, but rather expresses itself in a variety of ways, it is not surprising that this variety shows up in Muslim attitudes toward alcohol.

In those settings where Islam is most dominant, such as a village setting in a Muslim country, alcohol production and consumption are virtually nonexistent. At the other extreme, in settings where Muslims are small minorities in urban, non-Muslim environments without strong community support for abstinence, alcohol consumption does occur, although typically not to the level of that by the surrounding community. In Muslim cities with large numbers of non-Muslim visitors and workers, the high availability of alcohol contributes to usage by Muslims, even though sometimes it is unlawful for them (but not the foreigners) to drink it. Gender and age have also been factors in alcohol consumption because studies have shown that men are much more likely to drink than women and young adults more likely than others.

Migrants from predominantly Muslim settings to Europe and the United States have usually experienced conflicts in their social life due to the influences that encourage people to drink in order to be included and accepted. Islam as a global religion has demonstrated its flexibility to maintain its basic values, including its judgment on alcohol, while adapting itself to new environments.

In relation to the issue of alcohol use, Islam has taken the stance of total abstinence, a remarkably strong position given attitudes present elsewhere throughout the world. This approach, while not 100% adhered to by Muslims worldwide, has demonstrated its effectiveness in reducing significantly the production and consumption of alcohol by the faithful.

Notes

[1] Unless otherwise noted, all translations of the Qur'an from Arabic into English are my own.

[2] M. B. Badri, *Islam and Alcoholism: Islam, Alcoholism and the Treatment of Muslim Alcoholics* (Plainfield, IN: Muslim Students' Association of the U.S. & Canada, 1976), 16–18.

[3] For a detailed description of this step-by-step approach, see Taha Baasher, "The Use of Drugs in the Islamic World," *British Journal of Addiction* 76 (1981): 233–43; also cf. Badri, *Islam*, 19–29.

[4] The Qur'an 2:19.

[5] I will use the English word "God" instead of the transliterated "Allah" to avoid any suggestion that Muslims worship some deity other than the one other monotheists, such as Jews and Christians, worship. Arabic-speaking Christians pray to "Allah" just as Muslims do.

[6] The Qur'an 4:43.

[7] It is of interest in this time of multiculturalism to observe how Muhammad viewed the Bible. Statements in the Qur'an reflect some degree of ambiguity. On the one hand, he affirms that Jews and Christians are "people of the book," having received authentic revelations from God. "Those of you who have believed, believe in God, his apostle, the book which was revealed to his apostle, and the book which was formerly revealed" (The Qur'an 4:136). This former book refers to the scriptures of Jews and Christians: "We had Jesus, Mary's son, to follow in their [the Jews] footsteps, and he confirmed the Law which had come earlier. We gave him the

Gospel, which contained guidance and light" (The Qur'an 5:46). On the other hand, this affirmation is qualified, because in other statements the Prophet also points out that Jews and Christians have, over time, altered the original revelations so that their books, as they now stand, are not fully accurate. For fuller discussion, see A. James Powell, "The Qur'anic View of Other Divine Scriptures: A Translation of Sections from Writings by 'Afif 'Abd al-Fattah Tabbara and al-Ustadh al-Haddad," *The Muslim World* 59.2 (1969): 95–105, esp. 97–98.

[8] Dwight M. Donaldson, *Studies in Muslim Ethics* (London: SPCK, 1953), 14–59.

[9] The Qur'an 5:91.

[10] Badri, *Islam,* 4–5.

[11] Reported to be a comment by Muhammad as recorded in *The Hadith* by Ahmad, Abu Dawud, and Al-Tirmidhi.

[12] "Alcohol Cannot Be a Medicine," 1; Baasher, "Use of Drugs," 240.

[13] The issue of alcohol for Muslims touches the broadly sensitive area of conflicting worldviews, that of traditional Islam, and that of the modern western world.

[14] "Mahmoud" is a fictive character I have created for the purpose of rendering a faithful illustration of the research data.

[15] *Global Status Report on Alcohol* (Geneva: World Health Organization, 1999), 10–12.

[16] Ibid., 13.

[17] Ibid., 176, 181. The study in Egypt included 3686 male students in technical schools in Greater Cairo; the study in Morocco included 595 medical students (64% male, 36% female).

[18] Ibid., 13–16.

[19] Ibid., 24.

[20] Ibid., 29.

[21] Tamara L. Brown, Gregory S. Parks, Rick S. Zimmerman, and Clarenda M. Phillips "The Role of Religion in Predicting Adolescent Alcohol Use and Problem Drinking," *Journal of Studies on Alcohol* 62 (September 2001): 696–705.

[22] See pp. 48–49 in Michael Moore and Shoshana Weiss, "Reasons for Non-Drinking among Israeli Adolescents of Four Religions," *Drug and Alcohol Dependence* 38 (1995): 45–50.

[23] See pp. 63–64 in Hassaba Suliman, "Alcohol and Islamic Faith," *Drug and Alcohol Dependence* 11 (1983): 63–65.

[24] O. P. Kapoor, "Common Chronic Disease Patterns in the Arabian Gulf," *Bombay Hospital Journal* 43.3 (October 2001). Cited in Karima Burns, "New Year's Eve, Alcoholism and Muslims," 2. http://www.zawaj.com, Celebrating Non-Muslim Holidays. Cf. also Suliman, "Alcohol," 64–65.

[25] Talha Wadee, "Understanding the British Muslim," *Edges Magazine*, April/May 1999, 4.

[26] Bassam Tibi, "Muslim Migrants in Europe: Between Euro-Islam and Ghettoization," in *Muslim Europe or Euro-Islam: Politics, Culture, and Citizenship in the Age of Globalization*, ed. Nezar Al–Sayyed and Manuel Castells (Lanham: Lexington Books, 2002), 31–52. See especially pp. 45–49.

[27] Laurence Michalak and Agha Saeed, "The Continental Divide: Islam and Muslim Identities in France," in *Muslim Europe or Euro-Islam: Politics, Culture, and*

Citizenship in the Age of Globalization, ed. Nezar Al–Sayyed and Manuel Castells (Lanham: Lexington Books, 2002), 153–54. Dr. Michalak presented a paper at the meeting of Kettil Bruum Society in Paris, June 3–7, 2002, under the title "Alcohol and Islam: Alcohol Consumption among Tunisian Emigrants to France," which gives a thorough discussion of the matter. The paper has not been published, but Dr. Michalak was kind enough to allow me to read it.

[28] "Kareem" is a fictive character created for the purpose of rendering a faithful illustration of the research data.

[29] "Su'ad" is a fictive character created for the purpose of rendering a faithful illustration of the research data.

[30] Karima Burns, "New Year's Eve, Alcoholism and Muslims," at http://www.zawaj.com.

[31] Yehuda D. Neumark, Giora Rahav, Meir Teichman, and Deborah Hasin, "Alcohol Drinking Patterns among Jewish and Arab Men and Women In Israel," *Journal of Studies on Alcohol* 62 (2001): 443–47. While our specific interest is confined to alcohol consumption among Muslims, Neumark et al.'s study is informative in that it compares the behavior of Jewish and Arab adults in Israel.

[32] Moore and Weiss, 45–50.

[33] Baasher, "Use of Drugs," 237. Also cf. Badri, *Islam*, 44–51, who views Islamic punishment as akin to modern aversion therapy and commends it as useful.

[34] Judith K. Muhammad, untitled, http://www:islam-online.net; also Suliman, "Alcohol," 64.

[35] Badri, *Islam*, 30–35.

[36] Baasher, "Use of Drugs," 241.

[37] Suliman, "Alcohol," 64.

[38] A. M. Bilal, B. Makhawi, G. Al-Fayez, and A. F. Shaltout, "Attitudes of a Sector of the Arab-Muslim Poplation in Kuwait Towards Alcohol and Drug Misuse: An Objective Appraisal," *Drug and Alcohol Dependence* 26 (1990): 55–62.

[39] Alyssa, "Alcohol and Muslims." http://www:themodernreligion.com. See also Baasher, "Use of Drugs."

[40] Burns, "New Year's Eve," 2.

[41] Moore and Weiss, "Reasons," 49.

Bibliography

Alyssa, "Alcohol and Muslims." http://www:themodernreligion.com.

Baasher, Taha. "The Use of Drugs in the Islamic World." *British Journal of Addiction* 76 (1981): 233–43.

Badri, M. B. *Islam and Alcoholism: Islam, Alcoholism and the Treatment of Muslim Alcoholics*. Plainfield, IN: Muslim Students' Association of the U.S. & Canada, 1976.

Bilal, A. M., J. Kristof, and M. G. El-Islam. "A Cross-Cultural Application of a Drinking Behaviour Questionnaire." *Addictive Behaviors* 12 (1987): 95–101.

Bilal, A. M., B. Makhawi, G. Al-Fayez, and A. F. Shaltout. "Attitudes of a Sector of the Arab-Muslim Population in Kuwait Towards Alcohol and Drug Misuse: An Objective Appraisal." *Drug and Alcohol Dependence* 26 (1990): 55–62.

Brown, Tamara L., Gregory S. Parks, Rick S. Zimmerman, and Clarenda M. Phillips. "The Role of Religion in Predicting Adolescent Alcohol Use and Problem Drinking." *Journal of Studies on Alcohol* 62 (September 2001): 696–705.

Burns, Karima. "New Year's Eve, Alcoholism and Muslims." http://www.zawaj.com.

Donaldson, Dwight M. *Studies in Muslim Ethics.* London: SPCK, 1953.

Global Status Report on Alcohol. Geneva: World Health Organization, 1999.

Kapoor, O. P. "Common Chronic Disease Patterns in the Arabian Gulf." *Bombay Hospital Journal* 43.3 (October 2001).

Luczak, Susan E., Adrian Raine, and Peter H. Venables. "Invariance of the MAST across Religious Groups." *Journal on Studies of Alcohol* 62.6 (2001): 834–37.

Michalak, Laurence, and Agha Saeed. "The Continental Divide: Islam and Muslim Identities in France." In *Muslim Europe or Euro-Islam: Politics, Culture, and Citizenship in the Age of Globalization.* Edited by Nezar Al–

Sayyed and Manuel Castells. Lanham: Lexington Books, 2002.

Moore, Michael, and Shoshana Weiss. "Reasons for Non-Drinking among Israeli Adolescents of Four Religions." *Drug and Alcohol Dependence* 38 (1995): 45–50.

Muhammad, Judith K. untitled. http://www.islam-online.net.

Neumark, Yehuda D., Giora Rahav, Meir Teichman, and Deborah Hasin, "Alcohol Drinking Patterns among Jewish and Arab Men and Women in Israel." *Journal of Studies on Alcohol* 62 (2001): 443–47.

Powell, A. James. "The Qur'anic View of Other Divine Scriptures: A Translation of Sections from Writings by 'Afif 'Abd al-Fattah Tabbara and al-Ustadh al-Haddad." *The Muslim World* 59.2 (1969): 95–105.

Suliman, Hassaba. "Alcohol and Islamic Faith." *Drug and Alcohol Dependence* 11 (1983): 63–65.

Tibi, Bassam. "Muslim Migrants in Europe: Between Euro-Islam and Ghettoization." In *Muslim Europe or Euro-Islam: Politics, Culture, and Citizenship in the Age of Globalization.* Edited by Nezar Al-Sayyed and Manuel Castells. Lanham: Lexington Books, 2002.

Wadee, Talha. "Understanding the British Muslim." *Edges Magazine,* April/May 1999, 4.

Younis, Y. O., and A. G. Saad. "A Profile of Alcohol and Drug Misusers in an Arab Community." Letters to the Editor, *Addiction* 90 (1995): 1683–84.

5 In the Presence of the Divine: The Use of Hallucinogens in Religious Practice

John W. Gamble

To many in this country and in most western industrialized societies the use of a drug of any kind, much less one that the federal government has labeled illegal in religious practice may sound like a tremendous perversion of spirituality or worse simply satanic.[1] Rampant abuse of drugs, associated criminal behavior, and the lingering "sour taste" from this country's experience with hallucinogens during the 1960s and 1970s have led many to consider them as a possible vehicle leading to an encounter with the divine. There is, however, a long and honorable history of the use of hallucinogens for religious and healing purposes. That history stretches from the dim mists of prerecorded time down to the present.

Throughout this chapter the term hallucinogens will be used in referring to what are primarily plant-based substances that possess a mind-altering or psycho-active quality when ingested. However, over time, particularly in the United States, the terms used to designate these substances have gone through an evolution. In the 1950s, psychiatry used the term "psychotomimetics" in reference to the belief that these substances duplicated the condition of psychosis. In 1957, the Canadian psychiatrist Humphry Osmond, dissatisfied with that term, suggested "psychedelic" (meaning "mind manifesting") as a more appropriate term. This term caught the public's imagination and became common usage during the chaotic 1960s. In time that term came to carry so much cultural baggage both good and bad that R. Gordon Wasson, a key figure in the history of hallucinogen research, coined the term "entheogen" meaning "God within us." Wasson's suggestion was an effort to move the discussions of these substances into a serious and sacred arena. His term has caught on particularly in religious circles; however, the term "hallucinogens" continues in general usage, and for the purpose of this chapter will be used along with the term "psychoactive compound."

Perhaps the first question to be answered concerns a definition of "hallucinogens." Although the primary focus of this chapter will be on plant-based substances, several hallucinogenic compounds have been created in the laboratory, most notably LSD. *Webster's Ninth Collegiate Dictionary* defines *hallucinogen* as "a substance that induces hallucinations." And *hallucination* as "1: a: perception of objects with no reality usually arising from disorder of the nervous system or in response to drugs (as LSD); b: the object of a hallucinatory perception. 2: a completely unfounded or mistaken impression or notion."[2] These definitions fail completely to address the broad spectrum of experiences that characterize reports from those who have ingested hallucinogens. Schultes (1992) defines hallucinogens as "toxic," that is, they produce intoxication. Other than tobacco, none are known to be addictive. Ingestion produces changes in one's experience of their internal and external environment. These changes may include alterations in the perception of space and time, intensity of colors, and numinous experiences that appear to occur in a realm other than the one in which people exist in their day-to-day ordinary mundane lives. In the United States, these substances are defined as drugs, and are, for the most part, illegal to obtain or use except in the very specific situation of their use by certain religious groups. In addition, it is important to note that if misused or misidentified, they can be dangerous and possibly fatal.

The negative connotation associated with drugs in general and hallucinogens in particular forms one half of a division that manifest throughout the literature on hallucinogens. The other half of this division honors the anthropological findings of the use of these compounds by indigenous peoples, and a plethora of documents from our modern culture that relate hallucinogen use to profound spiritual experiences. This split tends to color much of the available literature on the subject. Many authors are either strongly for or against the government prohibition on the availability of hallucinogens for the exploration of their therapeutic and spiritual possibilities. Over and over again the history of hallucinogenic use has come into conflict with the church and what has come to be called the establishment which has included the medical profession, federal, state and local governments and their attendant legal systems.

Much of what we know regarding the use of hallucinogens for sacred purposes comes from the study of indigenous cultures. There have been decades of research in the areas of anthropology, ethnobotany, and ethno-pharmacology. However, for the most part, the general public has been ignorant of the details of this research. The indigenous view of plants in general, and hallucinogenic plants in particular, occupy a position that is foreign to the western mindset. Indigenous peoples see hallucinogenic plants as a particular gift from the gods, and as such their use is a sacred act allowing the person to appreciate and to enter the world of the supernatural. This is in counterdistinction to the western industrialized culture's tendency to apprehend and appreciate the divine through the concepts revealed in the documents passed down through the ages. Along with this distinction the use of psychoactive drugs in industrialized nations has been viewed as a form of recreation and as a way to ameliorate psychological stress.

There lies in these distinctions a greater overarching difference in cultural perception. That difference encompasses a definition of man's place in nature and all that it entails. The indigenous vision tends to see all of nature as divine and man's well-being in the world as dependent on the generosity and goodwill of the divine powers in nature. For the hunter-gatherers and pre-agriculturalists that well-being included and still includes not only the availability of food and shelter in a benevolent environment but such related matters as individual health and illness. All such items are viewed as dependent on the whim and satisfaction of the divine powers believed to control these necessities.

Conversely, while the western industrialized cultural view generally respects nature (although this is a source of vitriolic debate in many quarters), the power of scientific discovery has vastly reduced our apparent dependence on a capricious natural world that must be propitiated by technicians skilled in negotiating the unseen world of divine and malevolent spirits.

However, the negotiation and propitiation of a spirit world by indigenous peoples for the purpose of survival and well-being is hardly the whole story when we come to consider the use of hallucinogens in the apprehension of the divine. There are numerous descriptions from persons in our culture of sublime experiences that left users with a belief that they have obtained a glimpse of the divine and at the same time discovered a new understanding of the world and their place in it. These experiences are sufficiently common so as to constitute a significant possibility that appears inherent in the exploration of hallucinogen use. At the same time our culture has been inundated with descriptions exposing the trivial and destructive nature of hallucinogens.

Soma and the Vedic Hymns:
The Earliest Recorded Use of Hallucinogens in Religion

The earliest religious strivings for which we have complete texts are the Vedic Hymns from two thousand years before the Christian era. These hymns were sung by the Aryan tribes that migrated to northwest India. The Vedas comprise ten books totaling 1,017 hymns. The hymns demonstrate an evolution over time and an increasing sophistication in religious thought and appreciation of the divine. These early manifestations of the human endeavor to enjoin with the divine along with the Upanishads and the Bhagavad-Gita are the foundation of the modern Hindu religion and have also strongly influenced Buddhism. Although many researchers believe that psychoactive compounds were known and used by early man, it is here in the Vedic Hymns that we find the first known use of hallucinogenic substances in a spiritual context. The hymns come to us today from the mists of prehistory by virtue of an extraordinary oral tradition. The Vedas distinguish themselves from an earlier, more primitive religion, in their appreciation of otherworldly gods who are, in the words of Rabindranath Tagore, Olympian-like.

The Vedas extol a special beverage called Soma which was a god, a plant, and the juice of a plant. At times the hymns present Soma as a vehicle for encountering the divine as in the following passage:

> We have drunk the Soma; we have become immortal;
> we have gone to the light; we have found the gods,
> What can hatred and malice of a mortal do to us now, O immortal one?[3]

However, at other times, Soma is spoken of as a god in its own right. In fact, Soma is generally considered by scholars to have been primarily thought of as a god by the worshipers.

> Like ornaments vying for the neck of a winner,
> like the cries of men contending for light,
> so our songs strive for Soma who,
> in accordance with his choice,
> is purified by waters as a sage.
>
> His wisdom is like an enclosure for rearing of cattle.
> It is he who has revealed the abode of immortality.
> All worlds have expanded for him who found the light.
> Our songs increasing like cows in the pasture,
> Hail aloud the sacred Drop with deep devotion."[4]

The Hymns of the Veda precede the Upanishads by several centuries. In these later meditations we find the Indian spiritual focus increasingly moving to a contemplation of the essence of the divine within man. Because the primary characteristic of the hallucinogenic experience is a profound emphasis on one's internal psychic landscape, these later developments were no doubt prompted by the hallucinogenic Soma experience. It is here in the emphasis on contemplation and the far reaches of the contents of consciousness that we find India's great gift to the world of spiritual endeavor as manifested in Buddhism, Hinduism, and the various forms of Yoga.

The composition of Soma remained unknown until recently. Sometime in the first century BCE the real Soma had disappeared from Vedic ritual and the name came to be applied to a host of other substances. The question of the actual source of Soma fascinated scholars for years. Numerous substances had been suggested as possibilities in an effort to find the original Soma. However, each failed to provide a satisfactory match to the experiences detailed in the hymns. An example is Rabindranath Tagorei's definition as: "The fermented juice of a plant used in Vedic ritual, and also deified."[5] It is thus equated with an alcohol-type preparation.

The story of the discovery of the plant from which Soma was derived is as strange as the many issues surrounding these substances. R. Gordon

Wasson was a retired vice-president with J. P. Morgan & Co. in New York. He and his Russian-born wife, a pediatrician, were aware of scientific research investigating the indigenous Mexican peoples' use of sacred mushrooms in religious rituals. In 1953, they traveled to Oaxaca, Mexico and for the next two years befriended the Indians of that region. Finally, in 1955, Wasson with a companion was allowed to participate in a mushroom healing rite. Wasson described the experience as profound and soul shattering. He wrote of being reminded of the *agape* or eucharistic meal of the early Christians. Wasson published his experiences on May 13, 1957, in an article in *Life Magazine,* with the striking title of "Seeking the Magic Mushroom." Despite that rather sensational initial publication, Wasson was a meticulous and critical scholar and researcher who continued his investigations into the use and source of hallucinogens known to ancient and indigenous peoples. Turning his attention to the question of Soma, Wasson concentrated on information contained in the Vedic Hymns. In 1968 he published *Soma: Divine Mushroom of Immortality.* Wasson's research had convinced him that the mushroom fly agaric (*Amanita muscaria*) was the Soma of the Vedic Hymns. Wasson hypothesized that the Aryan peoples coming from the Northwest brought their shamanic ecstatic techniques with them into the Indian subcontinent.

This theory coming from such an unlikely source was initially greeted with a considerable degree of skepticism. However, it is now generally accepted that the psilocybin mushroom fly agaric was the source of the Vedic Soma. As a result of his investigations Wasson has offered the theory that these experiences of early man under the influence of psychoactive substances that produced intense experiences of a numinous nature and altered perception may have been the beginning of the belief in another more sublime otherworldly place; in short, a heaven. The effect of Wasson's discoveries and his attendant publications was to inform the general public of the existence of natural substances that produced powerful mind-altering effects. That information laid some of the groundwork for later popular interest in hallucinogens. At the same time Wasson's work served to invigorate the field of ethnobiology (the study of plant use by indigenous people) and ethnopharmacology and in so doing brought to the foreground the work of men such as Richard Evans Schultes of Harvard. Schultes had been studying the role of hallucinogens in indigenous religions in the South Americans for some time. The other effect of Wasson's publishing in a popular periodical was the beginning of regular visitations by people from the United States seeking mushroom experiences. It should be noted that the controversy that continues to exist today regarding the nature of Soma centers around the issue of whether or not fly agaric is the source of Soma rather than whether Soma was based on a hallucinogenic plant substance. The later point is fully accepted by modern scholars.

In modern times, Indian spiritual teachers tend to downplay the use of psychoactive substances in the pursuit of the divine. However, there is evidence that these plant preparations continue to play a part in the spiritual practices of some sects and their seekers. In their book, Schultes, Hofmann, and Ratsch include photographs of yogis and sadhus or "holy men" of India smoking hallucinogenic substances as part of their preparation for spiritual practices.[6]

The effects of hallucinogenic compounds have most certainly been known and used to varying degrees by primitive peoples as well as more civilized peoples in a variety of early cultures. However, an interesting study by Brunner of the literature of ancient Greece and Rome to determine the possible use of marijuana, found no conclusive evidence suggesting use for purposes of intoxication in these societies.[7]

The Middle Ages

The European historical past concerns us in two significant areas when we come to a consideration of the use of plant hallucinogens. In both considerations we encounter the approbation of the church and what we now call the establishment. We will encounter these two entities united against the use of hallucinogenic substances down through the ages. The first area of contention involved the capacity of hallucinogens to induce a worldview that was perceived in Europe as threatening the established church's power. The second area involved the New World. Here the capacity of hallucinogens to sustain a particular cultural and religious vision was perceived as a threat to the success of imposing a different spiritual orientation, and a worldview that would allow for the subjugation and exploitation of the native peoples.

The issue of witchcraft is complicated in a number of ways. The first complication involves the question of the nature of that religion. Certainly the worship of the devil qualifies as a form of religious endeavor. However, what we know of witchcraft is unclear regarding the focus of worship and actual rituals that involved the use of hallucinogens. Much of the Middle Age information concerning the use of psychoactive plant preparations in witchcraft comes from church documents. With respect to the church's position, there exists a serious debate as to whether witchcraft actually existed or whether it was a creation wholly of the church. The idea that witchcraft and witches were a covenant fiction invented by the church and confirmed through the use of torture and fear is appealing to some, not least for its value in condemning the excesses of the Inquisition and also because the behaviors to which people confessed were on the surface quite implausible. In addition, it is difficult to separate what came to be called witchcraft from shamanic animistic healing that had existed in Europe before the time of recorded history. Despite these issues the church's traditional designation of certain individuals as practicing a form of worship that was heretical and anti-Christian in nature will be accepted for the present purposes, and the documents derived from church-based observations will be accepted also. At the same time, though, the designation of some persons as witches, and their practice as witchcraft, required a church-based definition along with that of the prevailing power establishment.

Although initially the experiences contained in the church documents appeared to historians as generally implausible, modern investigation of hallucinogenic substances has changed that view. It is now recognized that the psychic effects of hallucinogenic ingestion suggest that the reported experiences were not only plausible but quite likely. Despite this possibility the question of the religious content of the rituals that are alleged to have occurred remains unclear. In many instances it appears that those singled out as witches were relatively isolated women who may have been involved in healing work in the community and who at the same time were perceived as strange. These perceptions of strangeness would not have been unusual with regard to an isolated woman living alone in communities where superstition abounded.

Harner cites a number of examples of church-based observations and descriptions of so-called witchcraft descriptions. The original texts are in Latin and clearly illustrate the confusion and lack of sophistication on the part of the alleged hallucinogen user and the attitudes of the church toward the phenomenon. A typical passage follows:

> Elizabeth Style said: "Before they are carried to their meetings, they anoint their foreheads and Hand-writs with Oyl the Spirit brings them (which smells raw) and then they are carried in a short time, using these words as they pass, *Thout, tout a tout, tout throughout and about.* And when they go off from their meetings they say, *Rentum, Tormentum* ... all are carried to their several homes in a short space." Alice Duke gave the same testimony, noting besides that the oil was greenish in color. Ann Bishop, the Officer of the Somerset covens, confessed that "her Forehead being firs anointed with a Feather dipt in Oyl, she hath been suddenly carried to the place of the meeting. ... After all was ended, the Man in black vanished. The rest were suddenly conveighed to their homes."[8]

Similar passages read:

> In rifleing the closet of the ladie, they found a Pipe of ointment, wherewith she greased a staffe, upon the which she ambled and galloped through thick and thin, when and in what manner she listed.

> But the vulgar believe, and the witches confess, that on certain days or nights they anoint a staff and ride on it to the appointed place or anoint themselves under the arms and in other hairy places and sometimes carry charms under the hair.[9]

Ciruelo provides the following in the early seventh century:

> Witches, male and female, who have pact with the devil, anointing themselves with certain unguents and reciting certain words, are carried by night through the air to distant lands to do certain black magic. This illusion occurs in two ways. Sometimes the devil really carries them to other homes and places, and what they see and do and say there really happens as they report it. At other times they do not leave their homes, but the devil enters them and deprives them of sense and they fall as dead and cold. And he represents to their fancies they go to other houses and places and do and see and say such and such things.

But nothing of this is true, though they think it to be, and though they relate
many things of what passes there. And while they are thus dead and cold they
have no more feeling than a corpse and may be scourged and burnt; but after
the time agreed upon with the devil he leaved them, their senses are liberated,
they arise well and merry, relate what they have done and bring news from
other lands.[10]

From the above and many similar descriptions it is clear that the
church authorities did realize that, for the most part, actual travel and
meetings did not occur.

The debate over the existence of witches and their worship activities
notwithstanding, the church aggressively responded to what it perceived
and then defined as the threat. Along with the medical authorities, the
church repressed the acts of healing that occurred outside its authority.
Michelet provides the following quote from church authorities, "that if a
woman dare cure without having studied she is a witch and must die."[11]

With the suppression of the practice of unsanctioned healing the
church successfully asserted its authority both as the purveyor of healing
experiences and of the only legitimate access to the supernatural. The use
of hallucinogenic plants among peoples in Western Europe subsided as
did the phenomenon of labeling certain members of the community
witches. The designation was to resurface again at various times, most
notably in the United States during the Puritan period. There is no
suggestion that the latter labeling involved the use of psychoactive
plants. By the same token those involved in the modern form of
witchcraft or Wicca religion do not appear to use hallucinogens in their
worship rituals.

The identity and properties of the plants that made up the "Oyls" and
concoctions of the Middle Age European witchcraft are well known. The
definitive source book, *Plants of the Gods*, refers to them as the "hexing
herbs."[12] The Mandrake (*Mandragora*) along with Black and Yellow
Henbane (*Hyoscyamus niger* and *Hyoscyamus albus*) and Belladonna
(*Atropa belladonna*) constitute the primary ingredients of the witchcraft
preparations. All four species of plants have a long history of use in
sorcery and magic. However, the effects of these plants are reported to be
so powerful that they not only precluded the possibility of a shared group
experience, they also very likely precluded engaging in a formal ritual

experience. An individual's experience under the influence of a powerful hallucinogen is profoundly idiosyncratic. Harner suggests that formal rituals took place in meetings at which hallucinogens based on these plants were not used.[13]

Interestingly, the medieval superstitions surrounding these plants continue to echo in our modern world. The reader may recall seeing in the second episode of the popular movie series *Harry Potter* the scene in which the young students are being instructed on the proper precautions to use when dealing with the Mandrake plants. The students all don earmuffs in order to insulate themselves from the cries of the plant as it was removed from its pot.

There exist some modern descriptions of the effects of using preparations made from these plants. These descriptions generally correspond to the ones found in the documents from the Middle Ages. Harner quotes the German scholar of the occult Kiesewetter as follows: "... rubbed it on his forehead and armpits and had colleagues do the same. They fell into a twenty-four hour sleep in which they dreamed of wild rides, frenzied dancing, and other weird adventures of the type connected with medieval orgies."[14]

Shamanism

The definitive early source on Shamanism, *Shamanism: Archaic Techniques of Ecstasy*, was written by Mircea Eliade in 1951. At that time, Eliade wrote: "He (the shaman) is a visionary and inspired. However, the basic experience is ecstatic, and the principle means of obtaining it is, as in other regions, magico-religious music. Intoxication by mushrooms also produces contact with the spirits, but in a passive and crude way. ... This shamanic technique appears to be late and derivative."[15] This was written before the work of Wasson and the many other ethnobotanists and ethnographers whose work has now demonstrated that hallucinogens played a definitive role in the shamanic religions of the old world and new. Furst reports that Eliade had changed his mind before his death and saw no difference between a shamanic trance chemically induced or induced by other means.[16]

Shamanism is an animistic religion that characterizes spiritual life among indigenous hunter/gatherer/fisher-peoples around the globe since before recorded history up to the present. It has also been found active among herdsman and planter preindustrial peoples. It is difficult to give the modern readers, steeped as they are in an industrial/postindustrial culture, immersed in the rational world of concepts, trained and constrained to view "what is outside" the psyche as the only real, a flavor for the world vision that characterizes indigenous peoples involved in shamanic religions. In the first place, life is profoundly nature dependent not just for survival but for all aspects of well-being. This is a world inhabited by spirits and energies that have an immediate impact on the well-being, or lack thereof, of the peoples. These indigenous peoples move in a universe whose manifestation in their interior psychic life is as real as the physical universe they move in. Alberto Volloldo made the following observation, "the indigenous priest-shaman is a person of the percept while we in industrialized societies are a people of the concept."[17] That is to say that the dominant mode of involvement of the shaman priest in the realm of the divine spirit world is to literally see and experience that which cannot ordinarily be apprehended. Conversely, members of industrialized societies usually understand their environment in terms of a series of rational cause-and-effect concepts. For an indigenous person, there is no abrupt distinction between the inner and the outer world. The shaman is the principle actor in this world. It is the shaman who functions as the intercessory between the people and the supernatural forces that so closely abound their life. He or she is diviner, seer, magician, poet, singer, artist, prophet of game and weather, keeper of tradition, healer of bodily and spiritual ill.

There are numerous paths to the role of shaman including heredity or appointment by the tribe, but in the most common instance a man or woman is "called." This call most often manifests through a dream. However, before the dream the shaman-to-be may stand out in some way from the other members of her or his village. It is not usual for a shaman to have had a significant illness in youth. Eliade compares the shaman to monks and mystics and saints within Christian churches characterized by a powerful religious bent. The training of the shaman includes the acquisition of the traditional techniques, the names and functions of the spirits, an appreciation for the mythology of the tribe and the secret sacred language. In addition the shaman will frequently be required to undergo demanding and dangerous experiences as part of his or her initiation and learning. Eliade notes that "the shaman may influence the religion of the peoples, but neither the ideology nor the mythology and rites are the creation of the shaman."[18] The shaman is an actor in an ongoing established mythology and religion.

Often, but not in all instances, the primary tool of a shaman in his or her work with the supernatural forces is the use of a sacred plant hallucinogen. This plant induces in the shaman the altered state that allows the performance of the tasks of intercession with the gods. Regarding these hallucinogenic plants Furst writes, "the hallucinogenic plant is believed to contain a supernatural transforming power over and above the life force or "soul stuff" that in animistic-shamanistic religious systems inhabits all natural phenomena, including those we would classify as inanimate."[19] Again, he notes that "... in the preindustrial or tribal world, psychotropic plants are sacred and magical, they are perceived as living beings with supernatural attributes, proving for certain chosen individuals such as shamans and under certain special circumstances for ordinary people as well, a kind of bridge across the gulf that separates this world from Other worlds. Nowhere in the indigenous world do we find these plants used as a means of escape from the culture, instead they reinforce the cultural perspective."[20]

Modern anthropological and ethnobotanical research has determined a veritable cornucopia of hallucinogenic plants that have been in use the past hundreds of years by indigenous peoples of the Americas. Ceramics date the use of psychoactive compounds in the Americans from between 100–200 BC. The name of R. Gordon Wasson emerges again along with others who worked to determine the actual hallucinogenic plants that have been used historically by indigenous peoples in sacred rites in this hemisphere. Ololiuhqui, the sacred hallucinogen of the Aztecs, has been identified as the seeds of a certain morning glory plant. Ayahusca or yaje, known as the vine of the soul for its capacity to reveal to its users truths that are believed to be crucial for their well-being, is used by shamans and curers in the Amazon jungle. The Indians of the rain forest are also known to prepare and use powerful hallucinogenic snuffs.

Further north in more arid climates the hallucinogenic cacti San Pedro (*Triochocreus pachano*) and Peyote (*Lophophora williamsi*) have ancient histories of use for sacred ritual purposes by the indigenous peoples of the Americas. Natural tobacco must also be included in the list of sacred plants. Indigenous peoples consider tobacco a special gift from the gods. Tobacco is intoxicating when taken in large doses and interestingly is the only one of the plant products in regular sacramental use that has addictive properties. Its use includes actual ingestion by the shaman or an initiate, and in the form of smoke, as a supernaturally charged substance, that renders those items on which it is blown divinely charged. The smoke is believed to bring divine healing to those infused with it by the shaman. In fact, so many psychoactive plants are known and used in religious ceremony by indigenous peoples in the Americas compared with the Old World that Schultes and La Barre hypothesize that the reasons for this abundance of knowledge and use in the New World would have to be cultural rather than botanical. La Barre notes that American Indian survival in the New World as essentially Paleo-Mesolithic Eurasiatic hunters depended on the effectiveness of their shamanistic religion which required the used of hallucinogenic plants. In short, they were "culturally programmed" to explore the new environments for the appropriate sacramentals. In contradistinction to Old World, the New World never knew "the intolerant fanaticism that is the hallmark of some of the Old World religions, particularly Christianity and Islam, both of which massively transformed the areas in which they took hold."[21]

All of that changed with the arrival of the Spanish at the end of the fifteenth century. The arriving Spanish, charged as they were to seek wealth and convert the natives to Christianity, used the most egregious means in their attempt to accomplish these ends. Much of the information we have on this period concerning Indian use of hallucinogenic plants comes from Spanish authors among them Ruiz d Alareon's (1629) *Tratado on Idolatries and Superstitions,* of the Indians of Morelos and Guerrero. The Spanish quickly realized that the Indian use of plant hallucinogens was a crucial element in their religious and cultural foundation. They noted that the magic plants were more than a tool for communication and were in fact viewed as a divinity and object of worship. Curiously, the Spanish accepted the Indians' description of the effects of the plants. However, because Christ was absent from any of the reported experiences, they reasoned that the experiences and their use was the work of the Devil in his efforts to prevent the Indians from coming to Christianity. The Catholic Church under the Spanish called the hallucinogen peyote the diabolical root and equated its consumption with cannibalism. In 1616 the Holy Inquisition of Mexico issued a proclamation ordering the persecution and excommunication of those who, "under the influence of 'herbs and roots' with which they lose and confound their senses, and the illusion and fantastic representations they have, judge and proclaim afterwards (these illusions) as revelations, or true notice of things to come."[22] In their zeal to stamp out these practices and to lead the Indians to Christ, the Spanish employed as punishments for engaging in hallucinogenic-based ritual public flogging and being burned alive. Of this Colonial period Wasson wrote, "There runs a note of somber poignancy as we see cultures in a duel to the death—on the one hand, the fanaticism of sincere Churchmen, hotly pursuing with the aid of the harsh secular arm what they considered a superstition and idolatry and, on the other, the tenacity and wiles of the Indians defending their cherished plants."[23]

In the final analysis perhaps one could say that both sides had their way but the cost to the Indians was terrible. Today the indigenous people of the Americas continue the use of hallucinogenic plants in their religious life having, as we shall see, integrated them into their Christian acculturation. The sacred Ololiuhqui seeds, known as the "semilla de la Virgen" (seeds of the Virgin), are an example of that integration.

The American Experience with Hallucinogens in the 1950s, 1960s, and 1970s

Albert Hofmann was a Swiss researcher working for Sandoz Pharmaceuticals Co. in Basel, Switzerland. In 1938, Hofmann synthesized LSD while searching for a respiratory stimulant. Five years later he accidentally exposed himself to the drug. The effects were astonishing and Hofmann realized that he had discovered a drug that might have significant promise as a research and therapeutic tool focusing on the human mind. LSD, in contrast to plant hallucinogens, is a synthesized compound. It was the subject of serious research in the United States and Europe throughout the 1950s and 1960s. Numerous articles appeared in scientific journals detailing the promise and excitement that accompanied that research. Although the focus of the majority of the research was psychological/psychiatric in nature, the religious/spiritual nature of the psychedelic experiences continued to manifest itself and at times became the actual focus of the research. Hofmann had exhorted researchers and clinicians to administer LSD under strict medical supervision and only after intense psychological preparation. This remained the general state of affairs until the 1960s.

Aldus Huxley had suggested the relationship of hallucinogenic substances and modern religious experience to the popular imagination in 1954 with his book the *Doors of Perception.* Huxley described his experiences with the hallucinogenic drug mescaline and advocated it as a vehicle for "vitalizing" religious life. Interest in religion and hallucinogens gained momentum with Wasson's article in *Life Magazine,* in 1957. Alan Watts furthered that interest. Watts had become well known in the United States as an interpreter of eastern spirituality to an increasingly larger audience. Born in England, Watts emigrated to the United States in 1938, where he was ordained as an Episcopal priest. He left the Christian ministry in 1950 and from then on wrote, taught, and lectured on both radio and TV on eastern religion in general and Zen Buddhism in particular. In 1960 Watts published a seminal essay describing his experiences with the synthesized hallucinogen lysergic acid diethylamide .25 or LSD. Watts noted in his article that "for more than thirty years I have been studying the causes, the consequences, and the conditions those peculiar states of consciousness in which the individual discovers himself to be one continuous process with God, with the Universe, with the Ground of Being."[24] Watts goes on in his article to tie the experiences encountered under the influence of LSD with that numinous state of consciousness that has been the focus of his studies. Watts ends his article with a discussion of opposition to the use of psychedelic drugs including a rather vitriolic focus on traditional religious and secular attitudes of western society. In a footnote he observes "American Indians belonging to the Native American Church, who employ the psychedelic peyote cactus in their rituals, are firmly opposed to any government control of this plant, even if they should be guaranteed the right to its use. They feel that peyote is a natural gift of God to mankind and especially to natives of the land where it grows, and that no government has a right to interfere with its use."[25]

All of this might have been no more than an interesting discussion that touched a relatively small minority of readers of religious texts had it not been for developments at Harvard University. Sandoz Laboratories had actively marketed LSD to researchers since 1947. In 1960 Timothy Leary established the Psychedelic Research Project at Harvard. Leary was a popular professor in the psychology department and a respected researcher who had published in various journals. He enlisted Richard Alpert, a Stanford educated psychologist who taught and conducted research in the Department of Social Relation and the Graduate School of Education. From 1960 to 1963, Leary and Alpert conducted research using LSD. Leary had received permission from the State Commission of Correction to give a hallucinogen to thirty-five inmates of the Concord State Reformatory. Following the experiment he reported that the convicts were having religious experiences. Understandably, his work was controversial. Walter Houston Clark, Professor of Psychology and Religion at Andover Newton Theological School in Newton, Massachusetts, and former dean and professor at Hartford School of Religious Education, was called on to confirm the religious nature of their experiences. In doing so, Clark began his own fascination with the religious possibilities of hallucinogens.

In 1962, Leary's student Walter Pahnke conducted an experiment known as the "Good Friday Experiment." The experiment had as its central focus the religious/spiritual possibilities of an hallucinogenic episode using psilocybin (an extract of psychoactive mushrooms). Pahnke was a physician and minister working on his doctorate in religion and society at Harvard University. He began his experiment by defining mystical consciousness as having the following characteristics: unity, transcendence of time and space, deeply felt positive mood, sense of sacredness, objectivity and reality (a sense of certainty that the experience is real), paradoxicality (opposites are felt to be equally true despite violating the laws of logic), alleged ineffability (language inadequate to describe the experience), transiency, and persisting positive changes in attitude. During the experiment he administered the hallucinogen to ten of twenty Protestant divinity students. The other ten students received what they expected to be an inactive placebo, but was in actuality a capsule of nicotinic acid that caused a feeling of warmth and tingling. All of the students were randomly chosen and unaware of whether or not they received the active compound or the supposed inactive substance. The subjects were located in a chapel that was connected to the main sanctuary by speakers. They then received over the speakers the two and a half hour Good Friday service. Following the experience and six months later the subjects were asked to write a description of their experiences, fill out a questionnaire, and participate in an interview. Pahnke concluded that results strongly supported the hypothesis that a hallucinogen can help support mystical experiences when used by religiously inclined people in a religious setting. Walter Houston Clark wrote of the experiment, "There are no experiments known to me in the history of the scientific study of religion better designed or clearer in their conclusions than this one."[26] Pahnke had planned a long-term follow-up to his experiment, but was killed in an accident before this could occur. In the meantime Timothy Leary's work, and the whole issue of LSD research in general, fell into disrepute.

In psychiatric research and treatment settings the use of LSD had gone through a number of models to explain the effects. The psychiatrist Humphrey Osmond pioneered the use of LSD in treating alcoholics (a notably intractable treatment population). He observed that the distinguishing factor in whether or not the treatment was a success was whether the patient achieved a transcendent and mystical state of consciousness. In an effort to broaden the psychiatric conception of hallucinogenic drug treatment and experience Osmond coined the term *psychedelic* referring to what he defined as the "mind-manifesting" attributes of the drug. Osmond was intrigued with the results of his work with LSD and became a proselytizer for the possibilities he felt were inherent in the drug experience. In 1957, he wrote that psychedelics would soon become a tremendous boon to humanity and "have a part to play in our survival as a species."[27] These words of high expectation characterized the wild exuberance that had begun to swirl around the use of LSD and other hallucinogens. During the course of their investigations Leary and Alpert at Harvard had become convinced that LSD and related hallucinogens contained the possibility of transforming the human psyche in very positive ways with a concomitant transformation of society. The two expressed their thoughts in what might be best described as adolescent superiority. In 1962, they wrote, "Make no mistake, the effect of consciousness-expanding drugs will be to transform our concepts of human nature, of human potentialities of existence. The game is about to be changed, ladies and gentlemen. ... These possibilities naturally threaten every branch of the Establishment. The dangers of external change appear to frighten us less than the peril of internal change. LSD is more frightening then the Bomb!"[28] Leary began to publicly urge the youth of the nation to use hallucinogens to expand their consciousness by challenging them to "Tune in turn on and drop out." He toured the country giving talks about the benefits of hallucinogenic experience and in so doing garnered extensive publicity.

Quite predictably there was a powerful backlash not only to the excesses of Leary and Alport, but also to the rhapsodic musings of therapists such as Osmond. Before the backlash, though, the religious or mystical potential of hallucinogens had been picked up and institutionalized in a rash of newly developed cults and churches. Some of these churches such as the Church of the Awakening, were very serious efforts to incorporate the psychedelic experience into a formal religious ritual. The physicians John and Louisa Aiken founded the Church of the Awakening in 1958 following the accidental death of two of their sons. In the late 1950s and early 1960s the church began to incorporate the use of peyote in their services. In 1963, the church was incorporated under the laws of the state of New Mexico as a nonprofit religious organization, and the psychedelic experience was named as a sacrament of the church. Other so-called churches where less religiously serious and more interested in the recreational aspects of hallucinogenic drug usage. All sought to take advantage of the legal protection being sought by Native Americans for their use of the cactus peyote in their worship services. Not only had LSD been co-opted by a number of cults and New Age–type churches, but the youth of the society at large had discovered the drug and its extraordinary effects. The Czech physician-researcher Stanislav Grof came to the United States in 1967 to continue his work with hallucinogens. To his astonishment, he found a situation that he described in that year:

> Black-market LSD seemed to be readily available in all parts of the country and for all age groups. Self-experimentation with psychedelics flourished on university campuses and many large cities had their hippie districts with distinct drug subcultures. ... At the same time the psychedelic movement was profoundly influencing contemporary culture: music, painting, poetry, design, interior decorating, fashion, movies, theater, and television plays.[29]

This situation activated the church/establishment alliance in vigorous opposition to the use of hallucinogens for any purpose. The psychiatric profession took harsh umbrage at the enthusiastic endorsements of clinicians such as Osmond and researchers such as Leary and Alpert. Their interpretations had blurred the lines between science and religion as well as sickness and health. Their advocacy of personal use of the drugs further obscured these distinctions and added confusion between clinicians and their patients and teachers and their students. Roy Ginker, president of the American Medical Association, castigated those professionals who endorsed the use of hallucinogens and accused the U.S. Food and Drug Administration of not protecting the public. However, psychiatry was not the only element in society that became alarmed. The vast majority of the established order of the country began to call for curbs on the drug excesses. In 1965 Congress passed the Drug Abuse Control Amendment putting tight restrictions on hallucinogenic research. In 1970 Congress passed the Comprehensive Drug and Abuse Prevention Control Act that made the possession of most known hallucinogens an illegal act. As the backlash gained momentum, Leary and Alpert were fired from Harvard, and Leary was arrested and jailed.

The Modern Situation

The use of hallucinogens in religious ceremonies continues in the present both in the United States and in many indigenous cultures, particularly in the western hemisphere as well as in Asia and Africa. Furthermore, there is a very real continuing interest in the use of hallucinogens in some elements of mainstream religion.

The beliefs of the Native American Church blend fundamentalist Christian elements with pan-Native American moral principles. The hallucinogenic cactus peyote became the official sacrament and is considered divine by the members of the church. Peyote is a small spineless North American Native of the Chihuahua desert. It is found from the Rio Grande drainage basin in Texas southward into the high central plateau of Northern Mexico. The Harvard ethnobotanist Schultes called peyote a veritable factory of alkaloids.

The use of peyote was essentially unknown in the United States until the late 1800s. During this time the Native Americans were losing their land and witnessing the disintegration of their way of life. The use of peyote spread among tribes with the aid of Native American practitioners who traveled throughout the Southwest holding ceremonies and a Smithsonian Institute archeologist, James Mooney. Mooney became convinced of the need to unite the Indians and to protect their legal right to worship peyote. In 1918 Mooney wrote the charter for the Native American Church. Predictably the use of a hallucinogenic plant as a sacrament engendered the united opposition of the church and power establishment resulting in stiff legal opposition. A series of court struggles followed. In 1940, the church was declared illegal by the Navajo tribal council as a potentially harmful influence on Native Americans and as an affront to the Christian religion. In 1967, the tribal council reversed its decision. In 1960, an Arizona judge ruled that the Native Americans were guaranteed access to the peyote sacrament under the First and Fourteenth Amendment rights. In August 1978, the Ninety-Fifth Congress by joint resolution passed the American Indian Religious Freedom Act guaranteeing American Indians, Eskimo, Aleut, and Native Hawaiians the right to exercise their traditional religious beliefs and practices. This right included the use of hallucinogenic substances as a sacrament. Presently the Native American Church claims in excess of a quarter of a million members.

Several other modern movements have claimed an hallucinogenic sacrament. An additional example is the Peyote Way Church, which was established in 1978. The church presents itself as "a non-denominational all race Peyotist Religion."

> The church's web site states that, "Peyote is a spiritual medicine. It can bring us in touch with the God within us, our Heavenly Father and our Heavenly Mother. ... When we eat the Peyote we experience time and eternity, and it is from that vantage that, the next day we can live our life in a very positive and non-trivial way, realizing that this day could be our last and that everyone around us is our brother and sister and we need each other. Rabbi mother S. Kent, Klondyke Arizona.[30]

Despite the legal acceptance of the Native American Church's right to their use of peyote, struggles over the use of hallucinogens as a religious sacrament continue.

In May 1990, in *U.S. versus Boyll,* against Robert Boyll a non-Native American was dismissed. The decision was upheld by the Tenth Federal District Court of Denver. Boyll had been arrested following a pilgrimage to Mexico to obtain peyote for himself and members of the congregation with whom he worshiped.

The Rastafarian religion, originated in Jamaica (although not limited to it), is a messianic movement dating back to the 1930s. Rastafarians believe that the only true God is the late Ethiopian emperor Haile Selassie. Rastafarians use the hallucinogen marijuana as a sacrament, which they believe is the biblical weed of wisdom. Reggae, the popular music of the movement, is well known in the United States. Rastafarians have at times been associated with a revolutionary thrust in Jamaica.

In Brazil, the Centro Espirito Beneficente 'Unido do Vegetal (Beneficent Spiritual Center Union of the Plants) has as its primary sacrament a tea made from the Ayahuasca vine, which is known as Hoasca in Portuguese. The church, founded in 1961, comprises a blend of traditional and cultural specific spiritual beliefs. The church claims membership in the thousands. It has been a positive influence in areas of the country that were known for their violence and lawlessness. Participants in the services believe that the plant is an ally when used in a reverential way that can open one to Divine consciousness.

Some of the literature involving the use of hallucinogenic substances has focused on the possibility that there are references to such use in the

Christian Bible. This idea is held by the members of the Ethiopian Zion Coptic church as support for their use of marijuana in ritual. In 1988, the church published a pamphlet through Beacon Press titled "Marijuana and the Bible." There have been other efforts to find the use of hallucinogens in the Bible. Dan Merkur authored a piece entitled, "Manna, The Showbread, and the Eucharist: Psychoactive Sacraments in the Bible."[31] The piece argues that the manna from Heaven was a hallucinogen. The French author Daniele Piomelli published a letter in the journal *Nature* suggesting that the ecstatic trance life of Saint Catherine of Genoa could be explained through her conscious or accidental use of a hallucinogenic plant. However, these efforts have never been entirely convincing and have not received wide currency in the literature on hallucinogens.

Present Indigenous Use of Hallucinogens

Indigenous use of hallucinogens generally differs markedly from that found in contemporary church worship. Contemporary church use of hallucinogens involves the use of the psychoactive substance by the general congregation (in some instances approval is required by a designated church authority). The worshipers then have their own individual psychic experience in a group in the sacred space. Group worship and ritual generally occur prior to the hallucinogen taking full effect and after the intense effects have worn off. We may find a somewhat similar scenario in some indigenous cultures. However, usually a hallucinogen is used primarily by the shaman curer/priest to access the realm of the supernatural for the purpose of effecting a cure, divining the future, appeasing the spirit powers, or otherwise obtaining information needed by the group for its members' survival.

The Huichol Indians of Mexico live in a rather isolated territory in the Sierra Madre Mountains. Their culture and religious beliefs have remained quite intact due to their isolation and to the relatively minor influence of the Spanish. The cactus peyote has been the essential sacrament of the Huichols for hundreds of years, and it is this plant hallucinogen that evolved into the sacrament of the Native American Church. Peyote continues to this day as the divine sacrament of the

Huichols. The ingestion of the peyote during a religious ceremony enables the shaman as well as the ordinary Huichol "to find his life." That is to say that the sacrament attunes the partakers to their symbolic cultural existence. It is used mainly in a ceremonial context and is considered essential for these ceremonies. However, because the cactus is not native to their territory, the gathering of the plants requires a lengthy pilgrimage. The pilgrimage involves a journey three hundred miles northeast of their homeland and occurs on an annual basis to this day. However, part of the journey today may be made by car, public transport, or on foot. The Indians see the journey as a sacred task. All Huichol hope to make this journey at least once in their lifetime.[32]

Glascoe et al. explored the indigenous use of the coca plant (*Erythroxylon coca*). Chewing the leaf of the coca plant is an honored and ancient tradition among the Quechua-speaking Indians of Peru and other indigenous tribes in South America. Although not a hallucinogen per se, coca is a stimulant producing a mild mind-altering experience. On occasion the taking of large quantities of the plant have been used to induce visions. The practice of chewing coca should not be confused with the use of the drug cocaine. The mild intoxication that results from the chewing of the coca leafs is a very far cry from the powerful effects of the highly refined drug that comes from the plant and that causes such havoc in the industrialized cities of the western hemisphere. Among the Indians the coca plant is seen as a divine gift and, in addition to the practice of chewing the leaves, the leaves themselves are used in spiritual ceremonies. One of the primary purposes of plant usage is the mediation between the Quechua-speakers' relationships with the ultimate forces that populate and animate the universe. In addition, the general practice of chewing coca eases social intercourse and the subjective response to illness and fatigue. Beyond this everyday use of the plant, certain individuals become skilled in the use of the plant in a shamanic context, including the foretelling of the future and communicating with the supernatural forces of nature.

In 1978, Richard Cowan, Douglas Sharon, and F. Kaye Sharon along with the Peruvian healer Eduardo Calderon created a film documenting a day in the life of a Calderon, who used to be a Peruvian curandero or healer. In 1982, they followed the film with the book *Eduardo El*

Curandero: The Words of a Peruvian Healer. The book augmented the information provided in the film. Both film and book provide an important view of the amalgam of Christian teachings, traditional shamanic techniques, and the use of an hallucinogen in a curing ceremony. In his healing work Eduardo embodies the core indigenous shamanic belief of a power that pervades the environment and tends to be focused in particular sacred places and objects. Although the power is present for everyone, it is the shaman who commands and works with this power. The hallucinogen employed by Eduardo is the San Pedro cactus. San Pedro has been known and employed in healing and spiritual ceremonies for centuries in Latin America. Eduardo's healing strategy involves bringing into meaningful interaction the forces of good and evil in symbolic ritual. His work with these forces allows the patient to balance the disharmonies in his body and psyche. Much as an officiant in a traditional Christian church would call on the divine presence, Eduardo addresses God, the Virgin Mary, and the saints of the Roman Catholic faith with forms that include The Hail Mary and the Our Father as he creates a sacred space and charges the objects that he will use in the ritual healing. As the ritual proceeds he consecrates the mixtures to be drunk by calling and petitioning God to bless them. Eduardo also addresses the forces of nature, the mountains and lagoons, streams, gardens of magical plants, shrines and curanderos of the past and present. The actual curing ceremony occurs after the imbibing of the consecrated San Pedro and other mixtures.

The details provided in these documents are typical of the healing and ceremony work that continues to this day in indigenous cultures whether these cultures are located in isolated rural areas of Third World countries or in a modern urban city where indigenous people have gathered to look for work and a better life. As the anthropologist Marlene Dobkin de Rios has noted, many Latinos remain culturally rooted in the indigenous folk traditions of their homelands, even when they may have migrated to urban industrial cultural areas. Dobkin de Rios emphasizes the shaman—curandero's use of the symbolic images of spirit allies to interact with and to transform the symbolic worlds of their patients. "By placing the blame for illness or feelings of bad luck onto the shoulders of antagonist or evil spirit the healer transforms the patients free-floating anxiety into straightforward fears that can be faced, managed and dismissed."[33]

Dobkin de Rios notes that the issues of indigenous healing are characterized by complexities and subtleties that transcend the hallucinogenic journey. In fact, I was present at a ceremony in the Peruvian Amazon during which the hallucinogen Ayahuasca was used to set the stage and support a treatment involving a young woman from a nearby village. The curandero ended the session by diagnosing the patient as having been hexed and by indicating that the perpetrator of the hex would know his, the curandaro's rage and vengeance. The following day he explained to the visitors from the industrialized United States that he did not actually believe that the patient had been hexed; rather, she was suffering from symptoms that resulted from a former employment she had held. However, the hexing explanation fit her conception of what had happened to her, and thereby allowed for the healing to take place.

Dobkin de Rios provides an interesting contrast between a Christian church–based healing ceremony and an indigenous ceremony. The church ceremony took place in a town in northern California in a small church. Dobkin de Rios described the preacher stirring the congregation into a state of excitement such that "within twenty minutes people in the room went into trance states, fell to the floor, spoke in tongues and finally became unconscious. One woman was apparently healed of a crippling disease."[34] Dobkin de Rios noted that the emotionality of the evening was pronounced. In contrast a ceremony in Peru involved the drinking of a foul-smelling and -tasting hallucinogen, the manipulation of objects on a mesa (altar), the singing and chanting of songs and a restrained ritual exorcism. In the Christian ceremony the minister had involved God's grace to cure illness, and in the indigenous ceremony the curer was said to contact the supernatural to intercede on behalf of the patient and effect a cure. Both of these methods of spiritual cure are very much present in our world today.

Twenty-four to twenty-seven years after the original Pahnke Good Friday Experiment, Rick Doblin interviewed, tape-recorded, and re-administered Pahnke's one hundred-item follow-up questionnaire to sixteen of the original subjects in the experiment. Of the remaining three subjects one was deceased, one could not be located, and one declined to participate in the follow-up. The results were striking. All seven hallucinogen-receiving subjects that participated in the follow-up continued to consider the original experience mystical in nature and to have made a valuable contribution to their spiritual life. None of the placebo subjects considered their experience of significant value. Interestingly, the follow-up also uncovered an adverse reaction suffered by one of the hallucinogen-taking subjects that had not been reported in the original data. This reaction was not reported to have lessened the impact of the experience for that subject.

Shamanism has captured a large segment of the public imagination. The primary seminal event was the publishing of a series of books by Carlos Castanada reportedly detailing his experiences with a native shaman. Castanada's work has engendered considerable controversy regarding his purported experiences with hallucinogenic plants providing descriptions that echo the wild rides and visions of the Middle Age witches. Despite the controversy over the authenticity of the experiences, his books had a significant impact on the generation that came to age during the 1960s through the 1980s and continues to this day. A review of the journal *Shaman's Drum*, Number 58, 2001, revealed ads for, among other things, a color video on the "Secrets of Soma," showing how to prepare the *Amanita muscaria* (fly agaric) mushroom, a publication offering an "Overview of Huichol Shaman Culture," and a series of workshops in which participants can "Experience Huichol Shamanism." The more adventurous can travel to the Peruvian Amazon jungle to work with, and be involved with, the shaman and Ayahuasquero Don Agustin Rivas.

The Future

In the past few decades there has been an effort to integrate the knowledge and skills of traditional healers into the mainstay western vision of treatment. In 1975, the United Nations World Health Organization (WHO) began just such an initiative. It recognizes that in most developing countries traditional healers constitute the major health resource for a significant portion of the population. In the western hemisphere the WHO's regional office for the Americas, the Pan American Health Organization, has continued with the efforts of integration. These efforts, coupled with the anthropological work of many scientists, have resulted in an increasing respect and acceptance of traditional healing methods. This change has been accompanied by a growing interest in the therapeutic possibilities of hallucinogenic substances. However, the work of traditional healers and western research has demonstrated that the use of these substances without recognition of the cultural/symbolic context that the patient inhabits can result in disappointing and possibly injurious results.

For the first time since the euphoric and chaotic 1960s, the United States Food and Drug Administration has approved the use of hallucinogenic substances in formal well-controlled investigations designed to assess the risk-benefit ratio of particular substances. Research has begun onpatients suffering from terminal conditions, intractable pain, and addiction problems. However, as Charles Grob warns, in order to realize the potential of these extraordinary substances, researchers and therapists must adopt a cautious, controlled, scientifically valid approach to this work if it is to be allowed to proceed. Here, Grob refers to both the reckless experimental procedures and the messianic proselytizing that characterized hallucinogenic research in the United States in the 1960s.[35]

On another front, there has been a significant increase in interest in hallucinogens by some mainstream religious organizations. It may well be that this interest has never really abated but instead gone underground and there is now a sense that public discussion is, if not wholly acceptable, at least not dangerous. In 1995, the Chicago Theological Seminary and the Council on Spiritual Practices invited a group of theologians, clergy, mental health professionals, transpersonal psychologists, and other professionals who shared an interest in hallucinogens to a weeklong conference. Participants discussed their past experiences with hallucinogens and speculated on both the religious value of such substances and their future potential for religious and therapeutic use. The book *Psychoactive Sacramentals* emerged from that conference. Participants at the conference used the term *entheogens,* meaning "God within us," exclusively in place of hallucinogens.

The participants sounded a cautionary note in some of their presentations. Several authors observed that in and of themselves the use of hallucinogens does not lead to religious experience and development or make spiritual endeavors more likely to be successful. For that matter the use of hallucinogens does not automatically lead to general maturity or cultural intelligence. The psychologist Charles Tart noted that the use of entheogens does not guarantee a God-within experience, nor do they automatically guarantee growth or love or light or revelation.

Despite these cautionary notes the participants were universally enthusiastic concerning the possibility of hallucinogens as a sacramental adjunct to religious worship. Albert Hofmann the discoverer of LSD noted that his discovery was not the product of planned research but something that came to him in the form of a serendipitous gift. It is his belief that the discovery of LSD and its action were given by a higher power who felt that it would be beneficial to humankind. The transpersonal physician researcher Stanislav Grof noted that the hallucinogenic experience revealed extraordinary healing and transformative potential that had to be normal, but usually dormant, constituents of the human psyche that is "infinitely larger than we could ever have imagined."[36]

At the same conference Rev. Aline Lucas, a graduate from Harvard Divinity School, practicing priest and dean of St. Thomas College at the time of the conference, discussed a liturgy that involves the use of hallucinogens. The Rev. Mike Young noted the irony that at this time it is illegal for him to administer a hallucinogenic sacrament while it could be quite legal for a scientist to administer a substance that could very likely lead to a religious experience if done in an appropriate setting. Finally, Brother Steindl-Rast, a brother in the Benedictine Monastery of Mount Savior, discussed sacramentals as natural things through which faith encounters God's power. God chooses the means of that encounter.

Conclusion

It seems that western industrial society is at a turning point where there is a willingness to again open the Pandora's Box of hallucinogenic substances for consideration and experimentation. With the advent of postmodernism, with its respect for multiple epistemologies, there has been a growing public interest in the historical and present ways in which indigenous peoples construe their world and their place in it.

In 1958, Walter Houston Clark wrote:

> But there is no doubt that the drugs (hallucinogens) and their religious use constitute a challenge to the established churches. Here is a means to religious experience that not only makes possible a more vital religious experience than the churches can ordinarily demonstrate, but the regeneration of souls and the transformation of personality are made possible to an extent that seems far more reliable and frequent than what the ordinary church can promise.[37]

Such a statement today would be certain to reignite the hostilities of the established church and its historical ally, the power establishment. The question of why these non-addictive substances, which are traditionally used for experiencing idiosyncratic altered states of consciousness, should engender such a sense of threat is interesting. There is no question that they have been viewed as a threat in the past and no doubt will continue to be so in the future. One reason certainly has to do with the nonordinary world that is revealed under their influence. A world that in many respects has the potential to suggest not only a degree of personal empowerment but of personal access to the world of the divine.

The move to renew experimentation will be accompanied with a strong degree of oversight and caution on the part of the researchers and therapists. On the religious front, there will continue to be a degree of reckless enthusiasm and at the same time a consideration tempered by serious spiritual longings and respect for the use of hallucinogens over the millennia of time. Unfortunately, in many respects, the industrialized societies are lacking in that historical cultural framework that informs indigenous man in the use of these substances. These societies' fast-paced, nature-distanced life ill prepares people for an appreciation of a powerful plant-based sacrament. Instead popular music, obsessive exposure to television images, and demanding work ethic predisposes the general member of today's society toward a psychedelic experience. That is an experience of whirling colors, intense sounds, excitement, and flowing entertainment. As the American anthropologist Peter Furst has written, "It is clearly society not chemistry, that is the variable, since the same or chemically similar drugs can function so differently in different cultural situations, or be venerated over centuries as sacred, benign, and culturally integrative in some contexts, but regarded in others as inherently so evil and dangerous that their very possession constitutes a serious crime."[38]

Notes

[1] Countries in other parts of the world vary both with respect to their laws on the use of various drugs, but on their enforcement attitudes. Hallucinogenic drugs were openly available in coffee houses in Amsterdam in 2002.

[2] *Webster's Ninth New Collegiate Dictionary.* (Springfield, MA: Merriam-Webster, 1987), 548.

[3] Wendy Doniger O'Flaherty, *The Rig Veda, An Anthology* (London: Penguin, 1981), 134.

[4] Raimundo Panikkar, *The Vedic Experience: Mantramanjari* (Delhi: Motilal Banarsidas Publishers, 1983), 822–23.

[5] Murry, followed by Glanvil (1681), cited in Michael J. Harner, *Hallucinogens and Shamanism* (London: Oxford University Press, 1973), 130–31.

[6] Richard Evans Schultes, Albert Hofmann, and Christian Ratsch, *Plants of the Gods: Their Sacred, Healing, and Hallucinogenic Powers* (Rochester, VT: Healing Arts Press, 1992).

[7] Theodore F. Brunner, "Marijuana in Ancient Greece and Rome? The Literary Evidence," *Journal of Psychedelic Drugs* 9.3 (1977).

[8] Harner, *Hallucinogens,* 139.

[9] Ibid.

[10] Ibid., 134.

[11] Cited in Charles S. Grob, *The Heffter Review of Psychedelic Research* 1.8 (1998): 53.

[12] See Schultes, Hofmann, and Ratsch, *Plants of the Gods.*

[13] Harner, *Hallucinogens,* 139.

[14] Ibid.

[15] Mircea Eliade, *Shamanism: Archaic Techniques of Ecstasy* (1951; reprint, Princeton, NJ: Princeton University Press, 1974), 223.

[16] Peter T. Furst, *Hallucinogens and Culture* (San Francisco: Chandler and Sharp, 1976), 15.

[17] Alberto Volloldo, personal communication, 2002.

[18] Eliade, *Shamanism,* 224.

[19] Furst, *Hallucinogens,* 15.

[20] Ibid., 6.

[21] Ibid., 7

[22] F. Guerra, "Mexican Phantastica—A Study of the Early Ethnobotanical Sources on Hallucinogenic Drugs," *British Journal of Addiction* 62: 171–87.

[23] Gordon R. Wasson, "Ololiuhqui and Other Hallucinogens of Mexico," in *Summa Anthropologica en homenaje*, ed. Roberto J. Weitlaner (Mexico City: Instituto Nacional de Antropologia E Historia, 1967), 329–48.

[24] Alan Watts, "Psychedelics and Religious Experience," in *Psychedelics: The Uses and Implications of Hallucinogenic Drugs*, ed. Bernard Aaronson and Humphry Osmond (New York: Doubleday, 1970), 131.

[25] Ibid., 144–45.

[26] Walter Houston Clark, *Chemical Ecstasy: Psychedelic Drugs and Religion* (New York: Sheed and Ward, 1969), 77.

[27] Humphry Osmond, "A Review of the Clinical Effects of Psychotomimetic Agents," *Annual New York Academy of Science* 66 (1957): 418–34.

[28] Timothy Leary, and Richard Alport, "The politics of consciousness," *Harvard Review* 1.4 (1967): 33–37.

[29] Stanislav Grof, *Realms of the Human Unconsciousness: Observations from LSD Research* (New York: Viking, 1967), 1.

[30] From the church's Web site, January 2002.

[31] Dan Merkur, "Manna, The Showbread, and the Eucharist: Psychoactive Sacraments in the Bible," in *Psychoactive Sacramentals: Essays of Entheogens in Religion*, ed. Thomas B. Roberts (San Francisco: Council on Spiritual Practices, 2001), 139–47.

[32] For a complete description of the Huichol pilgrimage and associated rituals, see Furst, *Hallucinogens*, 120–32.

[33] Marlene Dobkin de Rios, "Translating Peruvian Healing Practices into Counseling Techniques," *Shaman's Drum* 62 (2002): 35.

[34] Marlene Dobkin de Rios, "Hallucinogenic Ritual as Theatre," *Journal of Psychedelic Drugs* 9.3 (1977): 265.

[35] Grob, *Heffter Review*.

[36] Stanislav Grof, "The Potential of Entheogens as Catalysts of Spiritual Development," in *Psychoactive Sacramentals: Essays of Entheogens in Religion*, ed. Thomas B. Roberts (San Francisco: Council on Spiritual Practices, 2001), 34.

[37] Walter Houston Clark, "The Psychedelics and Relition," in *Psychedelics: The Use and Implications of Hallucinogenic Drugs*, ed. Bernard Aaronson and Humphry Osmond (New York: Doubleday, 1970), 194.

[38] Furst, *Hallucinogens*, 17.

Bibliography

Aaronson, Bernard, and Humphry Osmond. *Psychedelics: The Use and Implications of Hallucinogenic Drugs*. New York: Doubleday, 1970.

Aiken, John W. "The Church of the Awakening." In *Psychedelics: The Use and Implications of Hallucinogenic Drugs*. Edited by Bernard Aaronson and Humphry Osmond. New York: Doubleday, 1970.

Brunner, Theodore F. "Marijuana in Ancient Greece and Rome? The Literary Evidence," *Journal of Psychedelic Drugs* 9.3 (1977).

Callaway, Matthew. "Stonehenge and Sacred Ms: The Inspiration Behind the Circles of Stone." *Shaman's Drum* 58 (2001): 21–33.

Castaneda, Carlos. *A Separate Reality.* New York: Simon and Schuster, 1971.

———. *Tales of Power.* New York: Simon and Schuster, 1974.

———. *The Teachings of Don Juan: A Yaqui Way of Knowledge.* New York: Ballantine, 1969.

Clark, Walter Houston. *Chemical Ecstasy: Psychedelic Drugs and Religion.* New York: Sheed and Ward, 1969.

———. "The Psychedelics and Religion." In *Psychedelics: The Use and Implications of Hallucinogenic Drugs.* Edited by Bernard Aaronson and Humphry Osmond. New York: Doubleday, 1970.

de Rios, Marlene Dobkin. "Hallucinogen Ritual as Theatre." *Journal of Psychedelic Drugs* 9.3 (1977): .

———. "Translating Peruvian Healing Practices into CounselingTechniques." *Shaman's Drum* 62 (2002): 29–39.

Doblin, Rick. "Pahnke's Good Friday Experiment: A Long-term Follow-up and Methodological Critique." In *Psychoactive Sacramentals.* Edited by Thomas B. Roberts. San Francisco: Council on Spiritual Practices, 2001.

Eliade, Marcea. *Shamanism: Archaic Techniques of Ecstasy.* 1951. Reprint, Princeton, NJ: Princeton University Press, 1974.

Furst, Peter T. *Hallucinogens and Culture.* San Francisco: Chandler and Sharp, 1976.

Grob, Charles S. *The Heffter Review of Psychedelic Research* 1.8 (1998).

Grof, Stanislav. "The Potential of Entheogens as Catalysts of Spiritual Development." In *Psychoactive Sacramentals: Essays of Entheogens in Religion.* Edited by Thomas B. Roberts. San Francisco: Council on Spiritual Practices, 2001.

———. *Realms of the Human Unconscious: Observations from LSD Research.* New York: Viking, 1967.

Guerra, F. "Mexican Phantastica—A Study of the Early Ethnobotanical Sources on Hallucinogenic Drugs." *British Journal of Addiction* 62: 171–87.

Harner, Michael J. *Hallucinogens and Shamanism.* London: Oxford University Press. 1973.

Hofmann, Albert. *LSD- My Problem Child: Reflections on Sacred Drugs, Mysticism and Science.* Los Angles: J. P. Tarcher 1983.

———. "LSD as a Spiritual Aid." In *Psychoactive Sacramentals.* 121–125.

Hruby, Paula Jo. "Unitive Consciousness and Pahnkey's Good Friday Experiment." In *Psychoactive Sacramentals.* Edited by Thomas B. Roberts. San Francisco: Council on Spiritual Practices, 2001.

Huxley, Aldous. *The Doors of Perception and Heaven and Hell.* New York: Harper Collins, 1954.

Leary, Timothy, and Richard Alport. "The politics of consciousness." *Harvard Review,* 1.4 (1967): 33–37.

Lucas, Aline M. "What Is Enthology?" In *Psychoactive Sacramentals.* Edited by Thomas B. Roberts. San Francisco: Council on Spiritual Practices, 2001.

Macnicol, Nicol, ed. *Hindu Scriptures: Hymns from the Rigveda, Five Upanishads, The Bhagavadita.* New York: E. P. Dutton, 1957.

Merkur, Dan. "Manna, The Showbread, and the Eucharist: Psychoactive Sacraments in the Bible." In *Psychoactive Sacramentals*. Edited by Thomas B. Roberts. San Francisco: Council on Spiritual Practices, 2001.

O'Flaherty, Wendy Doniger. *The Rig Veda: An Anthology*. London: Penguin, 1981.

Osmond, Humphry. "A Review of the Clinical Effects of Psychotomimetic Agents." *Annual New York Academy of Science* 66 (1957): 418–34.

Pahnke, Walter N. "Drugs and Mysticism." In *Psychedelics: The Use and Implications of Hallucinogenic Drugs*. Edited by Bernard Aaronson and Humphry Osmond. New York: Doubleday, 1970.

Panikkar, Raimundo. *The Vedic Experience: Mantramanjari: An anthology of the Vedas for Modern Man and Contemporary Celebration*. Delhi: Motilal Banarsidas Publishers, 1983.

Piomelli, Daniele. "One Route to Religious Ecstasy." *Nature* 349 (1991): 362.

Roberts, Thomas B. *Psychoactive Sacramentals: Essays on Entheogens and Religion*. San Francisco: Council on Spiritual Practices, 2001.

Schultes, Richard Evans, Albert Hofmann, and Christian Ratsch. *Plants of the Gods: Their Sacred, Healing, and Hallucinogenic Powers.* Rochester, VT: Healing Arts Press, 1992.

Smith, Huston. "Do Drugs Have Religious Import? A Thirty-Five Year Retrospect." In *Psychoactive Sacramentals*. Edited by Thomas B. Roberts. San Francisco: Council on Spiritual Practices, 2001.

Steindl-Rast, David. "Psychoactive Sacramentals." In *Psychoactive Sacramentals*. Edited by Thomas B. Roberts. San Francisco: Council on Spiritual Practices, 2001.

Tagore, Rabindranath. In *Hindu Scriptures*. Edited by Nicol Macnicol. New York: E. P. Dutton, 1957.

Tart, Charles. "Psychoactive Sacramentals: What Must Be Said." In *Psychoactive Sacramentals*. Edited by Thomas B. Roberts. San Francisco: Council on Spiritual Practices, 2001.

Von Glascoe, C., D. Metzger, A. Palomino, Ernesto Vargas, and Carter Wilson. "Are You Going to Learn to Chew Coca Like Us?" *Journal of Psychedelic Drugs* 9.3 (1977):

Wasson, Gordon R. *Soma: Divine Mushroom of Immortality*. New York: Harcourt Brace, 1968.

———. "Ololiuhqui and Other Hallucinogens of Mexico." In *Summa Anthropologica en homenaje*. Edited by Roberto J. Weitlaner. Mexico City: Instituto Nacional de Antropologia E Historia, 1967.

Watts, Alan. "Psychedelics and Religious Experience." In *Psychedelics: The Uses and Implications of Hallucinogenic Drugs*. Edited by Bernard Aaronson and Humphry Osmond. New York: Doubleday, 1970.

Young, Mike. "If I Could Change Your Mind." In *Psychoactive Sacramentals*. Edited by Thomas B. Roberts. San Francisco: Council on Spiritual Practices, 2001.

Part II

Alcohol in Historical Context

6 Monastic Moonshine:
Alcohol in the Middle Ages

Deborah Vess

I am the vine, you are the branches: Those who abide in me and I in them bear much fruit.

John 15:5

"A man had two sons; he went to the first and said, 'Son, go and work in the vineyard today.' He answered, 'I will not,' but later he changed his mind and went. The father went to the second son and said the same; and he answered, 'I go, sir,' but he did not go. Which of the two did the will of his father?" They said, "The first."

Matthew 21:28–31

They are truly monks when they live by the labor of their hands.

The Rule of St. Benedict, chapter 48

My first college level teaching position was at a monastic-sponsored school, Benedictine College in Atchison, Kansas. After the first faculty meeting I attended, I watched with amazement when the dean, herself a Benedictine nun, along with several assistants, brought out huge barrels packed with ice and beer and other alcoholic beverages. I could not help but chuckle as many of the monks proceeded to take an extra beer or two and stuff them into the deep recesses of their habits for later enjoyment. As a medievalist, it was natural for me to see these monks as icons of a past age, continuing a very long, intimate, and productive relationship between monasteries and alcohol.

The shape of the famous *bocksbeutel*, a squat, flagon-shaped green or amber bottle used for wine in the Franken region of Germany illustrates the extent to which consumption of alcoholic beverages was an omnipresent aspect of medieval monastic life. The name of the bottle comes from the German word for a male goat, *bock*. Although the shape of a goat's scrotum allegedly inspired the bottle's shape, many think that the ease with which monks could tuck them underneath their habits more correctly explains the practical shape.

In fact, one of the popular conceptions of monastic life in the late Middle Ages was that monks and nuns had become lax in their observance of discipline. This was especially true of the Reformation era, when many visitations of religious houses resulted in accusations of monastic corruption. Among the charges was wanton consumption of wine and other alcoholic beverages. Popular songs of the Middle Ages reflect these attitudes. The monks of Saint Nicholas at Angers, for example, made a particularly famous wine, La Roche aux Moines. This monastery was the home of the infamous Abbot Adam, celebrated in a ninth-century song as the "purple abbot." The abbot "had such a mighty thirst" that "never did a day or night go by, but it found him wine-soaked and wavering even as a tree that the high winds sway." The abbot so loved the fruit of the vine that his skin had become purple, or "deep tanned with wine." The poet humorously relates that he was so thoroughly soaked from his years of excessive imbibing that "as to body was he incorruptible."[1]

The ribald Renaissance author Rabelais, who in his lifetime was first a Franciscan friar and then a Benedictine monk, satirized the monastic love of wine in *Gargantua and Pantagruel* when he had Pantagruel set off on a quest not for the Holy Grail, as in Arthurian legend,[2] but for the Oracle of the Divine Bottle. Friar John, a companion of Pantagruel, makes the apt remark that "no man of honor hates a good wine; which is a monkish saying." John's love of wine makes him "a true monk if ever there has been one since the monking world monked its first monkery."[3] According to an old monk's prayer, "He who drinks wine sleeps well. He who sleeps well cannot sin. He who does not sin goes to heaven. Amen."

Even in modern times, one of the founders of Benedictine life in America, Boniface Wimmer, inspired controversy when his superiors chastised him for operating a brewery in Indiana. Nevertheless, this did not stop him from founding another more famous one at St. Vincent's Abbey, in Latrobe, Pennsylvania. Such activities led more puritanical Americans in the nineteenth century to label the Benedictines as the Order of Sacred Brewers.[4] Monastic love of the brew and the profit that may come from it still linger on in contemporary imagination, as in the riotously funny novel *God Is My Broker*. Here, Brother Ty, seeking refuge from an addiction to the bottle, enters a monastery and financially transforms the community by reading Deepak Chopra.[5] Indeed, monasteries and alcohol complement one another like bread and butter, a relationship one can understand not so much through humor as through an examination of monastic spirituality. Wimmer's brewery was a companion to the abbey gristmill, a symbiosis succinctly captured by one modern monk who reminds us that, "God made us to eat [and drink]. And there's something spiritual in that."[6]

Many of the portraits mentioned above are caricatures of monastic culture and overlook the deep spirituality and theology that was the basis of monastic consumption of the fruit of the vine. To begin with, a drunken monk was likely much more difficult to come by than these stories would suggest. Wine-makers sealed their products with wax before Dom Perignon discovered the cork in the eighteenth century. This made wine turn to vinegar very quickly and, consequently, medieval wine was not as strong as wines are today. Until the nineteenth century, people consumed wine immediately after production, directly out of wooden casks, again resulting in a weaker concoction. Such revisionist commentary, however, only scratches the surface, and one must turn to monastic spirituality to uncover the truths that these humorous stories contain. The monastic life was ideally an *imitatio Christi*. In the Mass, the central act of the Catholic liturgy, the host and wine become the body and blood of Christ.

The medieval iconographer often played on the association between the blood of Christ and the wine of the sacrament, as Christ is often shown standing on top of a vat of grapes, being squeezed by the wine-press with blood from his wounds flowing into the Church. From this point of view, Christ is the ultimate wine-maker and, therefore, it is not surprising that monastic houses devoted to the worship of the crucified Christ excelled in the production of the fruit of the vine.

Vineyards often serve as a metaphor for the kingdom of God in both the Old and New Testaments. In Isaiah 5:7, for example, the prophet likens the House of Israel to the "vineyard of the Lord of hosts." Similarly, Jesus, heir of the House of David, claimed to be the "true vine" and on several occasions likened his new spirituality to labor in a vineyard.[7] In Matthew, chapters 20 and 21, for example, Jesus told three parables about vineyard owners where he likened admission into the kingdom of heaven to those who were willing to toil in the vineyard. Jesus said, "The kingdom of heaven is like a landowner who went out early in the morning to hire laborers for his vineyard" (Matt. 20:1). Even those workers who came last were to be rewarded in the same way as those who came first, and even the son who originally declined to work but later toiled in the vineyard earned the approval of his father.[8] In another telling parable, Jesus discussed the case of a vineyard owner who rents his lands to tenants. When the owner sent his messengers and later his own son to collect rent, the ungrateful tenants refused to pay. Just as the vineyard owner ousts tenants who refuse to pay rent, the God would give the heavenly vineyards or his kingdom to "other husbandmen, which shall render him the fruits in their seasons ... the Kingdom of God shall be ... given to a nation bringing forth the fruits thereof" (Matt. 21:41–43). Christians were the new heirs to the Kingdom of God, and toiling in the vineyard of the Lord to bring forth new spiritual fruit was their task.

Clearly the monasteries literally enacted this imagery, as they owned the vast majority of vineyards in Europe during the Middle Ages. The great Benedictine house of Cluny in Burgundy, for example, was the largest landowner in France during the Middle Ages, and it owned all of the most productive and best vineyards. When the French Revolution erupted in the eighteenth century, Benedictines owned half of all the vineyards in France. Members of monastic communities planted many of their vineyards in locations strongly associated with the Christian tradition. The Benedictine monk Dom Perignon made one of the greatest discoveries in the history of wine-making, the use of the cork as a bottle stopper, at the monastery of Hautvillers in France. This monastery had as its most treasured relic the body of Constantine the Great's mother, St. Helena, whom tradition credits with the discovery in the fourth century CE of the true cross in Jerusalem. Hautvillers reflects the intimate connection between the cross, the blood of Christ, and the wine of the sacrament, as the labors of Dom Perignon in the vineyard of the Lord took place in the shadow of St. Helena.

The monasteries themselves often made the connection with wine-making and the blood of Christ explicit in their choice of names. One of the oldest monasteries in Switzerland, for example, bore the name of St.

Maurice, who is credited with having preserved the Holy Lance. The Holy Lance pierced the side of Christ making blood and water to flow together, and throughout history it has been a symbol of the redemptive power of the crucifixion and the Christian's death and rebirth through baptism. The emperor Constantine later possessed the Holy Lance, and a rather dubious tradition held that a nail, perhaps from the true cross, embedded in its head dated from the time of St. Helena. The monastery of St. Maurice owned many lucrative vineyards around Lake Geneva and produced a very fine white Yvorne wine from Chasselas grapes, known locally as Dorin grapes.

The hagiographers of St. Martin of Tours, the first monk to bring monasticism to France, strongly associate him with the vine. Tourangeots still celebrate St. Martin's feast by drinking wine, and they refer to excessive drunkenness even today as "St. Martin's sickness." The word for drinking alcohol is *martiner*, and to tap the wine barrel is still known as *martiner le vin*. The historian Gregory of Tours, himself a monk, relates that the relics of St. Martin worked a miracle reminiscent of the first miracle of Jesus, the turning of water into wine at the Wedding Feast of Cana. Gregory claimed that when a nun placed an empty wine jar next to St. Martin's tomb, each time she placed a single drop of holy water in it, the jar miraculously overflowed with wine. This story again points to the strong connection in the monastic life between the Gospels and the vineyard. St. Martin's earthly diligence in the vineyard of the Lord resulted in the domestication of the wild grapes of the Touraine forest and the development the Chenin Noir and the Chenin Blanc grapes, which wineries use most widely today for the famous white wines of Touraine and Anjou. St. Martin also planted the first Vouvray vineyard on a slope by Marmoutier. Vouvray depends on the sun and, consequently, the English still call summer Martinmastide. According to another legend, St. Martin's donkey while tethered once ate everything in the vineyard above knee level. The monks panicked, believing their crop had been ruined, and then were greatly surprised when they produced their best wine ever that year. The wine-makers of Touraine still grow their grapes near the ground. The inhabitants of Trier, Germany, still celebrate St. Martin's feast on the day young wine is tasted.[9]

One can better understand the stories above as lived expressions of the medieval method of exegesis, according to which the Scriptures contained multiple layers of meaning. The medieval theologian believed that Scripture taught literal as well as allegorical, tropological or moral, and anagogical truths.[10] St. Martin, as well as countless monks and nuns, took these parables and teachings of Jesus literally as they toiled physically in the vineyards and developed some of the most famous wines in the world. They also interpreted the Scriptures in their other senses as they spiritualized manual labor.

St. Benedict of Nursia is credited with writing the most influential Rule for monastics in the west. According to his teachings, "idleness was the enemy of the soul,"[11] and so he enjoined monastics to spend a third of their day in manual labor. For Benedict, those who would live the monastic life are "truly monks when they live by the labor of their hands."[12] Benedict also described the duties of various members and leaders of the community, including the cellarer, who had charge of dispensing goods. Benedict urged the cellarer to "treat everything as a vessel of the altar."[13] Benedictines applied this teaching to all things they touched, from the land worked in the fields to their own material goods. In fact, Benedict likened the way one behaves toward the material goods in one's care to the way one cultivates the spiritual tools given to them. Just as a soul is a sacred vessel to be lovingly polished,[14] so, too, one's care of material goods is to be equally reverent.[15] During work in the fields, monastics recited the psalms or someone read them aloud, creating a context in which work itself became another form of prayer. Dom Jean Leclercq describes medieval monastic *lectio*, or meditation on the Scriptures, as involving recitation aloud. Such meditation involved movement of the lips and, as one listened to "the voices of the pages," one literally "ate" the word and then spiritually digested it.[16] Scripture passed through the mouth physically and entered deep into the soul spiritually, thus harmonizing body and soul. This itself is a form of holy work, and the physical tilling of the vineyards or fields then serves as an allegory for the spiritual tilling of the soul.

The Benedictine motto of *ora et labora*, or "pray and work," does not represent two separate endeavors, but rather different aspects of a life devoted to seeking God. Prayer is a form of work, as Benedictines and other monastic orders recite the Divine Office several times daily; conversely, work is a form of prayer, as Benedictines treat everything as if it were Christ himself. Whatever one touched should be transformed into a holy vessel for God's work and, therefore, Benedictines developed a strong belief in stewardship of the earth. In this way, they explored, meditated upon, and enacted the parables of Jesus on vineyards in all their meanings, from the literal to the allegorical, to the tropological or moral, and to the anagogical interpretations.

As monasticism spread across Europe, monks and nuns in many locations followed the Rule of St. Benedict either in its entirety or in combination with other rules. Among the most important group of monks who adopted the Rule in its entirety were the Cluniacs, an order founded in the tenth century. While Benedict spoke of the need to balance work, study, and prayer during each day, he did not mandate that every group who adopted his Rule follow it to the letter. In fact, he understood that different conditions in different locations might result in diverse needs. Hence, communities often adapted the Rule to their own needs and preferences in their customaries. The Cluniacs tended to emphasize liturgy, or *ora*, over manual labor, *labora*. The Cluniac love of liturgy eventually consumed their day to the point where they engaged in the *laus perpetua*, a twenty-four–hour continuous recitation of the divine office. Nevertheless, the Cluniacs, who rarely got themselves dirty in the fields, wore black habits and were ironically known as the Black Monks of Benedict.[17] Even though Cluniacs did not often physically work in the fields, they still had a need for vineyards, as wine was required for liturgical events, such as the Mass. The historian Desmond Steward, himself a member of the Knights of Malta, estimated that a modern monastery of thirty uses 155 gallons of wine a year simply for sacramental purposes.[18] Medieval records indicate even greater use, as many monasteries were often larger than thirty members. In the ninth century, for example, the monastery of Saint Germain des Prés produced 11,000 gallons of wine a year. So important was wine for the monks who were ordained as priests to use in their required daily recitation of mass and for the distribution of unconsecrated wine to commoners after mass that one finds the yearly ritual of planting, pruning, and harvesting recorded in monastic foundation charters, such as that of the abbey of

Muri near Zurich. France became a center of wine-making in the Middle Ages largely due to Benedictine influence.[19]

In the eleventh century, the Black Monk Robert of Molesme and several of his followers believed their way of life to be too lax and began a movement based on a reinterpretation of the Benedictine Rule. They founded a *novum monasterium* or "new monastery" at a place called Cîteaux in France. Robert had a strongly ascetic and eremitical streak, and he and his followers interpreted the Rule of St. Benedict very literally. They wished to restore the balance of liturgical activities with manual labor. Although other monks, such as the Cluniacs, had neglected this kind of work, the Cistercians dedicated themselves to the revival of manual labor as a third of the monastic day. Treating the land as a "vessel of the altar," Cistercians reclaimed vast wastelands in places like York, England, which William the Conqueror ravaged during the Norman conquest. What once were the barren frontiers of Germany now were lush and fertile lands. In the Book of Amos, chapter 9 verse 14, it is prophesied that "they shall build the waste cities and inhabit them; and shall plant vineyards and drink the wine thereof." Linking the Old Testament to the New, the Cistercians founded their houses in the most desolate locations, and then turned these barren wastelands into fertile fields dotted with vineyards. Geraldis Cambrensis (Gerald of Wales) said of the Cistercians that, "Give these monks a naked moor or wild wood; then let a few years pass away and you will find not only beautiful churches but dwellings of men built around them."[20] Orderic Vitalis linked the Cistercian zeal for manual labor to Gospel imagery when he wrote that, "though evil abounds in the world, the devotion of the faithful in the cloisters grows more abundant and bears fruit a hundredfold in the Lord's field ... the swarm of cowled monks spreads all over the world."[21] Orderic praised Cistercian spirituality, remarking that "many who were parched with thirst have drunk from their spring; many streams have flowed out of it through all parts of France."[22] Despite a rigorous life of manual labor that must have left an obvious imprint on their bodies and clothing, they wore stark white habits and were consequently known as the White Monks.

During the next several decades, the Cistercian way of life grew in popularity to such an extent that some historians argue that "all Europe threatened to become Cîteaux."[23] The Cistercians were often at odds with the Cluniacs, and the most famous Cistercian, Bernard of Clairvaux, denounced Cluny as a "den of thieves." Bernard also denounced wine, but even within his own lifetime Clairvaux had a vineyard, and within just a few years owned thirteen of them. The Cistercians produced some of the finest wine in all Europe, such as Meursault, named for a village that the Cistercians first acquired in 1108. The village of Meursault is famous for its white wines. One of its most famous vineyards was Les Perrières. Wine from Meursault was a favorite of many notorious figures in European history, such as the Cardinal de Bernis, the abbé for Madame de Pompadours, who said that he celebrated Mass with Meursault so he did not grimace at the moment of communion when confronting the Lord.[24] The vineyard of Les Perrières belonged to the Cistercians until the French Revolution. The White Monks also influenced wine making in Germany and introduced the Blauburgundeer grape to the Rhine area. This grape is the Pinot Noir from which German wine-makers produce all red hocks and, ironically, none other than St. Bernard himself first brought it to the Rhine area from his homeland of Burgundy.[25] The Benedictine motto of *ora et labora* accounts for the success of both white and black Benedictine monks in the art of wine making.[26]

Although Benedict emphasized manual labor, he also discouraged his monks from excessive drinking. In chapter 40 of his Rule, Benedict wrote that, "indeed we read that wine is not a drink for monks, but since monks cannot nowadays be persuaded of this, let us at least agree to drink sparingly and not to take our fill, as 'wine maketh even the wise to fall away.' "[27] Benedict limited monks to a "half bottle," equivalent to half a pint of wine a day.[28] Benedict himself had a bad experience with wine earlier in his career, before founding the monastery of Monte Cassino. While a hermit at Subiaco, a group of unruly monks at Vicovara invited Benedict to serve as abbot. They were much like the sarabaites Benedict describes in the first chapter of his Rule, who refused to be governed by any sort of discipline.[29] According to tradition, when Benedict was about to drink a cup of wine that his charges had poisoned out of resentment for his attempt to impose monastic *askesis*, or discipline, on them, the glass shattered when he made the sign of the cross.[30]

On another occasion, a disciple rather humorously named Exhilaratus brought Benedict two wooden flasks of wine but kept one for himself. Benedict warned him to "Take heed, my son that thou drinkest not of that flagon which thou hast hidden in the bush: but first be careful to bow it down, and thou shalt find what is within it." When Exhilaratus returned to the hidden cask, he bent down and a snake emerged from the wine, a telling reminder of Benedict's hesitation in the Rule about the drinking of wine.[31]

Nevertheless, Benedict was devoted to the Eucharist. In fact, he died in front of the altar awaiting the reception of the consecrated host and wine. Fittingly, if one stands within the central court of the abbey of Monte Cassino today, very near a statue of Benedict commemorating his death, one can see the vineyards on the hill owned by the monks. Although Monte Cassino does not produce one of the better wines in Europe, they do produce wine for Mass, and their vineyards symbolize the sacramental nature of manual labor and the importance of wine in monastic life. This importance was clearly evident at the medieval Benedictine monastery of Norwich, where the nuns enclosed the vineyards within the cloister.

Benedict spoke of his Rule as "a little rule" for beginners,[32] and emphasized the need for constant vigilance against evil. Benedict taught his followers that upon reaching the end of his little Rule, they should start all over again. True monastic *conversatio,* the third vow or promise made by Benedictines, is never-ending. The word *conversatio* is related to the Latin word *conversare,* which is a frequentive form of the verb *convertere,* meaning "to convert." The use of the frequentive form calls forth the notion of a continuous conversion or turning of the will.[33] True conversion is not a single turning of the will, but one in which the will turns and turns again. Benedict also likened his famous steps of humility to the vision of Jacob, where Jacob saw angels ascending and descending the ladder to heaven. Conversion is a form of monastic stability, as one makes the firm commitment to turn the will toward God, even in the face of setbacks and difficult times. Benedictine spirituality emphasizes ordinariness and the idea that one does not find the Divine primarily in some remote, transcendent sphere, but in the immanent realm of one's ordinary, daily activities.

The Benedictine belief in treating everything as a vessel of the altar and in seeking God within the ordinary results in the prudent use of everything with which one comes into contact. For Benedictines, perfectly ordinary things become sacramental, and they applied this belief to the remnants of the wine-making process. Monks and nuns turned inferior wines into vinegar and inferior grapes into juice for pickling. They used the residue of the process for manure to fertilize their fields and made soap from the pips,[34] which they also used as chicken feed or even to flavor cheese. The monks used the leaves from the grapes to feed their cattle in the fall, and used vine wood for an aromatic fuel. Medieval people commonly used wine as a disinfectant and in England they used it as a remedy for sore throats. Just as the sacramental wine of the Eucharist heals the spirit, unconsecrated wine heals the body.

Among the most famous products of monasteries are liqueurs, which their makers originally intended as medications. People still use them for this purpose in parts of Europe today. In fact, in medieval times people often referred to liqueurs as the *aquae vitae* or "waters of life." Liqueurs were very expensive to produce and, consequently, were rarely found outside of monasteries before the seventeenth century. Even many of the most famous monastic liqueurs have their origin in the late Middle Ages or early modern period. *Affentaler*, marketed in bottles with a red-eyed monkey on the front, is a tonic wine for invalids. Its name comes from the name of the place in which it was made, Affental, which originally meant "ave tal" or "Hail Mary Valley." In German, however, the word *affe* means "ape." Hence, the unusual packaging. *Benedictine* is another example still in use today. The Venetian monk Dom Bernardo Vincelli first made the amber-colored liqueur in 1510 at the Abbey of Fécamp from a cognac base sweetened with honey. Twenty-seven plants and spices flavored the exotic drink, which was a favorite in the court of François I. Today a company markets it with the abbreviation DOM on the label, which stands for *deo optimo maximo*, or "to God the greatest good." While the original formula contained Chinese tea, the modern formula does not. The monks of Kloster Ettal in Bavaria, founded in

1330, make a jade green liqueur and the monks often put it into chocolates. They also make a yellow liqueur. The Cistercians of the abbey of Seanque in Provence, founded in 1148, produce La Senancole, a yellow liqueur. The Cistercian Congregation of Senanque make Lerina, flavored with over forty plants. The Cistercians of the Strict Observance, or Trappists, at Tre Fontane produce a yellow and green liqueur flavored with eucalyptus plants.[35]

Wines were by far, however, the more successful commodity of Benedictine monks and nuns. The twelfth-century visionary Hildegard of Bingen illustrated the monastic love of wine when she said that, AMann macht den Menschen gewund; der Wein macht den Menschen gesund ("Men hurt men, but wine heals them"). The nuns of Hildegard's monastery near Bingen still make wine today. Many monastic wines, like the liqueurs, were thought to have strong healing properties or to otherwise benefit the body. The best known wines of Hungary are Somló wines, produced at Somlovasarhely, a Benedictine nunnery founded by King Stephen. The nuns make the best Somló from the Furmint grape, and its wines include Juhfark, also known as Lamb's Tail. For years, every Hapsburg Archduke drank a glass on his wedding night in the hope that he would beget sons and not daughters.[36]

Another Hungarian monastic wine, Egri Bikavér, was indirectly responsible for a "miraculous" event. In the sixteenth century, the Turks suddenly abandoned their terrifying attack because they thought the Hungarians were drinking blood and retreated. In honor of this event, Hungarians also call the wine the "bull's blood from Eger." Benedictine monks who originally came from France first made Egri Bikavér starting in the eleventh century. Although it was considered a fine wine in the Middle Ages, today it is much less highly valued and considered only an average wine at best. In the Middle Ages it was full flavored and bodied, due to the mixture of Kadarka, Kékfrankos, and Médoc Noir (merlot) grapes. Some think the decline in its quality may be due to a greater preponderance of the Kékfrankos over the better Kadarka grape.

Sometimes the wines themselves had miraculous longevity, as for example, the famous bottle of 1772 Château-Chalon given to the French president in 1991. Benedictine nuns first made Château-Chalon, which today are the world famous classic wines of France. Château-Chalon is a remote village in the Jura region of eastern France. Today, a taste for fine wine is often a symbol of high breeding. Similarly, in the Middle Ages, a taste for fine wine was one of the many aspects of noble life. Château-Chalon wine was popular in the court of François I. Marshal Biron, who plotted the downfall of Henry IV during Reformation times, was reputedly obsessed with the wine. Even the wine-makers themselves, the nuns of Château-Chalon, had to produce sixteen proofs of their nobility to be admitted. Their best wine is a white savagnin, made from a fairly rare type of grape. The nuns first produced the wine when an abbess in the fourteenth century ordered her nuns to pick the grapes as late as possible. The nuns originally fermented the wine in vats carved out of natural rock, and they left the wine in its cask for six to ten years. A film of yeast, which prevents oxidation but allows for evaporation, covers the wine. It is a very strong, concentrated wine, rather dark yellow in color, with a nutty, rich taste that wine connoisseurs have compared to sherry.

Benedictines produced other famous wines not so much through monastic ingenuity as by accident, such as the world famous wine from Johannisberg. The vineyard at Johannisberg dates back to Carolingian times, and the first recorded harvest in 817 CE produced about 6,000 liters of grape juice. In 850 Rhabanus Maurus named the mountain Bischofsberg, or "mountain of the bishop." The vineyard of Johannisberg became the greatest vineyard in Rheingau, Germany. In 1130, the Archbishop of Mainz gave Benedictine monks the Priory of St. Alban in Mainz. The monks dedicated it to St. John and made wine throughout the late Middle Ages. Their finest wines, however, would not be made until after the dissolution of the Priory during the upheavals of the Reformation era. In 1716, the Benedictine abbot of the monastery of Fulda acquired the property and made its vineyards famous. The monks made the wine from Riesling grapes, and they became the first Germans to bottle their wines, producing a fine hock wine. According to legends, in 1775 the Prince abbot of Fulda forgot to announce the time for vendange. The monks at Johannisberg were frantic and sent a horseman to Fulda to remind the prince that it was time to harvest the grapes. On the way back, highwaymen held up the messenger, and the grapes had almost turned to raisins on the vine by the time he returned to the monastery. The monks were stunned to discover that the result of the *Spätlese* or late harvest was not a disaster, but rather an excellent dessert wine classified as *Beerenauslese* and *Trockenbeerenauslese,* two of the highest subcategories of *Qualitätswein mit Prädikat* ("quality wine with distinction" or "quality wine with special attributes"), the highest quality of wine as defined by modern German laws. Both of these wines are very sweet, very rare, and very expensive.[37] The wines from Johannisberg were so renowned that one abbot had a special cellar constructed at Fulda for his best Johannisberg. A secret cabinet administered the cellar, and hence, the Germans still describe some wines as *kabinett* wines. The term *Kabinett* refers to the lowest of six subcategories under the category of *Qualitätswein mit Prädikat.*[38]

Another famous monastic wine is Chablis, produced by the White Monks of the monastery of Pontigny. The Cistercians bought the vineyards there from the monks of St. Martin of Tours. They were the first to plant the white chardonnay grape, the basis of all fine white Burgundies today. The monks floated the wine down to Chablis on barges. Among the most famous vineyards of Chablis is Vosgros, which is classified today as a *premier cru* vineyard. It is one of about forty vineyards with this status that denotes wines second only to those of *grand cru* vineyards in quality. Similarly, the Cistercians acquired Clos de Vougeot in Burgundy in 1110 and got complete control of its vineyards two centuries later in 1336. They surrounded the 125 acres of vines there with a "clos" or high stone wall, thus creating the largest vineyard in Burgundy that produced the finest of all Burgundy wines. The Cistercians there produced both red and white wines, and connoisseurs consider the white wine inferior only to Chablis and Meursault. A story from the fourteenth century illustrates the extent to which many individuals valued the wine. The humanist Francesco Petrarch apparently faced a difficult task as he tried to persuade Pope Urban V to leave Avignon and return to Rome. The pope loved Clos de Vougeot wine, and it could not be easily found on the Italian side of the Alps. Often the success of monasteries producing fine wine was tied to political power, as when the Abbot Jean de Bussière sent thirty hogsheads of Clos containing about 228 liters each to Pope Gregory XI on the occasion of his election in 1371. Three years later the abbot became a cardinal. The saying, *qui bon vin boit, Dieu voit* ("He who drinks good wine, God sees") depicts the power of great wine to win great favors.[39]

Monks and nuns in the region of Burgundy produced many other fine wines. Among the finest and most expensive wines in the world are from the Burgundian monastery of Saint Vivant at Vosne-Romanée. One of its best known vineyards is romanée-saint-vivant, which produced a wine prescribed for Louis XIV. The French classify this vineyard today as a *grand cru* vineyard, the highest designation possible. Another famous Burgundian vineyard was located at Pommard. Pommard is a red wine made from the Pinot Noir grape. The Renaissance humanist Erasmus often criticized the emphasis on outer practice as opposed to inner spirituality and was an advocate for reform of the Church before the Reformation broke out. Erasmus was an Augustinian canon early in life and struggled with monastic abstinence. He loved Pommard so much that he once consumed it on a fast day. When criticized for his indulgence, he responded with the famous remark that "my heart is Catholic but my stomach is Protestant."

Because monastic life required a contemplative lifestyle devoted to prayer, royalty often patronized monasteries in return for their prayers. St. Carilef of Calais founded his community in a vast forest about thirty miles southeast of Le Mans after he saw a "little vine bathed in mysterious light." The blessed vine produced so much wine that the community was easily able to entertain the Merovingian King Childebert and his entire court. According to legend, the emperor Charlemagne gave the vineyards at Aloxe-Corton in Burgundy to the monastery of Saulieu in 775 CE, as a result of his wife's complaint about the red stains from wine on his beard. The monks there learned to produce a white wine, which has been renowned for centuries. In the Enlightenment, the wine was a favorite of the infamous agnostic Voltaire, one of the strongest critics of monks. Today, the French rank the vineyards as *grand crus*, the highest rank wines can attain. Connoisseurs consider wine from this region to be among the world's finest.

Royal patronage continued when one of Charlemagne's descendants, Charles the Bald, gave the vineyards at Chablis to his brother Eudes, who was then abbot of St. Martin's monastery at Tours. As noted earlier,

King Stephen of Hungary established the Benedictine nunnery that later produced Somló. The *Codex Laureshamensis* records an impressive list of vineyards all over South Germany presented to the monastery of Lrosch by nobles. In the ninth century, the abbey of St. Denis, which contained the tombs of many Merovingian and Carolingian rulers in the Middle Ages, owned numerous vineyards in the *Ile de France*, the *desmesne* of the King. It was at St. Denis in the thirteenth century that the young boy Stephen, one of the leaders of the Children's Crusade, appeared to King Philip to request his blessing on his ill-fated expedition. He claimed to have been inspired in his quest by a vision of Christ himself. Here, too, the Abbot Suger first developed the Gothic style of architecture. Similarly, the Cistercian monk Bernard of Clairvaux preached the Second Crusade to an assembly of royalty at a Benedictine community, whose tympanum proudly features intertwined vines.

The wines of St. Pourçain, an abbey in the Loire basin established in the sixth century, also illustrate the connection between monastic wines and royalty. Once when the saintly King Louis IX gave a banquet for his brother, what guests most remembered was the St. Pourçain wine. King François I also had a passion for the wine. One can imagine that there would have been considerable benefits for the abbeys when the courts favored their wines and the monks made the most of these gifts. The German King Otto II gave the monastery of St. Maximin large numbers of vineyards in 996; seven centuries later, records show the monks there planting 100,000 new vines.[40] Certainly it could not be said of monks that they did not produce the fruit of the fields described in the parables of Christ.

So favored were monasteries for their wine-making industries that medieval monarchs often exempted them from taxes on their wines. Monasteries were frequently deeply tied to feudal society. The Cluniacs, for example, owned many villages whose laborers helped to cultivate their vineyards. The wealthier the communities became through royal and noble patronage, the more they could control industry in their geographic regions. The Abbey of Marmoutier at Boire in Anjou, for example, had a monopoly on wine pressing. Local growers had no choice but to take their grapes to the abbey press. Indeed, by the French

Revolution in the eighteenth century, half the vineyards in France belonged to the Benedictines.

Many of these monasteries developed amazingly large and profitable operations, such as the Cistercian monastery of Clos Vougeot in Burgundy, which owned the vineyard of Château Canternac Prieuré. By the eighteenth century, the monastery had an annual income of 24,000 livres or over 1,000 pounds from its vineyards. The Benedictine abbey of Sainte Croix in Bordeaux bought the vineyard of Château Carbonnieux in the Graves region of Bordeaux, where they made a dry white wine. Thomas Jefferson once visited the abbey and reported that they made fifty tonneaux each year and sold them for 800 pounds each. Monastic enterprise often went beyond profit on the continent. A rather suspect but entertaining story has the monks smuggling their wine into Islamic lands. Since the Qur'an forbids the drinking of alcohol, the monks had disguised the wine by calling it *Eaux Minerales de Carbonnieux*. When the Turks captured a young French woman who had taken some of the wine into Turkey, she promptly gave the wine to the Sultan. The unsuspecting Turks drank it and were quite taken with this "mineral water." They subsequently wondered why Christians would drink wine when they had such wonderful water!

In the twelfth century the Cistercians of Kloster Eberbach acquired Steinberg, which had a vineyard on a hill. The monks cleared the woods there and planted a vineyard that covered sixty acres. The Cistercians at Steinberg produced another of the world's truly great wines, one of the dessert wines known as *Trockenbeerenauslese*. Steinberg was the biggest vineyard in Germany, as evidenced by reports from the sixteenth century of the size of their vat. The vat was twenty-eight feet long and nine feet high. Fourteen ropes held it together and it had an amazing capacity of 22,000 gallons. According to records from 1506, the abbey's warehouse in Cologne contained 150,000 gallons of its 1503–34 vintages. One wonders whether these medieval monks got the same financial advice as the mythical Brother Ty from the "Supreme Insider."[41]

In the Middle Ages, such financial success was often viewed with suspicion. In fact, the Benedictine Rule does not prohibit the community itself from ownership of goods or from profitable enterprises; it only forbids the individual monk to hold private goods.[42] Nevertheless, the financial success of communities often led to charges of corruption and lax discipline. In the eleventh and twelfth centuries as well as throughout the later Middle Ages, dissatisfaction with monastic life in the face of evolving social, political, and economic conditions created new forms of religious life. The wealth of the Cluniacs, for example, in part prompted the austerities of the Cistercian reform. The movements of the Central and late Middle Ages created many new religious orders, and these various groups, despite having origins in a desire for increased asceticism, ironically also contributed to profitable wine- and liqueur-making industries.

During the Crusades, which Urban II first preached in 1095, the pope gave the knights a way to make their furious warfare a holy occupation by fighting the Muslims and freeing the Holy Land. Several orders of military monks evolved, such as the Knights Templar. The Templars were warrior monks who pledged themselves to a life of prayer and austerity. Nevertheless, medieval people commonly used the phrase to "drink like a Templar" to refer to a huge thirst, and the phrase conveyed some of the success of the Templars at the art of viticulture. The vineyards of the Templars at Épernay produced a still champagne, which was considered one of the finest medieval wines. The Templars supported their activities in the Holy Land through vast estates in Europe. Their legacy lives on in the names of some modern vineyards of France, such as the Clos des Templiers, where wine-makers still produce the red wine Champigny in the Loire valley. Another military order, the Knights of St. John or the Hospitallers, had vineyards on Cyprus that produced Commandaria, a sweet brown wine drunk with four parts water to wine. It was also one of the most highly prized vintages in medieval Europe. Another of the new religious orders of the central Middle Ages, the Premonstratensians, also produced a wine on Cyprus known as Belpais. Only Commandaria could rival its quality.

The Carthusians, an eremitical order founded in the central Middle Ages at Le Grande Chartreuse by Bruno, once a canon of the Cathedral of Rheims, produced perhaps one of the most famous of all alcoholic beverages. The Carthusians did not follow the Rule of St. Benedict, but rather pursued the solitary life within individual cells clustered together known as Charterhouses. Their most famous product did not fall into their hands until the seventeenth century, when François-Hannibal d'Estrées, Marshall of the Artillery of France, gave to the Paris Charterhouse an exotic recipe of 130 herbs distilled in cognac. In 1737, the Prior of the Paris Charterhouse passed the recipe on to the Prior General of Le Grande Chartreuse. Since that time, the Carthusians have produced this mysterious liqueur, known as Chartreuse, a delectable green liquid whose ingredients the Carthusians still keep secret.[43]

The Franciscans were another new order that soon began to produce wine. They cannot be regarded as monastics per se, as they take no vow of stability. In the early years of the order, the friars minor led a mendicant life wandering from place to place and begging for their food. Although St. Francis led a life of great austerity, wearing a simple brown habit that he mended repeatedly, later medieval Franciscans earned a risqué reputation for their love of spirits. Chaucer lampooned a friar in the *Canterbury Tales* as one who "knew the tavernes wel in every town."[44] Some of these humorous commentaries on Franciscans continue today, as seen in the *Weasel Breweries*, a Web site devoted to the "Order of the Brewers Minor."[45] Whereas Chaucer and the authors of *Weasel Breweries* have created entertaining fiction, the thirteenth-century Fra Salimbene of Parma was an historic lover of wine and one of the first to write widely on the quality of various wines. The eighteenth-century Franciscan Friar Junipero Serra established a string of seventeen missions in the New World in California. Although he was over sixty and not in good health, Friar Serra built a winery in 1771 at the mission San Gabriel. The friars there aptly call its most famous vine Trinity vine. Although the vine likely dates from a later period, it does symbolize the contribution of Friar Serra to wine-making in the Americas. The Franciscans produce, among other wines, Angelica, which is a sweet dessert wine. Much of the modern California wine-making industry owes its origins to the Franciscans, and to other groups, such as the Christian Brothers. According to another tradition, it was a Franciscan Friar who first discovered the secret to making Scotch whisky.

Despite the many successes of the monastic and religious orders with the production of alcoholic beverages, there were a few well-known examples of failures. The wine from Saint Wandrille in Normandy, for example, was so foul that it became a synonym for anything nasty and distasteful in the Middle Ages. While the quality of Saint Wandrille's wine may have been suspect, the quality of monastic and religious life itself came under fire in the later Middle Ages. According to some writers, the monks began to love their wine perhaps a little too much. The Black Monks of Christ Church in Canterbury often bickered with the monks of Canterbury over status and privileges, and Gerald of Wales wrote that the monks there were corrupt as well in the excessively large quantities of wines they served at meals. Similarly, William the Conqueror founded Battle Abbey under less than holy circumstances as an act of penance for the slaughter that occurred during the Battle of Hastings. William founded the abbey on the precise spot where, according to tradition, King Harold died of an arrow wound through the eye. Whereas Benedict allowed only half a pint of wine a day, the abbot of the Black Monks of Battle Abbey permitted his monks in good health to drink a gallon a day and those in ill health to drink even more.[46] One of the more infamous and dubious stories of the late Middle Ages was that of the Cistercian abbot of Warden in Bedfordshire. In 1535, on the eve of the dissolution of the monasteries, visitors allegedly caught the abbot in the vineyard with a whore, a rather sad finale to one of the greatest epochs in monastic history.[47] Despite the dissolution, the infatuation of religious orders with wine and liqueur continued. As late as 1668, the Church condemned and suppressed the Gesuati because they apparently had no other interests nor served any other useful social or religious function than the making of alcoholic beverages.[48]

The Protestant Reformation succeeded in dissolving many of the great monastic communities in England and on the Continent. Later events continued to threaten monastic communities, such as the Thirty Years' War and the French Revolution. In the midst of such upheavals, some of the greatest monastic achievements in wine-making occurred. The Benedictine Dom Perignon was born in 1638, the same year as Louis XIV. At the age of nineteen, he entered the Benedictine Abbey of Saint-Vannes at Verdun. Nine years later, at the age of twenty-eight, he became the cellarer at Hautvillers. Before Dom Perignon, the monks at Hautvillers produced a *vin gris*; it was neither red nor white but somewhere in between. Dom Perignon used grapes from old vines, grapes with more tender skins and more responsive to the sun. He then developed a special technique of pressing the grapes and became the first to discover how to produce white wine from dark grapes. Dom Perignon had serious vision difficulties during certain periods of his life, and some argue these troubles helped to develop a keen sense of taste and smell. During a visit from two Spanish monks in 1698, he noticed that their water bottles were plugged with cork. Cork bottle plugs allowed for a better second fermentation, as the cork allowed oxygen in for the wine to breath, and so sparkling champagne was born. When Dom Perignon summoned his monks for the first taste of his wonderful concoction, he said, "Come quickly, I'm drinking stars!"[49] He died in 1715, in the midst of the Enlightenment, an age of questioning and skepticism about religion that would ultimately lead to the French Revolution.

No matter how much events of the early modern era threatened to dismantle the great monastic communities, they nearly always managed to survive and to resurface elsewhere under another guise. Many English monks and nuns refounded their communities on the Continent after Henry VIII dissolved them in the sixteenth century. The community of Westminster Abbey, for example, relocated to an abandoned collegiate church called St Lawrence at Dieulouard in France. When the French Revolution threatened them with dissolution once again, the community packed their bags and relocated back to England, where today they flourish as Ampleforth Abbey. Not only did the monasteries survive to see better times, but so did the wine that they made. One of the most appealing stories is that of the community of the Espirito Santo at Jerez. In 1812, when Napoleon's forces ransacked Montserrat, the industrious nuns at Jerez buried several precious casks of their famous amontillado under the cloister. New inhabitants discovered them a century later, and enough of the wine was left to reconstruct the solera, the Spanish system of blending and maturation.

Scholars have often argued that we owe the art of viticulture to monks.[50] After the fall of the Roman Empire in the western world, the spirituality of monks led to the successful and profitable cultivation of wine. Without them, the western world might well have never known the wonders of such fine wines as Château-Chalon or Chablis. Monastic and religious orders still make some eighty different wines throughout the world, from Europe, to Israel, to Greece. The numbers of saints revered as patrons of wine production illustrate the monastic influence on viticulture, such as St. Killian, an Irish saint who is a patron of wine growers in Franconi; St. Morandus, a Benedictine from the Rhine, who is the patron saint of Alsatian wine growers; and St. Roch, a Franciscan, who is a patron of wine growers. One of the most renowned wine-producing regions of France near Bordeaux still bears the name of St. Emilion, an eighth-century hermit whose piety attracted a group of followers who adopted the Benedictine Rule.

No matter what one's religious persuasion, modern connoisseurs still universally value and appreciate monastic wines and liqueurs. The author Norman Douglas, a professed atheist, once remarked, "No man of the world will scoff at monks' liquor."[51] Despite the often humorous association of alcohol with monastic corruption, one should also contemplate the extent to which the stories of late medieval bibulous monks also display the intense joy of life felt by monastics, a joy which flows from the true love of God. There is indeed something in the monastic production of alcoholic beverages that betrays the essence of Christian spirituality. One of the famous literary heroes of the novelist Saki (H. H. Munro), Reginald, put the matter somewhat humorously when he remarked, "people may say what they like about the decay of Christianity; the religious system that produced green Chartreuse can never really die."[52] On a more serious note, the monastic world in fact contributed mightily to the preservation and growth of Christianity. While monastic missionaries such as Boniface spread the word to unknown lands and other monks preserved the ancient world heritage through the copying of manuscripts, monks and nuns who produced wine and liqueur made their own unique contribution to the Christian tradition. Christ saw himself as the true vine, and his monastic followers saw themselves as custodians of his earthly vines, pruning them, mixing the juices from their grapes, and producing some of the most heavenly liquids on earth. Benedictines and other members of monastic orders listen to the Eucharistic prayer every day and to the words the priest utters over the wine: "Blessed are you, Lord, God of all creation. Through your goodness we have this wine to offer, fruit of the vine and work of human hands. It will become for us our spiritual drink." The monastic ethos of *ora et labora* is a powerful reminder that everything one touches may become a means by which to drink from the everlasting cup. Surely in their prayerful labors, the many monks, nuns, and members of the religious orders have created a better and more fertile vineyard on earth for all of us, one that is that much closer to the realization of the already-but-not-yet-present Kingdom of God.

Notes

[1] See Helen Waddell, *Medieval Latin Lyrics* (London: Constable and Company, 1966), 127. The poem appears in a ninth-century manuscript from Verona.

[2] In Arthurian literature, especially in its late medieval form, the quest for the grail was the quest for a vision of Christ and mystical union with the Divine. Sir Galahad could see the face of Christ in the grail.

[3] Rabelais, *Gargantua and Pantagruel,* trans. J. M. Cohen (London: Penguin Books, 1995), book I, chapter xxvii, 98. Although Rabelais calls John a "Friar," he says he is a "cloister monk." This means he could not have been a Franciscan but was rather a monastic. In that same chapter, John takes his staff and defends the monastery's vineyards from an army of 13,622 men who tried to ransack them.

[4] Colman James Barry O.S.B., *Worship and Work: Saint John's Abbey and University, 1856–1980,* 3rd ed. (Collegeville, MN: Liturgical Press, 1994), 13–15, 520. Archabbot Wimmer grew up in Bavaria, a region known for its fine beers. One can imagine the culture shock he must have experienced when he encountered American temperance movements. For an excellent discussion of Wimmer's brewery at St. Vincent's, see Omer U. Kline, O.S.B., *The Saint Vincent Archabbey Gristmill and Brewery, 1854–2000* (Latrobe, PA: St. Vincent's Abbey, 1996). The Trappists, or Cistercians of the Strict Observance, are better known than the Benedictines for their production of beer. See "Die Sechs Säulen der Trappistenbiere" ("The Six Pillars of Trappist Beer"), http://www.wu-wien.ac.at/usr/absatz/salzberg/trappe/ (accessed May 26, 2003).

[5] Brother Ty, Christopher Buckley, and John Marion Tierney, *God Is My Broker: A Monk-Tycoon Reveals the 7 Laws of Spiritual and Financial Growth* (New York: Random House, 1998).

[6] Father Robert Keffer, quoted in Jan Uebelherr, "Modern Monks to Grace Sparta with Elegant Restaurant," *Milwaukee Journal Sentinel Online,* August 2, 2000, http://www.jsonline.com/entree/cooking/aug00/monk02080100.asp. Father Robert is a monk at the Cistercian abbey of Our Lady of Spring Bank in Sparta, Wisconsin. Interestingly, he operates a restaurant in Sparta.

[7] Cf. Jesus's words in John 15:1: "I am the true vine, and my Father is the vinekeeper."

[8] For the parable of the sons, see Matt. 21:28–31.

[9] For various legends surrounding St. Martin, see Gregory of Tours, *The Four Books of the Miracles of St. Martin,* in *Gregory of Tours: Glory of the Martyrs, Translated Texts for Historians,* ed. Raymond van Dam (Liverpool: Liverpool University Press,

1989); Gregory of Tours, *Historia Francorum*, trans. O. M. Dalton (London: Oxford University Press, 1927); Sulpicius Severus, "Vita St. Martini," in *The Western Fathers*, ed. and trans. F. R. Hoare (New York: Sheed and Ward, 1954).

[10] According to this scheme, literal truths were signs of spiritual truths. The allegorical sense linked the Old Testament with the New Testament. For example, the parting of the Red Sea might be interpreted as a foreshadowing of baptism. According to the tropological sense, the literal words are taken in their moral sense. For example, commentators often saw the beauty of the Old Testament matriarch Rachel as a sign of the contemplative life. The anagogical meaning pointed to things beyond the world, such as when the city of Jerusalem is interpreted as a sign for the heavenly city of Jerusalem.

[11] Timothy Fry, O.S.B., et al., eds. *RB 1980: The Rule of St. Benedict in Latin and English with Notes* (Collegeville, MN: Liturgical Press, 1981), 48:1. Hereafter abbreviated as RB.

[12] RB 48:8.

[13] RB 31:10.

[14] The abbot's care for the souls of his charges is described in much the same way as the cellarer's care for the material goods of the monastery. "When [the abbot] must punish them, he should use prudence and avoid extremes; otherwise, by rubbing too hard to remove the rust, he may break the vessel," RB 64:12.

[15] For an excellent analysis of the parallels between Benedict's discussion of material goods and his discussion of spiritual tools, see Judith Sutera, O.S.B., "Stewardship and the Kingdom in RB 31–33," *The American Benedictine Review* 41.4, 357–78.

[16] Jean Leclerq, O.S.B., *The Love of Learning and the Desire for God* (1961; reprint, New York: Fordham Press, 1988), 15–17.

[17] So, too, were all other monastics who followed the Rule of St. Benedict but who were not members of the Cistercian order, or later, of the Cistercians of the Strict Observance, or Trappists.

[18] Desmond Steward, *Monks and Wine* (New York: Crown Publishers, 1979), 33.

[19] The methods of the Cluniacs had an influence even outside the order, such as when a peasant named Bertin copied them and developed a wine known as *campus bertinus*. Napoleon so highly prized this wine that he was not known to drink anything else.

[20] Geraldis Cambrensis (Gerald of Wales), *The Journey through Wales*, trans. Lewis Thorpe (Harmondsworth: Penguin Books, 1978), 104.

[21] Orderic Vitalis, *The Ecclesiastical History*, ed. and trans. Marjorie Chibnall, Vol. 4. (Oxford: Clarendon Press, 1973), 310–13.

[22] Ibid., 327.

[23] Dom David Knowles, *The Monastic Order in England*, 224.

[24] "C'est que je ne veux pas que le Seigneur me voie faire la grimace à l'instant de la communion."

[25] *Hock* is a term used to describe wine from the Rhine regions of Germany. The term is derived from Hochheim, a town in the Rheingau.

[26] For a general discussion of the history of French wines, see J. Jacquelin, *Les Vignes et les Vins de France* (Paris, 1960).

[27] RB 40:6–7.

[28] RB 40:3.

[29] RB 1:6–9.

[30] Benedict's biographer, Gregory the Great, records this story in Book II of *Dialogues*, chapter 3. An excellent modern commentary on this work is that of Adalbert de Vogüé, *Gregory the Great: The Life of Saint Benedict*, trans. Hilary Costello and Eoin de Bhaldraithe (Petersham, MA: St. Bede's Publications, 1963).

[31] Gregory the Great, Book II, chapter 18.

[32] RB 73:1.

[33] The derivation of the awkward Latin term *conversatio* used by Benedict in the Rule, is a hotly debated topic. See "Monastic Formation and Profession," in RB 45:8.

[34] The pips are broken grape seeds that can make wine very bitter.

[35] Monks built the abbey of Tre Fontane on the site of the martyrdom of St. Paul in Rome.

[36] Another region in Hungary famous for its wines is Pannonhalma-Sokoróalja. Monks first came here in 996 C.E., and settled on a hill called Saint Martin's Mountain. It is near the small village Pannónia. The first written record about viticulture in Hungary occurs in the foundation deed of the monastery of Pannonhalma. For a general history of Hungarian wines, see Z. Halsz, *Hungarian Wines through the Ages* (Budapest: 1962) and Alex Liddell, *The Wines of Hungary* (New York: Mitchell Beazley, 2003).

[37] Long after Napoleon took control of the property in 1806 CE, Johannisberg's legacy continued. In 1858, for example, it produced its first Eiswein or "ice wine." Johannisberg produces Eiswein by harvesting the grapes while they are frozen on the vine and then extracting the juice before they thaw. Because the water in the grapes is frozen, the juice has a very high sugar and acid content. Eiswein is a very sweet dessert wine. Johannisberg today has the largest collection of Riesling wines in the world.

[38] The famous Benedictine English missionary Boniface founded the monastery of Fulda, which administered Johannisberg. Boniface planted many vineyards during his travels on the continent, but in England itself, the wine-making industry did not develop as quickly or last as long as that in France or Germany. Most medieval consumers regarded English monastic wine as inferior to wine from the continent, and Boniface was the first monk to import German wines into England. In fact, their language highlights their veneration for the fruit of the vine in their word for October, "Wyn moneth," the month they gathered grapes. In 900 Alfred the Great made a law against damaging a vineyard requiring the guilty party to pay compensation for damages. The Domesday Book, a census taken after the Norman Conquest in 1066, listed thirty-eight vineyards. Only a dozen of these vineyards, however, belonged to the monasteries. Nevertheless, wine was just as important to the English monks as to those on the continent, and the Anglo-Saxon chronicle praises the Norman abbot Martin of Peterborough, as "he made many monks, and planted a vineyard and ... made the town better than it was before." Even in the twelfth century, however, King John imported wines from Gascony to England, using 1000 ships to ferry them across the channel. See James Ingram, trans., *The*

Anglo-Saxon Chronicle (1912; reprint, London: J. M. Dent and Sons, LTD., 1917), entry for AD 1137, 209.

[39] Since 1889, Clos has not been as great a wine as it was in the Middle Ages, possibly because those who later owned the vineyard divided it into sixty smaller ones.

[40] Royal and noble patronage helped to develop monastic wineries. In some cases, the monks adopted rather noble tendencies themselves, as the wine they drank reflected their own hierarchical practices. At St. Maximin, the abbot drank only the best wine produced by the monastery's vineyards and called his Abtsberg. The monks produced it from grapes grown on top of the hill. The choir monks came from nobility and were literate, as they had to recite the Divine Office. The choir monks at St. Maximin drank Herrenberg, produced from grapes lower down the hill. Young novices drank only Bruderberg, from lower on the hill. As monasticism evolved in the central Middle Ages, many monasteries, especially Cistercian monasteries, employed lay brethren to work their granges. These lay brethren could not read and so could not recite the Divine Office. The lay brothers drank wine from grapes on the bottom of the hill. They called their wine Viertelsberg, or "fourth rate" wine. At Clos Vougeot, a Cistercian monastery, the monks divided the vineyard. The top part produced the best wine, and the monks kept this wine. It was never sold, but sometimes given as a gift, presumably to those whose patronage might bring the community great benefits.

[41] The production of alcoholic beverages continues to be a big money-making venture for monasteries today. The Trappists, a seventeenth-century reform of Cistercian monasticism, are well known for their Chimay and Westmalle beers, among others. The founder of the Trappists was Armand Jean le Bouthillier de Rancé, who was originally of a noble family and a priest in the French court. In 1664 he entered the Cistercian Abbey of LaTrappe, where he instituted strict discipline and a set of reforms that became known as the Trappist movement. It is rather ironic, then, that modern Trappists have achieved some notable financial success in the beer-making industry. The Trappists are currently protesting the French tax on beers with more than 8.5 percent alcohol, as their revenues will decrease by 2.5 million euros a year or the equivalent of $2.63 million a year. The monks argue that this tax is a violation of the European free trade area, and they may have a point, as the French have not imposed a similar tax on wine with high alcohol content. See "Monks Insist on High-Alcohol Beer," *BBC News World Edition*, January 10, 2003, http://news.bbc.co.uk/2/hi/business/2645521.stm. Modern monks continue to be every bit as industrious as their medieval counterparts. Although the novel "God Is My Broker" portrays a humorous view of monastic industry, the ingenuity of modern monks almost equals the financial wizardry of Brother Ty. Modern monks have not only developed numerous industries, but they also market their wares on the Web for profit. One can visit www.monksonline.org and the modern Cistercians of Our Lady of Spring Bank will happily sell the casual surfer herbs, vitamins, health items, icons, Gregorian Chant and, through their special Web site, www.LaserMonks.com, laser art. The monks are quick to remind one that these are, of course, "products that promote peace and well-being."

[42] RB 33.

[43] Ever industrious, the Carthusians also bred mouser cats with short blue hair to protect the vines from mice. The cats are still known today as "Chartreux."

[44] Geoffrey Chaucer, *The Canterbury Tales*, ed. Edwin Duncan, The General Prologue, line 240, Available online at http://www.towson.edu/~duncan/chaucer/ (last accessed May 19, 2003).

[45] Kirk Humphries and Sandy Marshall, *Weasel Breweries: Reveries from the Monks of Ann Arbor Abbey*, http://www.weaselbreweries.com/monks.html (updated January 4, 2003). This order is, of course, entirely fictitious, but surely based on a longstanding association between Franciscans, or the Order of the Friars Minor, and alcohol.

[46] Many monasteries of the late Middle Ages allowed their members greater portions of both wine and food. While Battle Abbey allowed its monks a gallon of wine a day, the monks at the twelfth-century Cistercian abbey at Kirkstall began to eat more meat in the fifteenth century. The monks divided the refectory of the monastery in the fifteenth century to create a place where meat could be eaten on the ground floor. They called the room the *misericord* or indulgence, and also created a refectory above it for vegetarian meals, the normal diet of Cistercian monks. The alterations of the refectory were indicative of a more lax interpretation of the Rule of St. Benedict beginning in the fourteenth century. The Rule allowed meat to be eaten when illness or weakness demanded it, yet the rebuilding of the refectory at Kirkstall demonstrates that entire communities were being allowed to indulge in meat on a regular basis. Sources from Kirkstall show that the monks consumed meat as frequently as three times a week. The papacy supported these reforms, as when Pope Benedict XII in 1336 allowed healthy monks to eat meat in the infirmary with sick monks. Although one might be tempted to interpret these new practices as signs of a more lax lifestyle, Benedict was the first to urge his followers not to be too rigid in their implementation of his "little Rule." Benedict recognized the fact that not all communities would have identical needs. Variations in climate and even the physical health of the members might create the need for greater or lesser amounts of food (RB 36, 37, 39, 40). For a virtual tour of the ruins of Kirkstall, one of the best preserved Cistercian abbeys in Britain, cf. the Deborah Vess Web site, http://www.faculty.de.gcsu.edu/%7Edvess/ids/medieval/kirkstall/kirkstall.shtml.

[47] Although stories of monastic corruption abound in the Reformation era, scholarly studies suggest that these stories were greatly exaggerated. The studies of F. A. Gasquet, for example, clearly point to the overall integrity of monastic life in places such as England. One can attribute some of these stories to the desire of Henry VIII, who separated from the Roman Catholic Church, to confiscate monastic properties for financial gain. Gasquet rather poetically refers to the accounts of Henry's visitors as those of "perjured robbers." See F. A. Gasquet's *Henry VIII and the English Monasteries*, 2 vols., 6th ed. (London: John Hodges, 1895), 492. See also his *English Monastic Life*, 6th ed. (London: Methuen and Company, 1924). For a general discussion of the dissolution, see Dom David Knowles, "Suppression and Dissolution," in *The Religious Orders in England* (Cambridge: Cambridge University Press, 1961), 195–402.

[48] One should not confuse the Gesuati with the Society of Jesus, or the Jesuits.

[49] Although tradition credits Dom Perignon with the discovery of the method of producing sparkling Champagne, the first recorded production of sparkling wine fermented in bottles occurred in 1531 at the Abbey of Saint-Hilaire at Limoux in southern France, nearly a century before Dom Perignon's birth. This abbey was also a Benedictine monastery.

[50] The Comte de Montalembert first put forth the argument that monasteries preserved the art of wine-making in Λεσ Μοινεσ δε λoccident (Paris, 1860–77). Other scholars, such as William Younger, suggest that the wine-making industry was primarily driven by private enterprise. See his *Gods, Men and Wine* (London: 1966).

[51] Norman Douglass, *Siren Land*, quoted in Steward, 13.

[52] Saki (H. H. Munro), *Reginald on Christmas Presents*, from *Reginald*, in *The Complete Works of Saki* (Garden City, NY: Doubleday, 1976), 10.

Bibliography

Barry, Colman James, O.S.B. *Worship and Work: Saint John's Abbey and University, 1856–1980*. 3rd ed. Collegeville, MN: Liturgical Press, 1994.

Brother Ty, Christopher Buckley, and John Marion Tierney. *God Is My Broker: A Monk-Tycoon Reveals the 7 Laws of Spiritual and Financial Growth*. New York: Random House, 1998.

Cambrensis, Geraldis (Gerald of Wales). *The Journey through Wales*. Translated by Lewis Thorpe. Harmondsworth: Penguin Books, 1978.

Chaucer, Geoffrey. *The Canterbury Tales*. Edited by Edwin Duncan, The General Prologue, line 240. www.towson.edu/~duncan/chaucer/ (accessed May 19, 2003).

de Vogüé, Adalbert. *Gregory the Great: The Life of Saint Benedict*. Translated by Hilary Costello and Eoin de Bhaldraithe. Petersham, MA: St. Bede's Publications, 1963.

"Die Sechs Säulen der Trappistenbiere." ("The Six Pillars of Trappist Beer"). http://www.wu-wien.ac.at/usr/absatz/salzberg/trappe/ (accessed May 26, 2003).

Douglass, Norman. "Siren Land." In *Monks and Wine*. Edited by Desmond Steward. New York: Crown Publishers, 1979.

Fry, Timothy, O.S.B., et al., eds. *RB 1980: The Rule of St. Benedict in Latin and English with Notes*. Collegeville, MN: Liturgical Press, 1981.

Gasquet, F. A. *English Monastic Life*. 6th ed. London: Methuen and Company, 1924.

———. *Henry VIII and the English Monasteries*. 2 vols. 6th ed. London: John Hodges, 1895.

Gregory of Tours. *Historia Francorum*. Translated by O. M. Dalton. London: Oxford, 1927.

Halsz, Z. *Hungarian Wines through the Ages*. Budapest: 1962.

Humphries, Kirk, and Sandy Marshall. *Weasel Breweries: Reveries from the Monks of Ann Arbor Abbey*, www.weaselbreweries.com/monks.html (updated January 4, 2003).

Ingram, James, trans. *The Anglo-Saxon Chronicle*. 1912. Reprint, London: J. M. Dent and Sons, LTD., 1917.

Jacquelin, J. *Les Vignes et les Vins de France*. Paris, 1960.

Kline, Omer U., O.S.B. *The Saint Vincent Archabbey Gristmill and Brewery, 1854–2000.* Latrobe, PA: St. Vincent's Abbey, 1996.

Knowles, Dom David. "Suppression and Dissolution." In *The Religious Orders in England.* Cambridge: Cambridge University Press, 1961.

Leclerq, Jean, O.S.B. *The Love of Learning and the Desire for God.* 1961. Reprint, New York: Fordham Press, 1988.

Liddell, Alex. *The Wines of Hungary.* New York: Mitchell Beazley, 2003.

"Monks Insist on High-Alcohol Beer." *BBC News World Edition,* January 10, 2003. http://news.bbc.co.uk/2/hi/business/2645521.stm.

Rabelais. *Gargantua and Pantagruel.* Translated by J. M. Cohen. London: Penguin Books, 1995.

Saki (H. H. Munro). *The Complete Works of Saki.* Garden City, NY: Doubleday, 1976.

Steward, Desmond, ed. *Monks and Wine.* New York: Crown Publishers, 1979.

Sulpicius Severus, "Vita St. Martini." In *The Western Fathers.* Edited and translated by F. R. Hoare. New York: Sheed and Ward, 1954.

Sutera, Judith, O.S.B. "Stewardship and the Kingdom in RB 31–33." *The American Benedictine Review* 41.4, 357–78.

Uebelherr, Jan. "Modern Monks to Grace Sparta with Elegant Restaurant." *Milwaukee Journal Sentinel Online,* August 2, 2000, www.jsonline.com/entree/cooking/aug00/monk02080100.asp.

van Dam, Raymond, ed. *Gregory of Tours: Glory of the Martyrs, Translated Texts for Historians.* Liverpool: Liverpool University Press, 1989.

Vitalis, Orderic. *The Ecclesiastical History.* Edited and translated by Marjorie Chibnall. Vol. 4. Oxford: Clarendon Press, 1973.

Waddell, Helen. *Medieval Latin Lyrics.* London: Constable and Company, 1966.

Younger, William. *Gods, Men and Wine.* London: 1966.

7 The Spirits of Christmas: Christian Conviviality in the Age of Dickens

Gregory Pepetone

> But my song I troll out, for Christmas stout,
> The hearty, the true, and the bold;
> A bumper I drain, and with might and main
> Give three cheers for the Christmas of old!
>
> Charles Dickens ("A Christmas Carol")

For years, the consensus view of Charles Dickens's Christianity among academics was that it amounted to little more than a sentimental conviction that people should behave decently, coupled with what one critic characterized as his "jackdaw fondness" for church architecture. However, the Victorian world inhabited by Dickens, despite the humor, imagination, and emotional warmth with which he invested it, comprised a daunting panorama of widespread poverty, social displacement, and spiritual turmoil. These developments, in turn, posed a challenge to the validity and durability of the Christian faith. Could it withstand the combined assault of the various competing belief systems vying for the minds and hearts of Dickens's Victorian readers such as scientific materialism, capitalism, Utilitarianism, and nihilism? It could, according to Dickens, though he sought, almost literally, to cushion the effects of these troubling developments through providing his anxious audience with a mythic sanctuary in which domesticity, goodwill, and philanthropy prevailed. The outcome, as I hope to demonstrate, was a profound and compelling vision of Christian conviviality.

The spirit of Christian humanism developed in Dickens is exemplified by the cup of smoking hot Bishop that the reformed Scrooge shares with his impoverished clerk, Bob Cratchit (*A Christmas Carol*) and by the communal punch bowl shared at Dingly Dell (*The Pickwick Papers*), to cite only two of many well-known examples. Indeed, the pages of Dickens abound in food and drink to such an extent as to raise questions about his personal commitment to Victorian restraint and sobriety. Nor is this the only respect in which Dickens seems to be at odds with Victorian standards. His novellas and interpolated tales of the supernatural, for instance, are notably different from the run of Victorian ghost stories served up, like the Fat Boy's revelation in *Pickwick*, for the sole purpose of making one's flesh creep (though he was certainly capable of such Gothic confections as evidenced by his chilling short story, *The Signalman*). Instead, the phantoms that haunt the pages of *A Christmas Carol, The Haunted Man and the Ghost's Bargain,* and *The Chimes* are archetypes rooted in serious political and spiritual convictions.

Charles Dickens's literary celebration of drink and what Martin Luther King would later call "the beloved community" were the product of a Victorian counterculture that championed liberal options to the drab political, ethical, and religious conservatism that we now associate with Victorian England. In Dickens's case, this romantic counterculture saw the kindly and communal Spirit of Christmas as one viable alternative to the commercial spirit and religious narrowness that plagued his age[1] ... as it plagues our own. The Christian liberalism of Dickens was beset from within by dour Evangelicals and revisionist biblical scholars,[2] and from without by romantic bohemians, British jingoists, social Darwinists, and a new breed of social scientist who sought, like Mr. Gradgrind in *Hard Times*, to reduce the spiritual needs and complexities of the human condition to a set of inflexible facts and figures. In light of all this, the prevalence of alcohol in *A Christmas Carol* and other works by Dickens, despite the emphasis placed on sobriety by middle-class Victorians, obviously served as a poignant reminder of a world in which imagination, good cheer, and a widely shared commitment to the common welfare still held sway ... if only between the covers of a novel.

Communion and Community in Dickens

Romanticism is listed above as one of several challenges to the Christian ethos in the nineteenth century. This is true to the extent that it took the form of intellectual pride. Byronic or Faustian pride, which is ultimately a subset of Milton's Satanic pride, posits a belief in an innate superiority that places one beyond the reach of good and evil. This antinomian attitude is, in differing degrees, a commonplace of Romantic heroes such as Walpole's Prince Manfred, Byron's Manfred, Goethe's Faust, Hawthorne's Rappaccini, and Bronte's Mr. Rochester. In each case, these radical individualists are divorced from the common "herd," often in pursuit of admirable ends achieved through questionable means. They exhibit a sullen pleasure in their alienated status, though just as often they harbor a tacit resentment and longing for human companionship. Typically, they seek to satisfy this longing through a passionate sexual relationship in which the female who becomes a *figura Christi,* such as Manfred's Astarte or Rochester's Jane Eyre. In each case, the price exacted for their willful separation from both the Creator and his creatures is a spiritual taint amounting to damnation. Modern exponents of Christianity such as C. S. Lewis frequently remind us that redemption for the intellectual, the artist, the scientist, or the business tycoon is to be obtained on exactly the same terms as those that apply to everyone else. Such, however, was not the dominant view of those Romantics who gave precedence to the intellectual and aesthetic life over other, more "Philistine" vocations.

The origins of this Romantic heresy are complicated but pertinent to the secular heresies of scientific reductionism and political economy in opposition to which Dickens offered his mythic brand of Christianity. Ironically, the foundation of the nineteenth-century art religion was the concept of the artist as hero and prophet. This conception, formulated in tracts such as Schiller's 1797 essay *On Naïve and Sentimental Poetry,* pervades both the private and public discourse on aesthetics for more than a century. According to Schiller's Romantic ideology, artists, in retaining their intellectual integrity and emotional susceptibility, had escaped the spiritual fragmentation that was rapidly overtaking European civilization as a result of Enlightenment skepticism and the Industrial Revolution. That they were able to do so despite these dehumanizing influences meant that they should be viewed as roll models, much as scientists, media celebrities, wealthy businessmen, and professional athletes are often treated as a breed apart within our own culture.

According to Schiller, divinely inspired art was redemptive in nature in that it possessed a potentially therapeutic value for society. Its wholeness, or holiness (the two words share a common etymology), would redeem others from the damning narrowness of a reductive, overly rational philosophy; that is, from a secular emphasis on materialism, the anomie and ugliness of city life, and the evils of commerce and the vulgarity of politics. German theologian Friedrich Schleiermacher, who fraternized with Jena Romantics such as the Schlegel brothers, supplied a Christian underpinning for this Romantic credo. In his *On Religion* (1799), Schleiermacher emphasized the imminence of God and advocated an accommodation between Christian orthodoxy and the nineteenth-century *zeitgeist*. "What is revelation?" asks Schleiermacher. In response to his own rhetorical question, he states that "Every original and new communication of the universe to man is a revelation."[3] This definition enthusiastically embraces the divinity of inspired art. Later theologians, such as Karl Barth, would dismiss this accommodation as Culture Christianity. In retrospect, it was an uncomfortably short step from Schiller's estheticism and Schleiermacher's Culture Christianity to the proto–anti-Semitism of Wagner.

As the century progressed, however, it became increasingly apparent that a sizable portion of society shunned the art religion. Art patrons viewed artists as vendors and their art as a purchasable commodity. The fulsome claims on behalf of the spirituality of art (and the boorishness of those who pay for it) made by certain romantics were predictably dismissed as pretentious, self-serving, and subversive by the bourgeoisie. In response, artists became progressively disenchanted with a status quo that commodified artistic revelation while ignoring its increasingly strident Jeremiads against the commercial spirit. As the nineteenth century unfolded, the relationship between Romantic artists and their predominantly middle-class patrons became at first strained, then hostile, and finally, adversarial. The suspicions with which this newly moneyed class viewed the Romantic creed became a self-fulfilling prophesy in that more radical members of the Romantic tribe, presumably frustrated by their inability to effect social change, embraced a rhetoric premised on destruction rather than redemption. Eventually, their art-religious loincloths were exchanged for khaki fatigues and the red flag of revolution.[4]

Dickens, perhaps the most lionized literary artist of his day, seldom struck an affected pose, in either his life or his art. On the contrary, he explicitly renounced the Faustian proposition that artists and other intellectuals enjoyed a special dispensation, one that rendered them exempt from the moral and ethical restraints by which lesser mortals are bound. Dickens, while he saw ignorance and want as the besetting vices of his age, nevertheless understood that neither prosperity nor intellectual cultivation can satisfy the innate human hunger for God. Indeed, taking his cue from Christ, who often chose to associate with the lowly of this world, Dickens frequently reserves his highest praise for the simple and the uncultivated, such as Peggotty in *David Copperfield*.

In *The Haunted Man and the Ghost's Bargain*, one of Dickens's most atmospheric but lesser known Christmas books, the author presents a notable portrait of a Gothic hero, Redlaw, the misanthropic chemist. He is a proud and reclusive professor who confronts a familiar specter from Gothic folklore, his own shadow, or *doppelgänger*. Having experienced a shattering disappointment in love as a younger man, he asks to be released from his painful recollections by being freed of memory itself, a "gift" that he inadvertently bestows on all with whom he subsequently comes into contact. Like the hapless George Bailey in Frank Capra's Christmas classic, *It's a Wonderful Life*, he finds that erasing the past (or in this case, his painful remembrance of the past) turns his life, and that of his circle, into a veritable hell. One of the most persistent themes in Gothic literature is the potentially humanizing effect of memory coupled with imagination. The Gothic imagination sees this almost uniquely human faculty as a creative catalyst—a spiritual force for personal and collective growth. It is memory plus active imagination that permit us to transcend the Gothic dilemmas posed by our past misdeeds. By enabling us to reflect imaginatively upon our own past and to adjust our attitudes and behaviors appropriately, memory becomes not merely a stenographic record of an immutable experience but a potentially redemptive agency, one that can lead to repentance. As Redlaw affirms, "Christmas is a time in which, of all times in the year, the memory of every remediable sorrow, wrong, and trouble in the world around us should be active with us, not less than our own experiences."[5] The story concludes with this prayer: "Lord, keep my memory green."[6]

Tenniel's final illustration for the original edition, published by Bradbury and Evans in 1848, depicts Redlaw and his circle gathered at the Christmas table sharing plate and cup in a typical Dickensian ritual of conviviality. This tribute to human sociability, in which drink figures as a referent to both the holy communion—the Christian sacrament that binds humankind to God and His Church—and creaturely communion— a secondary social ritual binding the past to the present and one to all, is given a specifically religious bearing. Dickens invokes Matthew, chapter 19, verse 14, as Redlaw, in a silent gesture of commitment, lays hands upon an impoverished and uneducated orphan child recently brought under his care: "He laid his hand upon the boy, and silently calling Him to witness who laid His hand on children in old time, rebuking, in majesty of His prophetic knowledge, those who kept them from him, vowed to protect him, teach him, and reclaim him."[7]

Romantic Christianity Then and Now

If spiritual pride was the downside of Romanticism for Dickens, its upside was its persistent reminder that there was not only more in heaven and earth than is dreamt of by the Horatios of this world, but that there is more to life than money—much more. This was to become Dickens's central theme, sounded repeatedly from *A Christmas Carol* and *Dombey and Son* to *Great Expectations, Hard Times,* and *Our Mutual Friend*, his last completed novel. Though his vision dominated by the pursuit of wealth darkened over time, it remained consistent in its rejection of the Victorian consensus on behalf of a predatory capitalism combined with a dreary religious Calvinism. It was a consensus that drained life of its imaginative vitality, warmth, and purpose, according to Dickens. It was George Bernard Shaw who maintained that, properly understood, *Hard Times* is a more revolutionary track than *Das Kapital*. It is not, of course. As George Orwell and others have subsequently pointed out, Dickens was a moralist, not a revolutionary.[8] He sought to reform, not to destroy Victorian culture. Indeed, in many ways he typified its commitment to moral earnestness, civilized discourse, propriety, and a melodramatic sentimentality. In his earlier more optimistic works, especially *A*

Christmas Carol, he seems as concerned for the welfare of economic man as for those who are victimized by his inhumanity and narrowness of vision. In his later novels, however, Dickens feels personally threatened by the coldheartedness of the Utilitarian spirit and fearful of those who embodied it. Consequently, as Edgar Johnson points out, his earlier emphasis on saving economic man from himself, typified by Scrooge, shifts to an emphasis on saving society from economic man.

Despite popular opinion to the contrary, Ebenezer Scrooge is not essentially a miser like George Eliot's Silas Marner or Robert Louis Stevenson's Uncle Ebenezer in *Kidnapped*. He is primarily interested not in hoarding wealth but in conforming his life and habits to a stern economic philosophy. In short, he is a modern businessman who equates the common welfare with the pursuit of self-interest. According to this creed, the rich owe nothing to the poor beyond the payment of those taxes that support prisons, poorhouses, and other "charitable" institutions. In modern terms, Scrooge might be described as "a compassionate conservative," someone for whom the business of Victorian England is business and nothing beyond. "It is enough for a man to know his own business," states Scrooge, "and not to meddle in other people's. Mine occupies me constantly."[9] He simply asks to be left alone by those whose misguided philanthropy he interprets as a sentimental smoke screen for an antiquated religious superstition uninformed by the precepts of a sound political economy. To him, the well-intentioned but misguided meddlers of this world are what like-minded individuals would later refer to as "bleeding hearts." He does not begrudge, openly at least, the prisons and workhouses that supplied the principle resorts of the poor in nineteenth-century England. He simply thinks it would be preferable for his fellow citizens to earn their own way, and to permit nature to dispose of those too weak to prosper in the current economic climate, i.e., "to decrease the surplus population."

Underlying his economic conservatism is the burgeoning myth of social Darwinism, a myth that predated Darwin by several decades.[10] Scrooge accepts survival of the fittest as an economic as well as biological and ethical imperative. Consequently, he believes that "Greed, for want of a better word, is good," to cite Gordon Gekko from a memorable moment from Oliver Stone's film, *Wall Street*.[11] Indeed, it seems obvious to me that Ebenezer Scrooge would be a welcome guest at any modern Republican fundraiser or social function. Like his latter-day counterparts, Scrooge endorses the trickle-down theory of economics. As long as it is a trickle and not a gush (particularly one mandated by the federal government) and as long as "down" does not embrace too wide a field of humanity, Scrooge is content.

Is he happy and fulfilled in any fundamental sense? Of course not, because, as Dickens affirms unequivocally, the happiness for which humans were made—by a Creator whose Trinitarian nature is social in its very essence—is inseparable from approaching life with an open hand, an open mind, and an open heart. It is a by-product of the "wonderful unanimity" that the converted Scrooge is finally able to share with his nephew Fred. Essentially, his shriveled heart has failed to beat in sync with that of his fellow creatures, as Scrooge is reminded by the Spirits of Christmas Past (memory), Present (example), and Future (fear). Consequently, the choices he has made have turned his own life, and the collective life of a culture dominated by men of his convictions, into a brutal and inhospitable environment. In such an environment, as Dickens continually reminds us, nearly everyone's heart bleeds.

As evidenced by a string of capitalistic antiheroes in Dickens's novels written after *A Christmas Carol*, such as Paul Dombey, Mr. Podsnap (*Our Mutual Friend*) and Merdles (*Little Dorrit*), Dickens finally despaired of converting the commercial spirit of modern society to an acceptance of the humility implicit in the dead Marley's self-recriminating, "Not to know that any Christian spirit working kindly in its little sphere, whatever it may be, will find its mortal life too short for its vast means of usefulness."[12] Mr. Dombey, Dickens's next, and far more complex portrait of economic man, is as self-absorbed and consumed by a pharisaical sense of his own dignity as any puffed-up churchman, supercilious scientist, or egotistical artist. While Scrooge is perhaps as much sinned against as sinning, one can hardly imagine the elitist pride of Dombey bending to a self-effacing ethic of public service.

Nowhere in Dickens is the contrast between the human warmth of Christian conviviality contrasted more vividly with the frigid conceit and selfishness that lies at the core of the Victorian business ethic than in the christening of the infant Paul. "It might have been well for Mr. Dombey, if he had thought of his own dignity a little less," remarks Dickens, "and had thought of the great origin and purpose of the ceremony in which he took so formal a part, a little more."[13] He goes on to describe the dinner table, as always the ritualistic focus of Christian conviviality in Dickens, in terms reminiscent of the frozen heart of Hell in Dante's *Inferno*. The room temperature, the food, and the drink in this passage serve as objective correlatives to the spiritual hypothermia of the guests, starting with Mr. Dombey himself who is likened to a specimen of frozen gentleman hung up at a Russian fair. Dickens had used comparable imagery earlier to describe both the forbidding environment of London's commercial district and the spiritual condition of its inhabitants, such as his misanthropic hero, Scrooge. The weather in *A Christmas Carol*, for example, is said to be cold, bleak, biting, and foggy. Elsewhere in Dickens, as in *Bleak House*, fog serves as a pervasive metaphor of the isolating mental and spiritual confusion in which the citizens of an anomic society are constrained to grope.

Paul Dombey senior, like Scrooge, is an individual "who carries his own low temperature always about with him."[14] In contrast to the geniality and companionship to be found at the humble abodes of the Bob Cratchit and Scrooge's nephew, Fred, a companionship symbolized by a flaring hearth and steaming punch bowl, both the atmospherics and the alcohol at little Paul's christening are decidedly glacial: "There was a toothache in everything. The wine was so bitter cold, that it forced a little scream from Miss Tox, which she had great difficulty in turning into a 'Hem!' "[15] Despite his satirical tone, Dickens is conveying a serious theological message: The chalice of Christian fellowship, a tangible and visible symbol of an intangible and invisible reality, becomes, in this instance, an accurate thermometer of the chilling emotional climate in which the Dombeys, and those close to them, routinely exist.

It is only by breaking Dombey's petrified pride in such a way as to leave him pathetically dependent on the daughter he has wronged, that Dickens can conceive of him as a humble and contrite *homo ecomonicus*. Likewise, Pip (*Great Expectations*) is utterly disillusioned by the hidden truth behind his great expectations, namely that his pretensions to gentility and social respectability are predicated on the wealth of a criminal. By implication, the Victorian social structure itself is little more than a flattering self-delusion. Thereafter, the prominent economic men of Dickens's novels, such as Podsnap, are ruined by their own misguided values, not converted from them. In a sense, though Dickens's insights into both Victorian society and the human condition clearly deepened over time, he was ultimately constrained to present his affluent hero-villains as ruinous, unrepentant, and irredeemable, much as he had presented Ralph Nickleby at an earlier stage of his career. However, whereas Nickleby is portrayed as sinister, later capitalists and social climbers are depicted as victims of the very system they serve.

Perhaps this difference in perspective between Dickens's younger and older selves can be attributed to his growing sense that no one who benefits from living within a modern capitalist state is entirely absolved from the sins committed for the sake of national prosperity. Toward the end, he had seemingly come to question his own prospects of achieving, the affluence and social status for which he had worked so obsessively.

America is, in many ways, the Victorian England of the late twentieth and early twenty-first centuries. It is at once war-like and imperial yet supremely confident of its essential decency and peaceful intentions. It is favorable to small government when it comes to social welfare and public services and big government when it comes to military/intelligence appropriations. It is stinting in its support of countries it does not control or whose ideology it finds unacceptable but resentful of criticism from the international community. It is increasingly conservative in its religious orientation but excited about Las Vegas, which has been called, with some justification, the unofficial capital of the United States. These are but a sampling of the neo-Victorian antitheses or hypocrisies that characterize our own time and place. The last of these seeming contradictions, America's comparatively recent preoccupation with right-wing televangelism, deserves a closer look in relation to the Christian conviviality of Dickens.

Neo-Puritan Abstinence Versus Christian Conviviality

The neo-Puritan spirit of his day condemned not only the consumption of alcohol, which can, as Dickens fully realized, have sinister as well as sacramental import, but on occasion discouraged the wholly innocent pleasures and pastimes of the laboring classes, e.g., picnics and cricket matches, on the grounds that they were sacrilegious. One of Dickens's earliest publications entitled *Sunday under Three Heads* (1834), defended the rights of the people to socialize on the Sabbath against the efforts of churchmen and politicians to close or outlaw use of public facilities for the lower, though not the upper, classes. Dickens was quick to seize upon the hypocrisy implicit in this double standard and point out that its likely consequence would be to drive the respectable poor to the gin shops and other less wholesome resorts. He angrily excoriated the religious and political Pharisees of his day, reminding them that the Sabbath was made for man, not man for the Sabbath: "Your saintly law-givers lift up their hands to heaven, and exclaim for a law which shall convert the day intended for rest and cheerfulness, into one of universal gloom, bigotry, and persecution."[16] Though devoid of any notable literary merit, this political pamphlet is important, as one of Dickens's biographers points out in that, "It contains the core of that warmhearted humanism and humanitarianism that glowed within him throughout his entire life."[17] Nowhere are these qualities displayed more imaginatively than in his famed *kunstmärchen*, or artistic fairy tale, *A Christmas Carol*. In its pages, he commends the Christian conviviality of the Yuletide season as "a kind, forgiving, charitable, pleasant time: the only time I know of, in the long calendar of the year, when men and women seem by one consent to open their shut-up hearts freely, and think of people below them as if they really were fellow-passengers to the grave, and not another race of creatures bound on other journeys."[18]

The *Carol* belongs to an extremely select list of artworks whose reputation bridges the great divide between high culture and popular culture. Indeed, Dickens may be, if not the last of the great men as G. K. Chesterton maintained, at least the last great author of literature to span that psychological and cultural divide. Like all such works, its very familiarity tends to obscure its stature. Only against the backdrop of Dickens's other novels and stories does this mythopoeic masterpiece appear as a complex synthesis of Dickens's worldview, a concise testament to Victorian culture, and one of the most characteristic achievements of Christian romanticism. It has often been the subject of film adaptations, all of which omit most of its many pointed references to the Christian faith, implicit as well as explicit: "Why did I walk through crowds of fellow-beings with my eyes turned down, and never raise them to that blessed Star which led the Wise Men to a poor abode. Were there no poor homes to which its light would have conducted me!" Perhaps it is because they are unmistakable, as in the case of Jacob Marley's lament cited above—embarrassingly so to those who would separate the "warm-hearted humanism" of Dickens from its Christian moorings—that they are omitted. The cinematic tendency to ignore or belittle the obvious piety of Dickens says something about the ethos of the British and American film industry and popular culture in general. However, this disparagement of Dickens's alleged Culture Christianity did not begin with the filmmakers. As I recall, even so ardent a champion as G. K. Chesterton faults Dickens's commitment to Christian tradition on the curious grounds that he (Dickens) should not have found it necessary to rely on his own invention when depicting the supernatural. Such criticism not only misses the allegorical significance of the three spirits who conduct Scrooge on a guided tour of his own haunted psyche, it misses the effectiveness and originality with which Dickens was able to accommodate his Christian message to the Romantic sensibility of his contemporaries.

The somewhat obscure German literary genre *kunstmärchen*, represented by writers who are largely absent from the reading lists of World Literature courses, such as Chamisso and E. T. A. Hoffmann, belongs to the nineteenth-century cult of childhood. The Romantic identification of childhood with adult qualities of mind and spirit threatened by modern commercial culture, such as imagination and emotional vulnerability, is arguably one of the finest, most original flowerings of Romanticism—recent theories to the contrary notwithstanding. It clearly relates to the educational organicism of Frobel's *Kindergarten* movement as well as to the Romantic revival of interest in folklore and myth generally. All of these developments are, in turn, distant echoes of the passage from St. Matthew referenced by Dickens (*The Haunted Man and the Ghost's Bargain*) in which Jesus points to the spirit of childhood as a prerequisite for entrance into the heavenly kingdom. Dickens was clearly conversant with this and other biblical lore, as were his Victorian readers. Indeed, he contributed to the cult of childhood in a variety of published and private writings. One of these, a child's biography for his own family entitled *The Life of Our Lord*, was unpublished during his lifetime.

Just as his purpose in writing *A Child's History of England* was educationally preemptive, i.e., an effort to protect his own children from a too conservative, or Tory, interpretation of British history, his purpose in writing a child's history of Jesus was theologically preemptive, i.e., an effort to protect his family from a too conservative view of religion. In this intimate abridgment of scripture, he presumably included only those portions of the Gospels he deemed ethically as well as theologically important. The dedication, addressed to "My Dear Children," reads in part, "I am very anxious that you should know something about the history of Jesus Christ. ... No one ever lived who was so good, so kind, so gentle, and so sorry for all people who did wrong, or were in any way ill or miserable, as he was."[19] Dickens in particular and Victorian Christianity in general, have been justly criticized for emphasizing the gentle over the magisterial nature of Christ. Though the Lord and Savior that Dickens commends to his own children may or may not be a proper Victorian gentleman, he was clearly not a teetotaler. This is how Dickens relates the wedding at Cana:

> The first miracle which Jesus Christ did was at a place called Cana, where he went to a marriage-feast with Mary his mother. There was no wine; and Mary told him so. There were only six stone water-pots filled with water. But Jesus turned this water into wine, by only lifting his hand; and all who were there drank it.

Though he refers to this event as a significant turning point in the ministry of Jesus, there is no attempt to rationalize or shirk its implications. Christ provides wine, approves the custom of imbibing it at important social functions, and even partakes of it himself ("all who were there drank it").

With regard to his views on alcohol (and other consciousness-altering substances) and religion, the Christian imagination of Dickens steered a middle course between the Romantic license of men such as Byron, Coleridge, and DeQuincey and the Puritanical abstinence of men such as George Cruikshank, the illustrator of *Sketches by Boz* and *Oliver Twist*. Though in the case of certain literary celebrities, drug addiction had its origin in medical problems, the Romantics indulged in the use of drugs, including alcohol, primarily as a stimulant to their literary imaginations. In stark contrast to literary lions such as Thackeray, who took a lenient attitude toward drink, Cruikshank, with whom Dickens shared a long-standing personal and professional relationship, became a prominent figure in the "total abstinence" or teetotal movement. In a passage revealing Dickens's moderate stance with regard to this issue, Edgar Johnson writes:

> The artist, once a hilarious climber of lampposts and wallower in gutters, had now become a fanatical teetotaler and was using his etching needle to depict the horrors of alcoholism. He carried his mania even into social intercourse; dinning with Dickens, he snatched a glass of wine from a lady's hand, intending to throw it on the floor. 'How dare you,' exclaimed Dickens furiously, 'touch Mrs. Ward's glass? ... What do you mean? Because someone you knew was a drunkard for forty years, surely it is not for you to object to an innocent glass of Sherry!'[20]

In *The Pickwick Papers*, a work that helped to establish a strong association in the public mind between Dickens and drink, Dickens delights in poking fun at the fundamental tenet of the temperance movement. Like those today who would blame the proliferation of violence and political disillusionment on the entertainment industry, the champions of total abstinence in Victorian society insisted that alcohol was an ultimate rather than a proximate cause of social ills that temperance could not hope to solve. He makes his point satirically in the following testimonial which figures as part of the "Report of the Committee of the Brick Lane Branch of the United Grand Junction Ebenezer Temperance Association." It reads in part, "Betsy Martin, widow, one child, and one eye. Goes out charing and washing, by the day; never had more than one good eye, but knows her mother drank bottled stout, and shouldn't wonder if that caused it (immense cheering). Thinks it not impossible that if she had always abstained from spirits, she might have had two eyes by this time (tremendous applause)."[21]

Similarly to Cruikshank, Dickens was aware of the human depravity of alcoholism, as attested by his chilling portrayal of Bill Sykes in *Oliver*

Twist. He could hardly have been otherwise given his own premature introduction to the sordid realities of life inside a Victorian debtors prison (John Dickens, Charles Dickens's father, was sent to the Marshalsea prison when his son was a boy). In the course of researching his novels, Dickens personally investigated some of the more infamous warrens of London, such as St. Giles and the Seven Dials District. Consequently, he knew from firsthand observation that gin was more likely to serve as the opiate of the impoverished masses than religion. Frequently, it offered a respite from the filth, ugliness, and boredom of poverty that religion did not afford. In the following passage from *Bleak House*, a tactless female dispenser of "Christian charity," Mrs. Pardiggle, is confronted by an unemployed laborer who parodies her all too familiar litany of prying questions: "Look at the water. Smell it! That's wot we drinks. How do you like it, and what do you think of gin, instead! ... How have I been conducting of myself? Why, I've been drunk for three days; and I'd a been drunk four, if I'd a had the money."[22] As one of Dickens's biographers puts it, "The widespread assertion that drunkenness was the cause of many evils rather than a result of already existing ones angered him, as if eradication of a symptom in any way dealt with the disease. ... Beginning with his earliest sketches, he had unequivocally claimed that societies with high levels of poverty and ignorance created the conditions that encouraged high levels of crime and alcoholism."[23]

Though Dickens often treats the subject of drunkenness lightly—indeed, some of the most humorous passages in *Pickwick* and *David Copperfield* hinge on this subject—the bitter words from *Bleak House* quoted above are not the words of a man who underestimated the sinister aspects of drink on either individuals or society. As C. S. Lewis observes, "The jokes about drunkenness in *Pickwick*, far from proving the nineteenth-century English thought it innocent, prove the reverse."[24] Indeed, Dickens is careful to balance such jokes with graphic portrayals of abject poverty that, in Dickens's mind, was apt to be the ultimate cause of alcoholism. In the early pages of *The Pickwick Papers*, for example, Dickens follows the hilarity of Mr. Winkle's narrowly averted duel with Dr. Slammer—occasioned by an instance of drunken misbehavior and mistaken identity—with the pathetic interpolated tale of Dismal Jimmy's death-bed delirium tremens.[25]

In his own habits, Dickens veered on the side of self-restraint. Commenting on this seeming paradox with regard to food in terms that would apply equally to drink, one recent biographer comments, "But if food can be a register ... for something very close to the need for love, so also it can be a proper measurement of human pride and social respectability. The fact is that in the end it might be said to stand for anything and everything, and it is perhaps best to notice that its prominence in Dickens's early fiction captures if nothing else the primacy which Dickens afforded to the need for oral satisfaction of every kind. Eating. Drinking. Speaking. Yet there is a paradox: the man who expatiates so imaginatively on the delights of food was himself a very abstemious person. He drank and ate very little."[26]

So why did Dickens freely tolerate in others that which he did not practice himself, and if drink can stand for anything and everything, as Dickens's biographer Peter Ackroyd suggests, what precisely does it represent in Dickens? The answer lies in the incarnational theology that informs his art. Romanticism has been defined as the ability to see the extraordinary in the ordinary. If so, the Christian imagination of Dickens and the romantic imagination of his contemporaries have something in common, for it is a core precept of Christian theology that there is redemption in every human activity baptized by the Holy Spirit. St. Augustine boiled down the Decalogue to this simple but profound injunction: love God and do what you will. To the baptized imagination of Charles Dickens, the imbibing of spirits was inseparable from the spirit of Christmas because every supper at which human fellowship supplied the main course was the Last Supper and every cup of wine exchanged in a spirit of Christian conviviality was the Holy Chalice of Christ. He thus speaks of "that happy state of companionship and mutual good-will, which is a source of such pure and unalloyed delight ... that the religious belief of the most civilized nations, and the rude traditions of the roughest savages, alike number it among the first joys of a future condition of existence, provided for the blest and the happy."[27] Far from being the voice of a shallow Culture Christian, the voice of Dickens, both in his time and in our own, strikes an authentic note of moderation, prophecy, and Christian humanism.

Notes

[1] As noted in Walter E. Houghton's absorbing study of nineteenth-century intellectual history, *The Victorian Frame of Mind* (New Haven, CT: Yale University Press, 1957), the world of Dickens was one plagued by doubts and anxieties, including religious doubts spawned by scientific and philosophical skepticism.

[2] On the other side of the theological spectrum from these evangelicals, there arose exponents of the "higher criticism," a hermeneutical approach to the Bible that questioned the credibility of *Heilsgeschichte*'s most basic claims, including the historicity of Jesus.

[3] Friedrich Schleiermacher, *On Relegion: Speeches to Its Cultured Despisers* (1799; reprint, New York: Harper Torchbooks, 1958), 89.

[4] Jacques Barzun, *The Use and Abuse of Art* (Princeton, NJ: Princeton University Press, 1974).

[5] Charles Dickens, *The Haunted Man and the Ghost's Bargain*. In *The Christmas Books.* (Oxford: Oxford University Press/Penguin, 1971), 351.

[6] Ibid., 353.

[7] Ibid., 351.

[8] George Orwell, "Charles Dickens." In *A Collection of Essays* (Garden City, NY: Doubleday, 1954).

[9] Charles Dickens, *A Christmas Carol*. In *The Christmas Books* (Oxford: Oxford University Press/Penguin, 1971).

[10] C. S. Lewis, "The Funeral of a Great Myth." In C. S. Lewis, *Christian Reflections* (Grand Rapids, MI: William B. Eerdmanns, 1978), 82–93.

[11] *Wall Street*, dir. Oliver Stone. Twentieth Century Fox, 1995.

[12] Dickens, *Carol*, 62.

[13] Dombey, 57.

[14] Dickens, *Carol*, 46.

[15] Dombey, 57.

[16] Edgar Johnson, *Charles Dickens: His Tragedy and Triumph* (Boston: Little, Brown, and Company, 1952), 1:145.

[17] Johnson, 6: 147.

[18] Dickens, *Carol*, 49.

[19] Charles Dickens, *A Child's History of England*, 15.

[20] Johnson, 619.

[21] Charles Dickens, *The Pickwick Papers*, 459.

[22] Charles Dickens, *Bleak House*, in *The Oxford Illustrated Dickens* (Oxford: Oxford University Press, 1987), 107.

[23] Fred Kaplan, *Dickens: A Biography*. (New York: Avon Books, 1988), 198.

[24] C. S. Lewis, *Christian Reflections*, 78.

[25] The Stroller's Tale, chapters 2 and 3.

[26] Peter Ackroyd, *Dickens* (New York: HarperCollins Publishers, 1990), 248.

[27] Dickens, 374.

Bibliography

Ackroyd, Peter. *Dickens*. New York: HarperCollins Publishers, 1990.

Barzun, Jacques. *The Use and Abuse of Art*. Princeton, NJ: Princeton University Press, 1974.

Dickens, Charles. *Bleak House*. In *The Oxford Illustrated Dickens*. Oxford: Oxford University Press, 1987.

——. *A Christmas Carol*. In *The Christmas Books*. Oxford: Oxford University Press/Penguin, 1971.

——. *Great Expectations*. In *The Oxford Illustrated Dickens*. Oxford, Oxford University Press, 1987.

——. *The Haunted Man and the Ghosts Bargain*. In *The Christmas Books*. Oxford: Oxford University Press/Penguin, 1971.

——. *The Life of Our Lord*. Morristown, NJ: Silver Burdett Press, 1987.

Houghton, Walter E. *The Victorian Frame of Mind*. New Haven: Yale University Press, 1957.

It's a Wonderful Life. Dir. Frank Capra. Perf. James Stewart, Donna Reed. Columbia Pictures, 1946.

Johnson, Edgar. *Charles Dickens: His Tragedy and Triumph*. Boston: Little, Brown, and Company, 1952.

Kaplan, Fred. *Dickens: A Biography*. New York: Avon Books, 1988.

Lewis, C. S. *Christian Reflections*. Grand Rapids, MI: William B. Eerdmanns, 1978.

——. "The Funeral of a Great Myth." In C. S. Lewis, *Christian Reflections*. Grand Rapids, MI: William B. Eerdmans, 1978.

Orwell, George. "Charles Dickens." In *A Collection of Essays*. Garden City, NY: Doubleday, 1954.

Pepetone, Gregory G. *Gothic Perspectives on the American Experience*. New York: Peter Lang, 2002.

Robertson, C. K. "Ministers in the Movies." In *Religion as Entertainment*. Edited by C. K. Robertson. New York: Peter Lang, 2002.

Schleiermacher, Friedrich. *On Relegion: Speeches to Its Cultured Despisers*. 1799. Reprint, New York: Harper Torchbooks, 1958.

Wall Street. Dir. Oliver Stone. Perf. Michael Douglas, Charlie Sheen, Daryl Hannah. Twentieth Century Fox, 1995.

8 Southern Comfort: Indulgence and Abstinence in the South

Gary L. Abbott, Sr.

Developed in 1874 in New Orleans, there really is a Southern Comfort Liqueur. It is produced today in Louisville, Kentucky. In 1904 Southern Comfort introduced the St. Louis Cocktail, a glass of Southern Comfort with a twist of lemon. The drink's motto was: "Limit 2 to a customer (No gentleman would ask for more)."

However, the presence of a "southern comfort" was a factor in southern life long before 1874 ... as it still is today. The so-called "devil's drink" of alcohol is a part of life in the south, it always has been, and indications are it always will be. It has thrived amidst the Temperance Movement, Prohibition, and countless sermons from Bible belt pulpits. Not even the Baptists seem to have been able to turn it off.

After all, what could be more southern than a Mint Julep? It is the archetypical stereotype beverage for the southern aristocracy whose alcohol base is bourbon. "The Mint Julep was probably first made in Georgia although Virginia lays claim as well. Kentucky though, may very well take credit for its popularity. It is the official drink of the Kentucky Derby."[1] *Irwin S. Cobb's Own Recipe Book* (written for Frankfort Distilleries) offers a unique historical background to the julep. "Down our way we've always had a theory that the Civil War was not brought on by Secession or Slavery or the State's Rights issue. These matters contributed to the quarrel, but there is a deeper reason. It was brought on by some Yankee coming down south and putting nutmeg in a julep. So our folks just up and left the Union flat."[2]

Maker's Mark Whisky traces its origins to 1780 when a third-generation Scotch-Irish emigrant named Robert Samuels first made it for himself and a few friends. "It wasn't until 1840 that [the Samuels] family got serious about whisky distilling. And that's when Robert's grandson, T. W. Samuels, built the family's first commercial distillery at Samuels Depot, Kentucky. He was known as the 'High' Sheriff of Nelson County.

Thus began a long chain of Samuels who actually made money making and selling whisky."[3] So it was that the local sheriff birthed Maker's Mark!

Perhaps no story illustrates the alcohol schizophrenia of the American south better than that of Jack Daniel's Tennessee Whiskey. In the 1850s a Lutheran minister named Dan Call ran a store and made whiskey in the Tennessee mountains at Lynchburg. He hired a seven-year-old boy named Jack Daniels to work for him. "In September 1863, under pressure to devote his life to lifting spirits rather than selling them, Call sold his still to Jack who was just thirteen at the time."[4] Since that day Mr. Jack's whiskey has been produced at the same general location ... in a dry county.[5] They can make it, and you can drink it, but you cannot purchase it in Moore County![6]

Breweries, distilleries, and wineries are a significant presence numerically and economically all across the southern United States. Numerous producers of beverage alcohol are headquartered in the south. In addition to Southern Comfort, Maker's Mark, and Jack Daniel's, some other (though not an exhaustive listing) examples include: Anheuser-Bush in St. Louis, Missouri; George Dickel Whisky in Cascade Hollow, Tullahoma, Tennessee; Jim Beam Bourbon Whiskey in Frankfort, Kentucky; Pritchard's Whiskey in Kelso, Tennessee; Biltmore Estates Winery in Asheville, North Carolina; twelve wineries are listed in Maryland[7]; twenty-three wineries are listed in Tennessee[8]; seventy-eight wineries are listed in Virginia[9]; plus countless others.

Liquor stores at county lines and city limits all across the south highlight the lines of southern alcohol contradiction. They mark the distinction between "wet" (those that sell alcoholic beverages) and "dry" (those that do not sell alcoholic beverages). To further confuse things, some "wet" cities and counties allow only the sale of beer and wine, but not spirits; and some "wet" counties will only allow the sale of mixed drinks in restaurants that derive a set percentage of their sales from food.

The American south's indulgence in abstinence is an indulgence in a fantasy world where things are not always as they seem. It is a game of deception played by those who drink alcohol and those who do not. It is a Doctor Jekyll/Mr. Hyde mentality. Occasionally, they spar with each other, but mostly they just live with it.

The mixed signals regarding beverage alcohol are rooted in the very Bible that so influences life in the American south. The use and abstinence of beverage alcohol are reflected in the Bible itself. Each side of the debate/dichotomy can find ample proof texts for its point of view in Scripture. Even among Christians, there is much difference of opinion regarding what is said and not said, right and wrong, about alcoholic beverages. The Bible simply does not settle the issue.[10] Moreover, whereas some in the south really do not care what the Bible says, or does not say, this ambiguity is a major source of the south's love/hate relationship with beverage alcohol. If the Bible is held up as the dam to halt the flow of beverage alcohol, it is quite clear that there are many holes letting it through to quench the ever-present thirst demand.

However, there are three events involving Jesus Christ that relate positively to alcohol in the form of a beverage. The first is Jesus's first recorded miracle. It occurred at a wedding celebration at Cana in Galilee where he turned water into wine (John 2:1–11). The second has to do with the Last Supper, which is observed by all Christians as The Lord's Supper, or Holy Communion, or Holy Eucharist. At this pivotal and symbolic meal Jesus and his disciples drank wine (not grape juice); and he commanded succeeding disciples to also drink wine "in remembrance of me"[11] (Matthew 26:27; Mark 14:23; Luke 22:17, 20; John 6:53–56; 1 Corinthians 11:25–26). The third has to do with Jesus promising his followers that he would one day drink wine with them again "in my Father's kingdom"[12] (Matthew 26:29; Mark 14:25). Any serious discussion of these events among southern clergy and laity of various denominations/groups will reflect the very issue being addressed in this chapter.

Roman Catholics and Episcopalians do not espouse abstinence from beverage alcohol, although they would not endorse overindulgence. Remember, too, that wine is used in their regular observances of Holy Communion (Holy Eucharist); and even children would be served wine on those occasions as a part of worship. Even their clergy drink alcoholic beverages ... in public.

Most Protestant groups/denominations espouse an anti-alcohol stance, at least officially. For example, the largest group, the Southern Baptist Convention, lists seventy-four resolutions in opposition to beverage alcohol from 1886 to 1991.[13] The United Methodist Church lists twenty-three documents in opposition to alcoholic beverages,[14] and affirms "our long-standing support of abstinence from alcohol."[15] The Church of God (Cleveland, TN) states in its official positions that "a Christian must totally abstain from all alcoholic beverages."[16] The Christian Methodist Episcopal Church speaks to the alcohol issue in its Social Creed: "We condemn the use of alcoholic beverages. ... We condemn the sale and use of liquor as that which imperils the abundant life to which Christ calls us."[17] These examples do not include local and state conventions, associations, conferences, districts, camps, and individual churches. The Women's Christian Temperance Union, though founded in the north (Cleveland, Ohio, in 1874), has had a strong following in the south, helping to enact the Eighteenth Amendment, though its influence in the modern south is greatly diminished. Mother's Against Drunk Driving, founded in 1980, is headquartered in Texas, and is a strong force in the south today.

Many Christian pulpits in the American south still denounce it, although not as much as they once did. However, many Christians (as well as non-Christians) in the south consume beverage alcohol. They may support, at least passively (or don't ask don't tell), the official church positions, but they practice a lifestyle that is often very different. Many dear Christian ladies who make fruitcake during the Thanksgiving/ Christmas holiday season think nothing of sending someone to get them some (usually very specific) alcoholic beverage to season their cakes, while they would be horrified at the idea of simply having a drink. One United Church of Christ church in Tennessee is remembered as the home of a lady who was a staunch member of the Women's Christian Temperance Union while her grain elevator husband was selling grain to folks who were making the very product she so opposed.[18] One of the old jokes in the south raises the question of how one can tell a moderate Baptist from a fundamentalist/conservative Baptist. The answer is that the moderates speak to each other in the liquor store. Many people very active in churches officially opposed to beverage alcohol drink socially.

The most recent statistics (in gallons) from the National Institute on Alcohol Abuse and Alcoholism show that the south leads the country in beverage alcohol consumption[19]:

Total United States Consumption 6,951,376,000
Northeast Region	1,201,034,000
Midwest Region	1,644,623,000
South Region	2,563,551,000
West Region	1,542,166,000

Thus, 36.9 percent of all the beer, wine, and spirits consumed in the United States in 1999 were consumed in the south. A study by the Department of Health & Social Behavior of the Harvard School of Public Health indicates that alcohol consumption among selected college students and locations in the south seems to correspond with those in other parts of the country.[20] Alcoholics Anonymous chapters can be found all across the south today as a measure of alcohol's ongoing negative impact amidst its widespread respectability. So much for abstinence.

One source even suggests that the "Pilgrims chose to make final landfall at Plymouth, Massachusetts, even though their original destination was elsewhere, primarily because they were almost out of beer."[21] It is important to remember here that these were the Puritans. David S. Reynolds notes: "Since the founding of the thirteen colonies,[22] alcohol and inebriation have been important to American culture and mythology. ... The tavern and church stood as twin pillars of community life in the eighteenth century, suggesting townsfolk's equal devotion to spirits and the Spirit."[23] Taverns/bars and the church are still the twin pillars of community life in the south, as they are in the rest of the country. The production and consumption of beverage alcohol in the south and the building of churches are as old as the first white settlers. They just came with the people ... and they remain with them in an ongoing tension to this day.

The south's love/hate relationship with beverage alcohol is clearly seen in the noble experiment of Prohibition from 1920 to 1933. When the Eighteenth Amendment to the United States Constitution became law, fifteen of the thirty-six states ratifying it were from the south. In fact, the amendment was encased by the south with the first state to ratify it being Mississippi on January 18, 1918, and the last state to ratify was North Carolina on January 16, 1919.[24] When the Twenty-First Amendment became law repealing the Eighteenth Amendment, only ten of the southern states were among the thirty-eight ratifying it. The first southern state to ratify it was West Virginia.[25] Noticeably absent from the ratifying states were Mississippi, Georgia, South Carolina, North Carolina, and Louisiana.

Even in all of this, there is a mixed signal. All southern states were quick to ban alcohol. Even so, illegal alcoholic beverage production and distribution flourished. As it became legal again, five deep south southern states steadfastly refused to be a part of the legalization of a product that was a major economic force both fueling the economy of the region and robbing it of resources and tax dollars ... and making criminals of much of the population distributing and consuming it. The respectable folks in the south made it and drank it, but would not vote for it. They still make it—legally and illegally, and drink it, but often they will still not vote for it. There are still "dry" areas in the south today.

Illegal beverage alcohol, moonshine, has always flowed out of southern hills and backcountry as routinely as creek water. "Cosby, Tennessee, is known as the Moonshine Capital of the World."[26] "Moonshine Festivals" are scattered across the south in such places as Dawsonville, Georgia, and McMahan's Cove, Alabama. From 1999 to 2003 the Alabama event funded more than $30,000 in local college scholarships, with the awards ceremony held in the local high school.[27] "More than 300 wine festivals and events take place each year in Virginia."[28] Clearly, the presence and influence of alcohol continues to have an impact interwoven into the fabric of southern community life today in spite of some continued social and religious opposition.

Kenneth Copley, 61, of Centerville, Tennessee, "a churchgoing teetotaler," was granted a presidential pardon on December 24, 2002, for making moonshine when he was 20. The crime is a federal felony. Copley was "all but baptized in it. His daddy made it. His brother made it. His neighbors made it. A Hickman County commissioner brags he used to cook white lightning behind a local church—with the congregation's full knowledge. ... Much of the illegal whiskey-making was along the banks of Hassell's Creek ... named for Black Jack Hassell, the great-great-grandfather of James Hassell, a four-time-convicted, fifth-generation moonshiner—and first-term county commissioner."[29]

Amidst all the legal ebb and flow of beverage alcohol, illegal moonshine continues to flourish. In Rocky Mount, Virginia, several years ago government agents spoke of "a new generation of moonshiners who have transformed legendary woodman's skills into efficient distilleries, some capable of producing thousands of gallons of liquor a week" funneling thousands of gallons a year from Virginia to North Carolina.[30]

When I served on the ministerial staffs of nine Southern Baptist churches in two southern states (Georgia and Texas) from 1967 to 2001, church leaders drank alcohol in every church, in spite of the denomination's, and sometimes the church's, official opposition. In several churches, there had been generations of families who made homemade wine for The Lord's Supper (Holy Communion) with great pride; although by the time I was present the practice had ceased.

One south Georgia legend has it that the pastor of a small, county seat, First Baptist Church once swapped his pastorate for a jug of whiskey. It occurred one Saturday night in the 1920s or 1930s in a local hotel room. It seems that the pastor and a visiting evangelist were sharing the contents of a jug of whiskey as each told the other how the other "had it made" in terms of their ministerial occupations. One had a fixed, prominent, socially affirming situation and the other had the freedom to roam from place to place. So, they swapped jobs … right then and there. The pastor became an evangelist and the evangelist became the pastor of the First Baptist Church.[31] I do not know who got to keep the jug.

Alcohol consumption and abuse cross all racial, social, ethnic, professional, political, economic, and religious lines in the south as in other parts of the country. Many in education, health care, and law enforcement assert that the major drug problem in the south today is alcohol. It is easy to obtain (in spite of laws to restrict it) and relatively inexpensive. In the south, though, it is a part of the folklore.

Perhaps nowhere is the alcohol folklore more a part of the southern heritage than in the sport of automobile racing. Even as the popularity of NASCAR explodes on the modern scene, those who give it life speak with a drawl. Less than a handful of the champions since 1948 have come from north of the Mason-Dixon Line. The National Association for Stock Car Auto Racing was formed in 1948. However, the legend and lore of moonshine is, as Scott Oldham has written, "woven into the fabric of NASCAR."[32] Just notice the names on the cars and uniforms of the drivers. There is even a series of races known as the Busch Series. Alcohol is well represented in NASCAR.

Even as satellites beam the pictures to televisions around the world, the roots of stock car racing remain firmly imbedded in the alcohol lore of the south. During Prohibition the folks who made alcohol in the backwoods of the south used drivers with "souped-up, stock looking cars" that would outrun government agents to deliver their product across Georgia, Tennessee, and the Carolinas.

When Prohibition ended, the government chases faded away (though not completely). So, the good ol' boys started to race each other on the roads and short dirt tracks that became more common throughout the region ... a far cry from the big modern tracks of today. "By the late 1930's the cars made it to the beaches of Daytona, driven by guys like admitted shine runners Fonty Flock, Lee Petty, and Junior Johnson."[33] The race from moonshine to millions, redneck to popular icon, Tobacco Road to respectability was on. The south had risen again—and who knows where it will end.

It is a phenomenon not lost on Hollywood. "The first movie to link bootlegging with horsepower," Oldham notes, was probably *Thunder Road* in 1958, starring Robert Mitchum. ... The Burt Reynolds movie *Smokey and the Bandit*, and the television series *The Dukes of Hazard*, are more modern examples. ... Most recently, *Days of Thunder*, starring Tom Cruise made the connection. [Interestingly] Cruise's character celebrates his first NASCAR victory by drinking 'shine from a mason jar.'"[34]

In addition to NASCAR, the rest of the southern sports scene is caught up in the marriage of alcohol and life: from Busch Stadium in St. Louis, to Turner Field in Atlanta, and every other Major League Baseball stadium, to the sacred grounds of the Augusta National Golf Club during Masters week, to the "World's Largest Cocktail Party" at the annual Georgia-Florida football game in Jacksonville, to every National Football League stadium, to many tailgate parties outside all college and NFL stadiums.

This intermingling of alcohol and life is not just a reality in the world of sports. Southern cultural life shares in this relationship. Alcohol is a part of the southern music scene, especially in the two music venues originating in the south: country music and jazz.

Country music's lyrics and vocalists are loaded with alcohol songs like "Rocky Top," "White Lightin'," "Hello Wall," "East Bound and Down," "Pop a Top Again," "Whiskey River," "Mountain Dew," "She Couldn't Change Me," and the recent number one "Whiskey for My Men, Beer for My Horses." Singers such as Hank Williams, George Jones, Johnny Cash, Hank Williams, Jr., Willie Nelson, Troy Gentry, Eddie Montgomery, and Toby Keith have sung about and enjoyed beverage alcohol. Perhaps Steve Goodman wrote the "perfect country song" entitled "You Never Even Called Me By My Name" with a little encouragement from singer David Allen Coe. As the song says, it did not become the "perfect country song" until Coe complained after seeing the first verses that the song did not say "anything at all about mama, or trains, or trucks, or prison, or gettin' drunk." "Well," Coe continues, "he sat down and wrote another verse to the song and he sent it to me, and after reading it, I realized that my friend had written the perfect country and western song and I felt obliged to include it on this album. The last verse goes something like this:

> Well, I was drunk the day my mom got out of prison
> And I went to pick her up in the rain
> But before I could get to the station in my pickup truck
> She got runned over by a damned old train.[35]

Jazz was born and flourished in New Orleans and Memphis before reaching out to the rest of the country. Jazz hits included: "Rum and Coke," "Moonlight Cocktail," "Little Brown Jug," and "Straight, No Chaser," to name a few. Jazz musicians, too, such as Billie Holiday, Charlie Parker, Thelonius Monk, Benny Goodman, and others, have been known to enjoy what they sang and played about.

The alcohol industry sponsors theater and art in venues large and small all across the south. Alcohol is served in the Fox Theater in Atlanta and concert halls in every major southern city, as well as in smaller venues like the Old Opera House in Hawkinsville, Georgia. In grocery stores, bars, restaurants, liquor stores, convenience stores, country clubs, juke joints, country stores, hunting and fishing clubs, river trips, wedding receptions, private homes, and even church socials ... it is all there. High society, middle class, and poverty; in rural and urban settings; white, black, and Hispanic; religious and non-religious; young (legal and not legal) and old—all share in "southern comfort."

Perhaps a good illustration of this twisted phenomenon of alcohol consumption in the life of the south comes out of my own personal experience. My grandfather was a wonderful man. Papa and I were buddies and I loved him dearly. From my earliest memory, I recall that he enjoyed a late afternoon drink of Windsor Canadian Whiskey ... even though he was a Southern Baptist. Not every afternoon, but "from time to time." As he aged and I became an adult, I gave Papa a fifth of Windsor Canadian every Christmas ... put it right there under the Christmas tree without the complete approval of my grandmother. It was a simple joy for him ... and me. For many years I was a Southern Baptist clergyman, and would dare not be seen in a liquor store. So, I had to get Papa's friend, Buck Elliot, to go to the liquor store for me. One Christmas I decided that I was going to start purchasing Papa's Christmas present myself ... just like I did gifts for everyone else in my family. I was so nervous (and somewhat afraid that someone would see me) the first time I entered a liquor store, but the joy of handing Papa his Christmas present that year, and the few thereafter before his death, is a memory I will forever cherish. And to think, I almost missed it. And no, I don't think I did anything wrong. In fact, it is one of the right things I have done in my life. I just wish now I had done it sooner ... and more often ... and that "from time to time" we had had a drink together.

"Alcohol was consumed in all of the colonial settlements in America,"[36] and by 1830 "alcoholic beverages were served at virtually all social gatherings"[37] in the United States. That statement is equally as true today, even in the south ... especially in the south. Southern Comfort's St. Louis Cocktail motto was "Limit 2 to a customer (No gentleman would ask for more)." However, some did. And today throughout the southern United States, while many people do not drink beverage alcohol, many people are asking for more than two expressions of their favorite "southern comfort" on a regular, acceptable, and equal (and often higher) per capita basis than the rest of the country.[38]

Today I am an Episcopal priest. The change in my faith expression is much too complex for this discussion. However, I have found a somewhat cynical sense of joy in responding to many Southern Baptists (especially), and others as well, when they ask me why I made such a change. With a twinkle in my eye I think of Papa and say: "I got tired of closet drinking."

Here's to abstinence ... southern style!

Notes

[1] See http://cocktails.about.com/library/weekly/aa042200a.htm. Accessed July 14, 2003.

[2] Ibid.

[3] See www.makersmark.com/his_02high.htm. Accessed July 17, 2003. Today, Maker's Mark is headquartered in Loretto, Kentucky.

[4] See www.jackdaniels.com. Accessed June 26, 2003.

[5] The exception, of course, was during the years of Prohibition.

[6] A few collector bottles can now be purchased at the distillery through some special arrangement, but there are no other retail sales of Jack Daniel's elsewhere in Moore County.

[7] See www.marylandwine.com/wineries. Accessed July 10, 2003.

[8] See www.picktnproducts.org/wineries/directory.html. Accessed July 10, 2003.

[9] See www.virginiawineries.org. Accessed July 10, 2003.

[10] Some of the references reflecting negatively on alcohol include: Leviticus 10:8–10; Judges 13:4; Proverbs 20:1; 21:7; 23:29–32; Isaiah 5:11; Jeremiah 35:6; Luke 1:15; Romans 14:21; and Ephesians 5:18. Some of the positive references include: Matthew 9:17; Psalm 4:7 and 104:14–15; 1 Timothy 5:2–3; 2 Chronicles 32:28; and Zechariah 10:7. There are far too many references to list them all here.

[11] New Revised Standard Version, Anglican ed. (New York: Oxford University Press, 1998).

[12] Ibid.

[13] See www.sbc.net/resolutions/AMResearch.asp. Accessed June 26, 2003.

[14] See www.umc.org/Scripts/umcii.idq. Accessed June 26, 2003.

[15] See www.umc.org/abouttheumc/policy/social/I-alcohol.htm. Accessed June 26, 2003.

[16] See www.churchofgod.cc/behavioral_temperance.cfm. Accessed June 26, 2003.

[17] See www.c-m-e.org/core/Social_Creed.htm. Accessed July 14, 2003.

[18] While the author knows the name of the church and community, it is probably best to just leave it at that.

[19] See www.niaaa.nih.gov/databases/consum02.htm. Accessed June 26, 2003. Numbers may not sum due to rounding. Statistics based on 1999 numbers. These are the most current available as of June 26, 2003.

[20] Elissa R. Weitzmann, Alison Folkman, Kerry Lemieux Folkman, Henry Wechsler, *Health & Place*, March 2003. "The Relationship of Alcohol Outlet Density to Heavy and Frequent Drinking-Related Problems among College Students at Eight Universities." See www.elsevier.com/locate/healthplace. Accessed June 26, 2003.

[21] See www.angelfire.com/biz6/dcris/moonshine.html. Accessed June 26, 2003.

[22] Five of these were in the South: Georgia, Virginia, North Carolina, South Carolina, and Maryland.

[23] David S. Reynolds, *The Serpent in a Cup: Temperance in American Literature* (Amherst: University of Massachusetts Press, 1977), 2.

[24] The Southern states ratifying the Eighteenth Amendment were Mississippi, Virginia, Kentucky, South Carolina, Maryland, Texas, Georgia, Louisiana, Florida, West Virginia, Tennessee, Arkansas, Alabama, North Carolina, and Missouri. See www.usconstitution.net/constamrat.html#Am18. Accessed July 10, 2003.

[25] The southern States ratifying the Twenty-First Amendment were West Virginia, Arkansas, Alabama, Tennessee, Missouri, Maryland, Virginia, Florida, Texas, and Kentucky. See www.usconstitution.net/constamrat.html#Am21. Accessed July 10, 2003.

[26] See www.angelfire.com/biz6/dcris/moonshine.html. Accessed June 26, 2003.

[27] See www.moonshinefestival.com. Accessed July 1, 2003.

[28] See www.virginiawineries.org. Accessed July 10, 2003.

[29] Jeffery Scott, "Moonshiner Gets Presidental Pardon," *The Macon (GA) Telegraph.* January 13, 2003, 5B.

[30] Peter T. Kilborn, "U. S. Cracks Down on Rise In Appalachia Moonshine," *The New York Times,* March 23, 2000, late edition-final, A1, col. 4.

[31] Again, the author knows the location of the town where this story is told; however, it is probably best to leave the story as it is.

[32] Scott Oldham, "Good Ol' Boys Turn 50," *Popular Mechanics,* 1998, www.popularmechanics.com. Accessed June 26, 2003.

[33] Ibid.

[34] Ibid.

[35] See www.lyricsconnection.com/davidallancoe.com/lyrics/younever.htm. Accessed July 14, 2003.

[36] Peter McWilliams, "Prohibition: A Lesson in the Futility (and Danger) of Prohibition," *Ain't Nobody's Business If You Do* (New York: Procedure Press, 1996). See www.mcwilliams.com/books/ain't/402.html. Accessed July 10, 2003.

[37] Reynolds, *Serpent in a Cup,* 2.

[38] See www.niaaa.nih.gov.

Bibliography

Kilborn, Peter T. "U. S. Cracks Down on Rise in Appalachia Moonshine" *The New York Times.* March 23, 2000, A1.

McWilliams, Peter. "Prohibition: A Lesson in the Futility (and Danger) of Prohibition." *Ain't Nobody's Business If You Do.* New York: Procedure Press, 1996.

Oldham, Scott. "Good Ol' Boys Turn 50." *Popular Mechanics,* 1998, www.popularmechanics.com. Accessed June 26, 2003.

Reynolds, David S. *The Serpent in a Cup: Temperance in American Literature.* Amherst: University of Massachusetts Press, 1977.

Scott, Jeffery. "Moonshiner Gets Presidental Pardon." *The Macon (GA) Telegraph,* January 13, 2003, 5B.

9 Recovering Religion: The Complex Legacy of *Alcoholics Anonymous*

C. K. Robertson

It is a typical Saturday night at St. Gilbert's Church. The lot outside is full of cars, packed together side by side and bumper to bumper, with barely enough room for occupants to squeeze themselves out their doors without scratching the paint off of the adjoining automobiles. To any visitor driving up to the church, it might well appear as if a service is in progress, or perhaps a special teaching or some other "religious" event. However, it is religion of a different kind that draws the dozens of drivers and many others on foot or bicycle to St. Kevin's several evenings a week, for Saturday night is a meeting night for members of *Alcoholics Anonymous* (AA) ... and they would not miss a meeting if their lives depended on it. Indeed, if asked, many would say they do.

Together with *Al-Anon* and *Narcotics Anonymous,* AA utilizes church meeting space more often than the sponsoring parish itself. Arguably, the "congregation" that is present on Saturday night is far more faithful in attendance, far more committed to the group's precepts and procedures, and far more zealous in their appreciation of the organization than the congregation found inside the sanctuary on Sunday morning.

The reasons for such faithful devotion by members are, to them, seemingly obvious: AA works! As one proponent puts it, AA offers "a solid and selfless spirituality"[1] that many are seeking, "unadorned by the creed, code, or cult of religion,"[2] yet with principles that "permeate" our world.[3]

Others, however, are less generous in their comments, describing AA as "stubbornly resistant to change,"[4] and "more harmful than beneficial."[5] One critic offers what is probably the most accurate observation: "It works for those for whom it works."[6] This essay explores the complex legacy of a decades-old systematic program that continues to attract at one and the same time both the highest praise and the sharpest criticism.

"Not for Sissies"

On June 10, 1935, "Dr. Bob" met with Bill W. and admitted that he was powerless over his drinking problem and ready to follow the steps that the latter had been developing for his own recovery. Thus, today's members proclaim, *Alcoholics Anonymous* was born. Its birth, however, did not occur in a vacuum, for there were historical antecedents to AA that directly influenced the form this particular organization would take. These antecedents included the temperance movement and the evangelical revival movement, of which both Bill and Bob had personal experience.

As in Britain, from which the majority of the earliest colonists came, drinking in the United States in the nation's formative years was quite simply a fact of life. Even as every English village was guaranteed to be marked (and usually still is) by both a church and a pub, so taverns became a central part of many Americans' lives. People drank. Indeed, they drank quite a bit. By the early nineteenth century, the consumption of alcoholic beverages (usually beer or hard liquor) "rose to its highest per-capita levels in U.S. history," with an accompanying rise "in public drunkenness and violence."[7] Although many women as well as men drank, the former became increasingly frustrated with their husbands' neglect of home and family. More often than not, the men were to be found in the tavern. The "devil's drink" made many women organize and promote bold initiatives to be rid of their dependence on irresponsible men. It is small wonder, then, that groups such as the nineteenth-century Women's Christian Temperance Union (WCTU) pushed not only alcohol abstention but also issues such as women's suffrage.

Around the same period, Christian revivals were taking the ever-expanding country by storm. In western territories dotted with saloons, evangelical preachers proclaimed a message of public repentance and personal conversion that would later be mirrored in AA's twelve steps.[8] Consider Jonathan Edwards's list of steps or categories experienced by many converts in the days of the so-called Great Awakening: Awareness of the "dreadful nature" of sin, helplessness to change one's "miserable condition" without divine aid, "earnest concern" for salvation, and openness to whatever means God uses to bring about conversion.[9]

By the time Bill and Bob met, the "noble experiment" of Prohibition had come—with the Eighteenth Amendment in 1919—and gone—with the Twenty-First Amendment in 1933. Although "intoxicating liquors" had been outlawed during that twenty-four–year period, alcohol still flowed, albeit through illegal means. A kind of schizophrenia had developed in the nation. Even as many persisted in denouncing the evils of alcohol, others saw little problem with drinking. Unsurprisingly, people who came out of the revival movement fell into the former category, whereas members of churches that focused less on personal piety and more on church tradition—Catholics, Episcopalians, Lutherans—were in the latter category. There was little consensus in regard to drinking, and even less on how to deal with problem drinking, until Bill W. took the legacy of the temperance and revival movements and gave birth to the twelve steps of AA (see Figure 9.1 below).

The Twelve Steps of AA

1. We admitted we were powerless over alcohol—that our lives became unmanageable.
2. We came to believe that a Power greater than ourselves could restore us to sanity.
3. We made a decision to turn our will and our lives over to the care of God as we understood Him.
4. We made a searching and fearless moral inventory of ourselves.
5. We admitted to God, to ourselves, and to another human being the exact nature of our wrongs.
6. We were entirely ready to have God remove all these defects of character.
7. We humbly asked Him to remove our shortcomings.
8. We made a list of all persons we had harmed, and became willing to make amends to them all.
9. We made direct amends to such people wherever possible, except when to do so would injure them or others.
10. We continued to take personal inventory and when we were wrong we promptly admitted it.
11. We sought through prayer and meditation to improve our conscious contact with God, as we understood Him, praying only for knowledge of His will for us and the power to carry that out.
12. Having had a spiritual awakening as the result of these steps, we tried to carry this message to alcoholics, and to practice these principles in all our affairs.

Figure 9.1—The Twelve Steps of AA

The only requirement for membership, AA members assert, is "a desire to stop drinking." If this sounds simple, then it should be noted that from the very beginning, Bill was quick to state that his program of twelve steps to sobriety was "not for sissies." In those earliest days, his success rate was "very low," but Bill pressed on, at times for no other reason than the fact that sharing his program with others helped him maintain his own recovery.[10] The steps involved an admittance of a personal powerlessness over the problem, a trust in a Higher Power and commitment to the group to maintain sobriety, and an absolute conviction that being sober means total abstinence. Strict adherence to the steps was required. Spiritual discipline was necessary. It is this same program that is followed faithfully by many today. Sister "Molly Monahan," as one anonymous AA member and Roman Catholic nun calls herself, challenges those who disparage twelve-step programs: "Ask yourself whether ... you would be willing to go through the process."[11] The vast majority of people who begin attending twelve-step programs drop out within a year. Some claim the figure is as high as ninety to ninety-five percent, although the insistence on the anonymity of members makes this figure difficult, if not impossible, to verify.[12] Sister Molly admits that "some people come in and out of the program over and over again," never reaching lasting sobriety.[13]

For those who do stay with the program, *Alcoholics Anonymous* provides a kind of salvation. From the beginning, the battle with alcohol dependence was defined by AA in fairly black and white terms: "One drink, one drunk." A twelve-step proponent proclaims that "it only takes a slip in our recovery to return to a worse hell than the one we left."[14] This "hell" is something well understood by many in the United States. It has been estimated that more than 14 million Americans suffer from alcoholism or alcohol abuse.[15] According to the 1999 *Global Status Report on Alcohol* by the World Health Organization, the United States ranks 32 out of a total of 153 countries for recorded per capita consumption of pure alcohol per adult (15 years of age and over in 1996).[16] Although men are more than six times as likely to engage in heavy drinking as women,[17] in recent years the alcoholic beverage industry has used increasingly "aggressive" marketing strategies to attract more female drinkers, associating alcohol in advertisements with "glamour, independence, and liberation."[18] Similarly, despite the long held popular notion of old drunks lying on park benches, an image promulgated in movies and television, it is young people who "drink more heavily than the rest of the US population."[19] In other words, neither gender nor age is a determining factor in the evolution of an alcoholic. The elusive "alcoholic gene," long sought after by those arguing for a clear genetic predisposition toward alcoholism, remains in the realm of theory.[20] No one is automatically an alcoholic in the making. Similarly, no one individual is automatically immune, despite arguments that certain ethnic groups may be able to metabolize alcoholic beverages better than others. As one researcher warns, "If you're a drinking adult, chances are better than one in ten you're an alcoholic drinker."[21] For those who find themselves questioning whether they are in that latter group, the next step is problematic: Where does one turn for help?

"Don't Think, Don't Drink, and Come to Meetings"

Members of twelve-step programs insist that alcoholism should be understood as a disease. What is interesting, however, is that the steps themselves do not speak of recovery through medical treatment, but instead through a moral inventory, not through prescriptions but through conversion. This is where the revivalist roots of AA become most clearly evident.[22] "Don't leave before the miracle happens," initiates are exhorted. Physicians do not usually speak in such terms. Members are reminded that "the spiritual life is not a theory; we have to live it." This does not sound at all like your general practitioner. Indeed, it sounds far more like your local clergyperson. Thus, when proponents of the steps speak of alcoholism as a disease, it is crucial to understand what is meant by "disease." Dr. Edward Jelinek was an early advocate for "the disease theory," emphasizing the complete helplessness of an alcoholic in the face of a drink. Although his five categories of alcohol dependence have largely been ignored or forgotten, Jelinek's suggestion that some individuals are powerless before alcohol led to the AA concept of the need for help from a Higher Power outside oneself.[23] Abstinence became not simply one solution, but the only solution.

Long after the inception of AA, particularly in the last thirty years of the twentieth century, research on alcohol dependence and alcohol abuse dramatically increased. Dr. A. Thomas Horvath argues that "what most Americans believe about drinking problems and their treatment is substantially inaccurate."[24] Most of the research that has been fermenting in the past few decades has until very recently escaped the notice of the majority of Americans, and certainly of those seeking help with problem drinking. In one survey of 450 US alcohol treatment programs, "90 percent ... were based on the twelve-step program."[25] Popular culture, in the form of public forums, celebrity interviews, films, television, politics, and popular literature, only serves to bolster the idea "that AA is the only way to go."[26] There are, however, other voices that are demanding entrance into the conversation, though they have not yet "achieved the organizational power and influence needed to shape policy."[27] One controversial proponent for alternative approaches to alcohol treatment is Dr. Stanton Peele, who asserts that "every major tenet of the 'disease' view of addiction is refuted by scientific research."[28] He concludes that, because of the almost universal disregard of modern medical research by twelve-step advocates, "the most enlightened guidance on addiction has not been available to the many people it could help."[29]

What kind of "enlightened guidance" is available? One significant body of research concerns the treatment of alcohol problems with medicine. Medications being used or prepared for use at the present time include naltrexone, which "retards the mild euphoria of a drink, helping alcoholics imbibe moderately," and acamprosate, which, though widely used in Europe, failed to win US Food and Drug Administration (FDA) approval because of "inadequate data."[30] Twelve-step proponents insist that fighting substance addiction with other substances is illogical, but advocates for alternative forms of treatment ask: Why not try? With other problems labeled as diseases, every possible treatment is considered and "treatments are changed if they are not effective."[31] A failure to acknowledge the potential help that can come from medical treatment, these researchers state, is to "become stuck" with one solitary methodology,[32] one that is summarized as "don't think, don't drink, and come to meetings." Influential groups such as the National Council on Alcoholism "react sharply" to any other approach.[33]

Perhaps the biggest difference between alternative approaches and the twelve-step program lies in definition. For Bill W. and twelve-step proponents to this day, the definition of an alcoholic is clear: someone who is helpless before alcohol. Abstinence is required precisely because no middle ground is possible. The disease is overwhelming. "Controlled drinking" is an oxymoron. Recovery is a process, never a reality achieved in this life. "Always recovering, never recovered" is the only possible reality for the alcoholic.

For a growing number of people, there is another way of defining reality. Rather than view individuals as either one way or another— alcoholic or nonalcoholic, with no room for anything in the middle— these researchers point out the fact that, by definition, individuals struggling with alcohol addiction must have a part of themselves that remains nonalcoholic.[34] If this were not the case, if it is truly all or nothing, then alcohol really does have complete power over the individual and recovery is impossible. It is precisely because a person is both alcoholic and nonalcoholic at the same time, these researchers say, that abstinence is even possible. It also means that abstinence does not have to be viewed as the only possible solution to the problem.

"Natural recovery, maturing out, autoremission, spontaneous remission, and spontaneous recovery" are all terms used to refer to the resolution of alcoholism without traditional treatment.[35] For some, the solution begins with something as simple as a change in diet. A person's ability to metabolize alcohol is interrelated with food metabolism.[36] Advocates of a diet approach argue that alcoholics suffer from malnutrition and need to examine their eating habits just as much as their drinking habits. "Habit" is a key word for these researchers, who assert that alcohol addiction is a learned behavior and can indeed be changed.[37] New lists of steps, quite different from the long-standing twelve steps of AA, are being offered by more and more alcohol addiction counselors. These alternative sets of steps emphasize choice: "Know you can change. Unlearn learned behavior. Make a decision to change. Cope with cravings (or compulsions). Find something to replace the habit."[38] These new steps speak less about helplessness and more about self-confidence, less about the need for a Higher Power and more about "the key building blocks of life—friends, family, job, career, hobbies."[39]

If these habit-breaking lists sound at all familiar, it is because alcohol addiction is increasingly being viewed in terms similar to nicotine addiction. Most people agree that smoking is one of the most difficult addictions to break, yet only one out of twenty persons who have kicked the habit attributes success to a support group like AA.[40] Instead, they usually experiment with treatment aids such as gum or patches, and they talk much more about their willpower than about their helplessness!

The issue of definition is not a small one, and is worth exploring in greater detail (see Figure 9.2 below).

Abstinence-only Approach	*Alternative Approaches*
"One drink, one drunk."	Many factors contribute to addiction.
"Once an alcoholic, always an alcoholic."	It is possible to change and be cured.
"It's a disease."	It is a harmful habit that can be corrected.
"Utilize, don't analyze."	Explore all the facets of one's life.
"It works if you work it."	If one method does not work, try another.

Figure 9.2—Differences in Definition

One point on which everyone agrees is the need to let go of blame when addressing problem drinking.[41] Judgmental attitudes do not help anyone. Beyond this point, however, there are significant differences. On the one side, there is an almost total focus on the individual, on the addiction itself, on the individual's helplessness and need for outside help, and on the totally negative effects of alcohol.

On the other side, there is an awareness of the larger social network to which the individual belongs, on the individual's whole life and difficulties aside from the actual addiction, on the ability to choose to limit drinking and to call upon personal reserves of willpower and energy, and even on the potentially positive effects of alcohol.[42] For those who advocate alternatives to the twelve steps, the more familiar approach appears "religious and dogmatic," demanding of its adherents "strict adherence to group policy."[43]

"What You See Here, What You Hear Here, Remains Here"

If definition of the issues and solutions is a primary difference between twelve-step proponents and alternative approach advocates, it is due largely to the different demographics of the groups. It is argued that AA and similar groups contain an overwhelming number of "late-stage alcoholics, those who experience severe withdrawal symptoms when they try to quit."[44] These individuals, understandably find in their recovery group a fellowship of like-minded converts, all sharing a real experience of helplessness and desperate hope that marks them out as different from those outside the group. They speak in glowing terms of a "safety net" where they feel encouraged and supported, where they can see their "true self reflected from all sides."[45] From this insider vantage point, the fact that others do not understand them is proof that these others are outsiders, either because they are not alcoholics or because they are alcoholics in denial. How can the uninitiated possibly understand a program that only makes sense to those already working it?

If this sounds familiar to students of religion, it is probably because much of the language of twelve-step programs echoes that of sectarian churches and religious groups throughout the centuries. In his classic study of ecclesial models, *Christ and Culture,* H. Richard Niebuhr includes among his list of church-to-culture approaches a model he describes as "Christ against culture." Niebuhr states that this model has been exemplified through the centuries by groups such as Benedictine monastics, Protestant sectarians, and the Mennonites and Quakers, all groups that have in some way separated themselves from the encompassing culture "for it is in culture that sin chiefly resides."[46] At first glance, this may well appear to be an unfortunate and undeserved comparison for twelve-step groups. After all, members often contrast the inclusive, "all-encompassing" spirituality of AA with the "narrow and exclusive system of the religious."[47] Again, far from appearing overly focused on the religious, AA offers a haven for alcoholics who "have not yet come to a belief in God" or even "those who are atheists by conviction." For such persons, "the group itself may serve as a Higher Power."[48] It thus seems unfair to include twelve-step programs in a list of groups that are exclusivist and sectarian in nature.

Having said this, it is important to recognize the ways in which Niebuhr's words about "Christ against culture" do resonate with the ethos of AA and other twelve-step programs. First, such programs call for a clear public conversion, a temporal transition from one state of being to another. Jonathan Edwards, the preeminent preacher and theologian of the Great Awakening who advocated a religiosity quite distinct from the mainline church work of his time, observed in his 1737 *Faithful Narrative of the Surprising Work of God* that before conversion individuals "are sometimes brought to the borders of despair, and it looks as black as midnight to them a little before the day dawn in their souls."[49] There is little gray area involved in such conversions, and there is no question for the converted of the absolute need for moving from the realm of death into that of life. In a similar manner, the individual who stands before his or her fellows in a meeting and solemnly proclaims, "My name is ____ and I am an alcoholic" has made an essential and radical decision to embark on a new way of life, thereby affirming an absolute need for personal conversion from "the way of death ... the vicious course."[50] It matters little that this is only the beginning of a long journey with many road bumps and potholes along the way. It is a turning point nonetheless, a watershed moment to which one can later refer when faced with temptations.

Second, the twelve-step paradigm is theistic and salvific in general principle, if not in every specific member's mind. AA proponents such as Mel Ash may assert that "the God that can be named is not God,"[51] but the fact is that there is indeed some kind of acceptance of "the man upstairs" by the vast majority of AA members. More than this, there is a strong tendency toward finding salvation—that is, help in the midst of helplessness—through this God who cannot be named, but who looks suspiciously like the Judeo-Christian God of old-time revivalists. This is quite different from the largely humanistic and secular vocabulary of modern alternative models. The US judicial system appears to recognize this continued religious undercurrent in AA and similar organizations, as four higher courts before 2000 ruled that mandating attendance at twelve-step programs for individuals going through the judicial system violates First Amendment rights. The reason? The courts have claimed that the programs are considered "religious activities."

Third, twelve-step programs assume *absolute trust in, and obedience to, the new group into which one is initiated.* As noted above, the group itself often becomes the "Higher Power" for many, representing the authority so desperately sought by the lost and hopeless soul. Criticism or even questioning of the group and its methods may be met with strong resistance. One critique may be overly harsh in asserting that newcomers to twelve-step programs who do not echo the "party line" are "treated with knowing condescension or actively hazed."[52] However, it is accurate to state that the group acts as a self-regulating homeostatic system, maintaining its forms and procedures against any possible change or serious critique. AA has "remained basically the same since its inception."[53] Niebuhr notes that resistance to change is a serious difference between a religious system that grows and develops and a sectarian group that itself becomes idealized by its members, who dedicate themselves fully to it.[54]

This last point of comparison leads directly into the fourth, that twelve-step programs often breed a *suspicion about all outside programs and organizations that utilize a different approach.* Researchers Robert Granfield and William Cloud argue that the principles of the movement are presented by members with "exactly the degree of religious self-assuredness" displayed by nonsecular sectarian groups.[55] To a group that is, using Niebuhr's description, "against culture," mainline systems are by definition suspect because they "water down" the message of salvation, exchange a broad way for the narrow path, and suggest that there may be redemption in some manner outside the strict program established by the faithful. Niebuhr speaks of a "primitive, unconquerable tendency to think in terms of in-group and out-group, of self and other."[56] For the "true believer," there is no use in building bridges with those who are co-opted by the darkness, for they have already fallen from the one true path to life. There is but one road, one way, one truth, and any who speak otherwise are to be viewed suspiciously or avoided altogether.

In a similar way, there are many who have accepted without question that, for the person struggling with alcohol problems, AA is "the only way to go."[57] It is interesting to note that this opinion is as widely held among people who are outside the program as among those who are active members. Even the United States government, in the form of its courts, has long supported the primacy of the twelve-step program above any alternatives, although (as noted above) this tendency to mandate attendance in such programs has in recent years been vehemently challenged.[58] In spite of these challenges, it is still a fair assumption that the average American, if asked by someone seeking help with an alcohol problem, would be far more likely to suggest checking into a twelve-step program or a "ninety-day wonder" rehabilitation center than trying some of the alternative possibilities listed earlier in this chapter. Perhaps the local AA chapter is indeed the best approach for a particular individual; the point is that because there is so little knowledge of the wider spectrum of treatment possibilities, there is little chance for people to make any kind of educated decision about which direction to proceed. For some advocates of alternative approaches, the problem does not lie with twelve-step programs; after all, they are doing what they were created to do. Rather, it has been suggested that the silence of doctors, researchers, and the general population contributed for many years to the lack of alternative approaches to treatment that only now are gaining attention.[59]

The fifth and final point to be made here regarding a correspondence between twelve-step programs and Niebuhr's "Christ against culture" model is that *programs such as AA continue to focus on the individual's problem and the individual's redemption.* "Treatment of alcohol-related problems, including dependence, is a strategy typically targeted to the individual and not to the large population."[60] From the days of the Great Awakening onward, the strong emphasis placed by sectarian movements on evangelism and personal salvation has been matched by a tendency to downplay or even disparage both the social gospel ethic and the broad-based ecumenical approach of mainline churches. Individual sin and salvation—not issues of homelessness, Third World debt, education reform, health care—is the focus of the weekly sermon in evangelistic, revivalist churches. Similarly, to outsiders looking in, it might appear as if many members of twelve-step groups are focused solely on their own drinking problems and less on the "constellation of factors" in society that result in alcohol problems.[61] As with their revivalist counterparts, AA members may say that a person must work first on one's own self.

"Take What You Need and Leave the Rest"

I am aware as I write this that AA and other twelve-step programs have at times been criticized for being too self-centered, for engaging in navel-gazing and neglecting matters of social concern. ... What I do know is that sober members of *Alcoholics Anonymous* no longer contribute to the *deficit* column of the common good.[62]

There is no denying the remarkable benefit that countless individuals through the years have found through *Alcoholics Anonymous*, nor is there any good reason to do so. There is little need to reject the life-enhancing results that are borne out of the spiritual and moral discipline that AA promotes. As has already been said, the program "works for those for whom it works." However, what is being argued by a growing number of researchers is that there is often an inability or refusal by many individuals, both inside and outside the twelve-step system, to accept that there are other *equally valid* approaches to problems with alcohol. According to the 1999 Global Status Report on Alcohol, "recorded alcohol consumption among adults has fallen steadily in most developed countries since 1980."[63] Unlike other developed nations, however, in the United States, it has been total abstinence that often is seen as the only way to go.[64] Does it have to be all or nothing? In spite of the Big Book's flexibility toward other models—"If someone thinks he can do the job in some other way ... encourage him to follow his own conscience"—many proponents of the twelve steps fail to acknowledge other approaches to recovery from alcohol dependency.

The power of paradigm shifts often lies in their timing. Paul of Tarsus appeared on the scene in the first century when the Roman roads, the communication systems, the tolerance for new religions, and the *pax romana* all combined to allow for mass promulgation of his message of new life in Christ. In the sixteenth century, Martin Luther appeared with his now-famous 95 theses right when nationalism was on the rise and the corruption of the papacy under the Medicis was at its zenith.[65] However, it has been said that even a Reformation needs a reformation, as the new paradigm itself becomes stuck somewhere along the way. It is noteworthy that Thomas Aquinas's theological system, which the Catholic Reformers argued was the correct way over against the

Protestants, was itself seen as overly radical and even rejected by some bishops in Thomas's own lifetime. Even so, could Luther and other Reformers have possibly envisioned how "set" their reforming ways would often become for later generations? System change does not come easily, but once it is successful, then the new way often becomes a system to be clutched and defended at all costs.[66]

What the founders of AA gave our society was nothing short of remarkable: A novel approach to quitting drinking that drew upon the success of both the temperance and revivalist movements of previous generations. The twelve-step "reformation" has been successful for many. However, its ongoing success may lie less in a rigid affirmation of its efficacy for all who struggle with alcohol and more in an adaptability that recognizes the positive advances in alcohol dependency work that have occurred since AA's inception. It can be argued that the public relations success of AA itself has helped pave the way for further research and, yes, reforms. It would be disappointing if the twelve-step movement that consciously or otherwise helped foster new ways of looking at alcohol dependency did not itself benefit ultimately for the alternative methodologies that are now with us, probably to stay.

Notes

[1] Sister Molly Monahan, *Seeds of Grace: A Nun's Reflections on the Spirituality of Alcoholics Anonymous* (New York: Riverside Books, 2001), 4.

[2] Ibid., 169.

[3] Mel Ash, *The Zen of Recovery* (New York: Tarcher/Putnam, 1993), 56.

[4] Jerry Dorsman, *How to Quit Drinking Without A.A.*, 2nd ed. (Roseville, CA: Prima Publishing, 1997), 4.

[5] Stanton Peele, and Archie Brodsky, *The Truth about Addiction and Recovery* (New York: Fireside, 1991), 10.

[6] Ibid., 29. Lance Dodes echoes this statement on page 225 in his book *The Heart of Addiction* (New York: HarperCollins, 2002), immediately adding that the twelve-step program also has "significant limitation."

[7] Heather Ogilvie, *Alternatives to Abstinence: A New Look at Alcoholism and the Choices in Treatment* (New York: Hatherleigh Press, 2001), 25. "The average American citizen over age 14 drank more than twice as much as the average American adult today."

[8] Devon Jersild, *Happy Hours: Alcohol in a Woman's Life* (New York: Cliff Street Books, 2001), 6. "The twelve steps draw on the procedures of the evangelical Oxford group—giving in to God, listening to God's direction, checking for guidance, making restitution, and sharing."

[9] Jonathan Edwards, *The Works of Jonathan Edwards* (Edinburgh: Banner of Truth, 1974), II.267, cited in Michael Rusk's chapter on "The Great Awakening: American Religion Comes of Age," in C. K. Robertson, ed., *Religion as Entertainment* (New York: Peter Lang, 2002), 20.

[10] Ash, *Zen*, 55.

[11] Monahan, *Seeds*, 51. See also Sylvia Cary, *The Alcoholic Man*, 2nd ed. (Los Angeles: Lowell House, 1999).

[12] Ogilvie, *Alternatives*, 134. Although the author's claim may at first glance appear exaggerated, it is one with which many other researchers today concur.

[13] Monahan, *Seeds*, 31.

[14] Ibid., 57.

[15] Cf. http://www.niaaa.nih.gov, the site of the National Institute of Alcohol Abuse and Alcoholism, which includes information on clinical trials and the latest research.

[16] *Global Status Report on Alcohol* (Geneva: World Health Organization, 1999), 10.

[17] *Global Status Report*, 22. In 1995, the report shows that 55 percent of 8th graders (13 to 14 year olds), 71 percent of 10th graders (15 to 16 year olds), 81 percent of 12th graders (17 to 18 year olds), and 90 percent of college students had tried alcohol.

[18] Jersild, *Happy Hours*, 29. The author further reports that women who in younger years are abused, either sexually or physically, later become problem drinkers "in disproportionate numbers" (p. 31).

[19] *Global Status Report*, 22.

[20] This assertion comes from no less than the US Secretary of Health and Human Services. It has been suggested that there might exist a genetic trait that "protects certain populations from becoming alcoholic." Cf. Jersild, *Happy Hours*, 10: "Psychologists now know that there is no definable 'alcoholic personality,' though alcoholics may differ somewhat on certain personality scores."

[21] Dorsman, *How to Quit*, 2.

[22] Devon Jersild notes that the 1800s, the period of both the temperance movement and revivalism, was "a time of many contradictions." Cf. Jersild, *Happy Hours*, 43.

[23] Jersild, *Happy Hours*, 293: "The language of powerlessness is at the heart of AA."

[24] Cited in Ogilvie, *Alternatives*, ix.

[25] Cf. Anne M. Fletcher, *Sober for Good: New Solutions for Drinking Problems—Advice from Those Who Have Succeeded* (Boston & New York: Houghton Mifflin, 2002), 13.

[26] Ibid.

[27] Robert Granfield and William Cloud, *Coming Clean: Overcoming Addiction without Treatment* (New York: New York University Press, 1999), 11.

[28] Peele and Brodsky, *Truth*, 26.

[29] Ibid, 13.

[30] Peter Landers, Fighting Addiction with a Pill, *The Wall Street Journal*, February 20, 2003, D1.

[31] Dodes, *Heart of Addiction*, 8.

[32] Ibid.

[33] Granfield and Cloud, *Coming Clean*, 10.

[34] Dorsman, *How to Quit Drinking*, 14.

[35] Granfield and Cloud, *Coming Clean*, 7.

[36] Dorsman, *How to Quit Drinking*, 33. The author asserts that "when you stop drinking, you can heal much of the damage from the disease if you change your diet" (p. 30).

[37] Cf. A. Thomas Horvath's words, cited in Ogilvie, *Alternatives*, x.

[38] Dorsman, *How to Quit Drinking*, 35.

[39] Peele and Brodsky, *Truth*, 379.

[40] Granfield and Cloud, *Coming Clean*, xi.

[41] Jersild, *Happy Hours*, 17.

[42] On this last point in particular, advocates of alternative approaches argue that abstinence-only educational programs such as Drug Abuse Resistance Education (DARE) fail to recognize that drinking alcoholic beverages can be "a meaningful social activity." Cf. Jersild, *Happy Hours*, 201.

[43] Peele and Brodsky, *Truth*, 314.

[44] Ogilvie, *Alternatives*, 7.

[45] Ash, *Zen*, 216.

[46] H. Richard Niebuhr, *Christ and Culture* (San Francisco: Harper & Row, 1951), 52.

[47] Ash, *Zen*, 55. See also Hamilton B., *Getting Started in AA* (Center City, MN: Hazelden, 1995) and Friends in Recovery, *The Twelve Steps for Christians*, rev. ed. (Curtis, WA: RPI, 1994).

[48] Monahan, *Seeds*, 41.

[49] As cited in Michael Rusk, "The Great Awakening: American Religion Comes of Age," in *Religion as Entertainment*, ed. C. K. Robertson (New York: Peter Lang, 2002), 21.

[50] Niebuhr, *Christ and Culture*, 50.

[51] Ash, *Zen*, 215.

[52] Steele and Brodsky, *Truth*, 34.

[53] Dorsman, *How to Quit*, 4.

[54] Cf. Monahan, *Seeds of Grace*, 168: "I daydream at times about how some features of the fellowship [of AA] might be adopted and adapted by religious institutions."

[55] Granfield and Cloud, *Coming Clean*, x.

[56] Niebuhr, *Christ and Culture*, 116.

[57] Fletcher, *Sober for Good*, 13.

[58] Stanton Peele and Charles Bufe, with Archie Brodsky, *Resisting 12-Step Coercion* (Tucson: See Sharp Press, 2000), 12.

[59] Landers, "Fighting Addiction," D1.

[60] *Global Status Report*, 59.

[61] Ibid., 38.

[62] Monahan, *Seeds of Grace*, 128.

[63] *Global Status Report*, 2.

[64] Ibid., 22.

[65] E. R. Chamberlin, *The Bad Popes* (New York: Barnes & Noble Books, 1993), 243.

[66] Carl B. Broderick, *Understanding Family Process* (Cambridge: Cambridge University Press, 1993). Cf. also Edwin H. Friedman, *Generation to Generation: Family Process in Church and Synagogue* (New York: Guilford Press, 1985); Monica McGoldbrick, Randy Gerson, and Sylvia Shellenberger, *Geneograms: Assessment and Inventory* (New York: Norton, 1999).

Bibliography

Ash, Mel. *The Zen of Recovery*. New York: Tarcher/Putnam, 1993.

Broderick, Carl B. *Understanding Family Process*. Cambridge: Cambridge University Press, 1993.

Cary, Sylvia. *The Alcoholic Man*. 2nd ed. Los Angeles: Lowell House, 1999.

Chamberlin, E. R. *The Bad Popes*. New York: Barnes & Noble Books, 1993.

Dodes, Lance. *The Heart of Addiction*. New York: HarperCollins, 2002.

Dorsman, Jerry. *How to Quit Drinking without A.A.* 2nd ed. Roseville, CA: Prima Publishing, 1997.

Edwards, Jonathan. *The Works of Jonathan Edwards*. Edinburgh: Banner of Truth, 1974.

Fletcher, Anne M. *Sober for Good: New Solutions for Drinking Problems—Advice from Those Who Have Succeeded*. Boston & New York: Houghton Mifflin, 2002.

Friedman, Edwin H. *Generation to Generation: Family Process in Church and Synagogue*. New York: Guilford Press, 1985.

Global Status Report on Alcohol. Geneva: World Health Organization, 1999.

Granfield, Robert, and William Cloud. *Coming Clean: Overcoming Addiction without Treatment*. New York: New York University Press, 1999.

Jersild, Devon. *Happy Hours: Alcohol in a Woman's Life*. New York: Cliff Street Books, 2001.

Landers, Peter. "Fighting Addiction with a Pill." *The Wall Street Journal*. February 20, 2003.

McGoldbrick, Monica, Randy Gerson, and Sylvia Shellenberger. *Geneograms: Assessment and Inventory*. New York: Norton, 1999.

Monahan, Sister Molly. *Seeds of Grace: A Nun's Reflections on the Spirituality of Alcoholics Anonymous*. New York: Riverside Books, 2001.

Niebuhr, H. Richard. *Christ and Culture*. San Francisco: Harper & Row, 1951.

Ogilvie, Heather. *Alternatives to Abstinence: A New Look at Alcoholism and the Choices in Treatment*. New York: Hatherleigh Press, 2001.

Peele, Stanton, and Archie Brodsky. *The Truth about Addiction and Recovery*. New York: Fireside, 1991.

Peele, Stanton, and Charles Bufe, with Archie Brodsky. *Resisting 12-Step Coercion* Tucson: See Sharp Press, 2000.

Rusk, Michael. "The Great Awakening: American Religion Comes of Age." In *Religion as Entertainment*. Edited by C. K. Robertson. New York: Peter Lang, 2002.

10 Ecstasy and Horror: A Spirituality of Drinking

Michael Rusk

The tobacco products in my local supermarket in Leicester, England, are carefully guarded behind the checkout desk, which is itself in a little booth of its own. One has to ask for a packet of cigarettes before they can be placed in the shopping basket. Not so with wine or spirits: rows upon rows of bottles from every corner of the globe—choice wines from Germany, France, Italy, and Spain but also from further afield, California, Australia, South Africa, and Chile—wait invitingly to be placed directly into the shopping basket. Alongside the wines, there are cans of beer, and an array of spirits—the famous Scottish malt whiskey, vodka, martini, and sherry, to name but a few. In this country of abundance, the shelves are constantly refilled, giving the illusion that nothing has been taken from them. However, it is estimated that 6% of people's disposable income in the United Kingdom is spent on alcohol.

Tobacco products, by government order, carry an ever more lurid warning of the dangers of smoking: "Smoking kills"; "Smoking causes damage to your health and to those around you"; "You can get help to stop smoking!" This is not so with alcohol. There are some notices stating that it cannot be sold to persons under age 18, but there is no government health warning; no hint whatsoever that excessive use of alcohol can seriously damage one's health and even cause death. There is increasing publicity on court cases in the United States and in Europe where the giant tobacco companies are brought to account for failing to inform smokers of the dangers of their products. Such high publicity trials are often fronted by horrific pictures of former smokers now in the last throes of lung cancer. There is no equivalent mention of a similar approach to the drinks industry, no court cases publicized where someone dying of cirrhosis of the liver points the finger clearly toward the cause of their demise: alcohol.

The reason for this inequality of approach between alcohol and tobacco is quite simple. The British and Americans are in denial that their societies are afflicted with problems related to alcohol consumption. The reticence on the part of politicians, medical practitioners, police authorities, social workers, and religious leaders to highlight the growing statistical evidence that alcohol is a major problem in society, is startling. Why such silence? Why such reluctance to name an evil which is blighting society? There will be many reasons to explain the reticence and to account for the continued delay of the publication of the British government's "National Strategy on Alcohol." This essay, however, suggests that behind the present tolerance and acceptance of alcohol in western societies, there lies a hidden theological confusion, which fails to identify alcohol as both a blessing and a curse.

A Blessing and a Curse

The Jewish and Christian faith traditions identify and name what in the created order can be regarded as a blessing from God and therefore to be embraced, and what is to be acknowledged as a curse and therefore to be avoided. Generally, there is a clear distinction between the two: What is good and what is bad. This is clearly illustrated in the instructions given to the people of Israel, as they are about to enter the Promised Land:

> The land you are crossing the Jordan to take possession of is a land of mountains and valleys that drinks rain from heaven. It is a land that the Lord your God cares for; the eyes of the Lord your God are continually on it from the beginning of the year to its end. So if you faithfully obey the commands I am giving you today—to love the Lord your God and to serve him with all your heart and with all your soul—then I will send rain on your land in its season, both autumn and spring rains, so that you may gather in your grain, new wine and oil. I will provide grass in the fields for your cattle, and you will eat and be satisfied. (Deuteronomy 11:11–15)

Here the blessings of God are clearly enumerated: The land is fertile and productive. Among its blessings are rain, mountains, and valleys. Among its produce of good things, new wine is specifically mentioned along with the other vital commodities of life: grain and oil. The Promised

Land is therefore clearly portrayed as a place where vines thrive and where wine is produced. Wine therefore becomes a symbolic representation of the abundance and bounty of creation. Freedom from warfare and the ensuing conditions of peaceful farming permit the vines to flourish and therefore this is seen as part of the Shalom or peace of God. However, Deuteronomy also indicates the nature of a curse:

> See, I am setting before you today a blessing and a curse—the blessing if you obey the commands of the Lord your God that I am giving you today; the curse if you disobey the commands of the Lord your God and turn from the way that I command you today by following other gods, which you have not known (Deuteronomy 11:26–28).

Among the curses enumerated later in Deuteronomy, if the people fail to obey God's commands, specific mention is made of vineyards that fail to produce a good harvest due to an infestation of worms:

> You will sow much seed in the field but you will harvest little, because locusts will devour it. You will plant vineyards and cultivate them but you will not drink the wine or gather the grapes, because worms will eat them. You will have olive trees throughout your country but you will not use the oil, because the olives will drop off (Deuteronomy 11:38–40).

Here, again, wine is seen implicitly as a blessing from God, the reward for obedience to God's commands, and the reward, too, for the patient cultivation of the vineyard. The curse is when the harvest is blighted by pestilence, by the withholding of the earth's bounty.

Three important points emerge from this. First, that there is a clear distinction made in Deuteronomy on what is deemed a blessing and what is to be recognized as a curse. There is no such thing as "a mixed blessing." Second, wine is quite clearly classified as a blessing from God. The circumstances necessary for its successful production both in terms of a sign of the earth's well-being and of a stable, harmonious society, where vine cultivation can take place unimpeded, point to a society that is seeking and benefiting from God's grace and favor. Behavior patterns are crucial: The people of Israel, if obedient to God's laws and commandments, will experience blessings; if disobedient, the consequences will manifest themselves in the form of curses which will be in some form of natural catastrophe or disaster.

The challenge which theological reflection faces on the issue of alcohol is therefore to explore these issues. Is it possible for something such as alcohol to be regarded as both a blessing and a curse, rather than exclusively one or the other? Is there a theological problem that something as potentially lethal as alcohol should play such a fundamental role as a sign of God's blessing and kingdom? Is there a way in which behavioral attitudes can be used to enable one to move from viewing something not only as a positive benefit to society but also identifying it as a curse? However, before moving on to address these questions it is helpful to set out in what ways alcohol can be regarded as a blessing and in what ways it is quite clearly a curse.

Alcohol as a Blessing from God

I visit a friend in the beautiful historic cathedral and University City of Durham in the northeast of England. After lunch, my friend offers me a Drambuie—an expensive, Scottish liqueur. He pours the drink into two tiny glasses, which are then raised to celebrate our friendship, and we taste the sticky sweet-tasting alcohol, sipping it slowly over the next hour. This ritual of friendship reenacted two or three times a year when I visit, is highly significant on a number of levels. My friend, prior to being an Anglican, was a member of the Baptist church in his youth, where the drinking of alcohol was not approved of in any way. The raising of the glass of Drambuie is therefore a mark of his own spiritual pilgrimage, a sign of liberation from a narrower, more restrictive understanding of God, and an owning and rediscovery of his Scottish roots. For both of us, the drinking of the liqueur is a renewal of our friendship, an experience of communion, of true fellowship and joy.

The Theology of Taste

In *Jubilate—Theology in Praise*, David Ford and Daniel Hardy note, "The basis of Christian existence is not just a basis. It is also an environment of abundance created through this overflow of life, and giving reason for praise in all situations. ... What will that life be like?[1] This abundance and exuberance in life is exemplified in a poem by Patrick Kavanagh:

> O unworn world, enrapture me, encapture me in a web
> Of fabulous grass and eternal voices by a beech,
> Feed the gaping need of my senses, give me ad lib
> To pray unselfconsciously with overflowing speech.[2]

In answering the question, "What will that life be like?" it is important to emphasize that taste will be a vital ingredient of this life of overflowing abundance and praise. The God-given sense of taste is something to delight in. Food and drink are not just basic commodities to keep us alive, although that is their primary and most vital purpose. The gift of taste offers the possibility of enjoyment of differing types of food and drink. This aesthetic dimension to human existence is therefore of theological importance. God has created humanity with the sense of taste and that in turn opens up the whole realm of possibilities of delighting in different tastes and experiencing within that something of the praise of God. Psalm 34.8 captures this dimension of praise wonderfully: "O, taste and see that the Lord is good."

The use of our taste buds is kept to a minimum in most churches. It is true that in Holy Communion, the congregation tastes bread and wine, but aside from this and the occasional fellowship meal, the sense of taste is not usually drawn upon in a Christian setting. Other faiths such as Islam, Sikhism, and Judaism, are more successful in featuring meals as an integral part of religious experience.

It could be argued persuasively, however, that Christianity was never meant to be confined to a narrow, exclusive ecclesiastical experience; that Jesus in the Gospel narratives is regularly described as having meals in people's houses[3]; and that the kingdom of heaven is described in terms of a messianic meal.[4] Moreover, the history of the monastic tradition of the Christian church points to the importance of feast days when the monastic communities would enjoy a sumptuous feast in honor of a particular festival such as Christmas or Easter or a Saint's Day. The feast would have been regarded as an integral part of the religious life. It is reasonable to conclude, therefore, that part of the worship and praise of

God for the Christian, has logically been found in delighting in food and drink. This would imply that the great wealth of material produced on cookery and on beverages—from television programs to attractive books on food and drink—can all contribute to an experience of delight and praise and that experience can ultimately become part of the worship and praise of God.

In this respect, the distinctive taste of alcoholic beverages is important. To the true wine connoisseur, the taste of the particular vintage is all-important. Wine-tasting events flourish, as people develop skills at identifying the uniqueness of each wine, gaining skills at recognizing from what region and in some cases in what year it was produced. Similarly, the distinctive taste of various beers, ciders, and Scottish malt whiskies are widely documented and are a source of much animated discussion.

The importance of taste is well illustrated by the phenomenal success of the Japanese beer, Asahi Super Dry. Writing in *The Times,* Vernon Davis describes the beer as having "a clear, crisp, and refreshing taste, the result of adding rice and maize."[5] What is remarkable about Asahi Super Dry is that the distinctive taste was not stumbled on by accident, but was actually invented in response to market research. Leo Lewis, remarks on the "legendary status" of the beverage in the same article in *The Times*:

> Harvard Business School has devoted a teaching module to studying the Super Dry model and several Japanese universities have made Asahi Studies part of their management courses. … One of the secrets of Super Dry's success is that it was tailored to suit the Japanese market. Before a pint of the stuff was brewed, Asahi people visited pubs, restaurants, and parks asking drinkers what they wanted from a beer.[6]

The importance of how an alcoholic beverage tastes has significant ramifications. First there is a delight and pride in maintaining a particular taste. With the production of Scottish malt whisky, for example, there will be a long and treasured tradition, often a secret history passed from one generation of brewers to another, so that the whisky maintains its distinctive characteristics over the years. In wine-making the vagaries of the weather and its impact on the soil and grapes means a wider range of variety in any given wine. The extremely hot summer of 2003 raised high hopes in the German Rhineland and in English vineyards of producing particularly excellent wine. Considerable time and energy therefore is poured into how an alcoholic beverage tastes, and the ultimate aim of this is to provide delight.

Theologically, therefore, the celebration of the distinctive and delightful tastes of various alcoholic beverages can be legitimately regarded as an important foretaste of the Kingdom of God. This is particularly so, because Christianity is an incarnational religion, experiencing the presence of God in the materiality of our world, and finding within that materiality something of transcendence and transfiguring power.

Striving to Produce the Perfect Drink

The importance of taste, evoking delight and imparting pleasure, leads to the aspiration for perfection—the desire on the part of the producer to produce the perfect vintage; the ultimate draught of a particular brand of beer; the finest of Scotch or Irish whisky. This striving after perfection need not be dismissed simply as some unbridled hedonism, but it can actually be regarded from a Christian theological perspective as something entirely legitimate in the quest to reveal the purposes of God.

Some alcohol advertisements, of course, focus on the hedonistic benefits of their products—to be seen with one's beverage will win peer approval and will make one sexually desirable. Others, however, are more reflective. Of particular interest in this respect are the Guinness advertisements of recent years. One television commercial in the 1990s, for example, was filmed on a Hawaiian beach with a local surfer intent on waiting for the biggest wave so that he could enjoy the ultimate surfing experience. The aim of the advertisement was to turn the possible disadvantage of having to wait for a pint of Guinness stout to be poured into a positive advantage. The message of the advertisement was "good things come to those who wait." This commercial, which has been voted in one poll as the most popular ad ever, is not simply about patience. The colossal waves, the wild horses galloping through those waves, the patient waiting of the surfer on the beach; the final decision to enter the sea; and the sheer joy of exhilaration as he rides the ultimate wave, touch on the meaning and purpose of life at a deep and unconscious level. The power of the commercial is that it strikes the unconscious religious aspirations of the human soul as it strives for ultimate meaning, purpose, and perfection. It can, of course, be argued that the alcoholic beverage industry has the financial resources to pay for the best creativity in the advertising industry to promote its products. However, the fact that the focus of the Guinness advertisements is on the meaning of life is of profound significance: It is a striving after the ultimate, a desire for perfection, which is akin to religious feeling.

The exiled early twentieth-century Russian theologian, Sergii Bulgakov, writing on the destiny of creation, stresses that everything created is striving for a perfection and liberation in God. Because Christianity is an incarnational faith that looks for redemption in the materiality of the world, the eye of faith must look at the potentiality of everything to discern how this perfection can be reached. He writes: "Art, understood as a 'rebirth in beauty,' is a discovery through itself and so also *in* itself of the sophianic character of creation, a breaking through on-being or half-being into substantial reality."[7] Bulgakov here is referring primarily to the potentiality of the natural order, but his theology embraces the complete compass of human activity and productivity. In the divine wisdom (sophia) of God, everything ultimately discovers its own perfection for which it strives.

The sense of praise and delight, therefore, gained from appreciating a particular bitter beer, a malt whisky, or some other alcoholic drink, is not necessarily a misplaced form of worship. From the Christian theological perspective, the recognition that such and such a drink is perfect, perhaps divine in its taste, is an appropriate response to a faith that fills its redemptive dimension as an actual reality in the materiality of the world. Christianity finds perfection not in some Platonic abstraction of the perfect drink, but in an actual real drink that evokes a feeling of absolute perfection. It is legitimate to presume that the enjoyment of tasting such a drink is in itself a religious experience, offering a hint of ultimate perfection just as much as feasting upon a magnificent view with the eyes, or using the sense of hearing to be thrilled by wonderful music.

The whole process of the alcoholic beverage industry insofar as it is striving for perfection can be regarded as a blessing. The treasured traditions of the brewery or vineyard handed down with care and precision from one generation to another, sometimes for hundreds of years; the quality control in production; the bottling and corking; the whole distribution system, including the laborious lifting and rolling or kegs up and down from the cellar; to the serving of the drink in appropriate glassware. Countless people the world over are necessary for one person to be able to experience the perfect drink at the local pub.

The Blessing of the Sabbath Rest

It also should be noted that the recipient of the drink—the result of so much industry and care—is experiencing something of a Sabbath rest experience. The visit to the pub, or the glass of wine over a meal, is often enjoyed when work is ended, at a lunch break or at the end of the working day. The experience of rest is at the heart of the Jewish and Christian understanding of the Sabbath:

> By the seventh day God had finished the work he had been doing; so on the seventh day he rested from all his work. And God blessed the seventh day and made it holy, because on it he rested from all the work of creating that he had done (Genesis 2:2).

Chief Rabbi Jonathan Sacks describes the joy of the Sabbath from a Jewish perspective:

> Imagine the experience of coming home on Friday afternoon. The week has flown by in a rush of activity. You are exhausted. And there, in all its simplicity and splendor is the Sabbath table. ... Seeing that table you know that until tomorrow evening you will step into another world, one where there are no pressures to work or compete, no distractions or interruptions, just time to be together with family and friends.[8]

For many, however, the experience of real and genuine relaxation is to be found in a visit to a pub. The English country pub—often a building of great antiquity in a picturesque village; the working men's clubs in the north of England, the hub and center of the village, where the coal miners would gather at the end of a back-breaking week's work; the Royal British Legion Club where war veterans would gather and reflect on their wartime experiences; the upscale wine bar where successful young yuppies meet after a hectic week in a city's commercial quarter: all these meeting places provide the space to experience rest and renewal. Of course, it may not reflect the sanctity of the Jewish home on the eve of the Sabbath.

However, in the broader understanding of Sabbath as rest from industry and work—of taking time out to enjoy life and to experience life as a blessing—then indeed it is theologically possible to describe what was taking place as a kind of Sabbath rest. Moreover, just as in the Jewish home the wine is found on the table as a symbol of "blessing and joy," so also in the secular environment the consumption of alcohol is considered of fundamental importance, giving the raison d'être for the existence of pubs, working men's clubs, and bars in the first place.

The Pub as the Place Where Christ Is Found

The pub is a place of conversation, of friendship, of sharing. Pubs are sought out if "they have a good atmosphere," and the reference is not to the quality of the air but rather the quality of interaction, the overall ethos brought about by service, sometimes by live music, the nature of the welcome and the general friendliness and warmth of the hostelry. In a travel book on Ireland, Pete McCarthy describes one such positive experience in a pub/shop, as the bartender half-pours a pint of Guinness before pausing for a three-minute interval:

> This lets the stout settle. It also allows the barman to ask you who you are, where you're from, and why you're here. The other customers listen and nod. Then, he fills the pint, smooths off the head with a table knife with a parchment-coloured handle, and waits for you to take the first sip. The perfect evening, in the perfect pub. The kind of evening that leaves you with a warm feeling. Especially when accompanied by seven pints of Guinness.[9]

Christianity cannot be characterized either as an individual religion or a family religion. Rather its emphasis is on gathering people together in new groups and discovering a new fellowship and common bond of humanity that is transfigured by the power of the Spirit of God into the Body of Christ. The hallmarks of this new community are the fruits of God's spirit: "Love, joy, peace, patience, kindness, goodness, faithfulness, gentleness and self-control."[10]

Jesus demonstrated the signs of this kingdom by a lifestyle of celebration and joy. In the Fourth Gospel, water is turned into wine at a wedding in Cana of Galilee; later, Jesus is described as the true vine from heaven.[11] Matthew and Luke record how Jesus was criticized for both his lifestyle and the company that he kept: "The Son of Man came eating and drinking, and they say, 'Here is a glutton and a drunkard, a friend of tax collectors and sinners.'"[12] Moreover, Jesus's ministry was not confined to the synagogues. Rather, the gospel narratives recount him journeying from village to village in Galilee and encountering individuals both on the way and in their own homes. Table fellowship was as much of a feature of encounter with Jesus as the healing miracles and teaching that took place in the synagogue on the Sabbath. There is, therefore, in the example of Jesus's ministry a commitment to discover and to reveal the presence of God to all people in all circumstances. While Jesus lives his life as an expression of the will of God, there is a boundless, and some would have said a scandalous freedom, as to where and with whom that life expressed itself.

The model of the life of Jesus presents a challenge to the Christian church that it must not confine itself within its ecclesiastical walls but rather engage with the wider world. Places where alcohol is served—pubs, inns, clubs, bars, restaurants, and hotels—are often places where there is a high emphasis on service. The customer is waited on and served. The whole notion of service, of waiting upon another, is seen as a Christ-like attribute. Just as Christ washed the disciples' feet, so the waiter who serves you at a table, or the barmaid who pulls your pint, is demonstrating how humanity can live by the self-giving of one to the other.

Second, pubs are often places where compassion and real listening can take place. Over a drink (perhaps because of a drink, inhibitions are lowered) anxieties, worries, intimate secrets are often shared. The public house is a place of interaction; of acceptance; of mutual exchange. All this can, of course, be said of church communities, but it is important that the church doesn't necessarily create an alternative community and identify that as the Kingdom of God. The existence of communities of love, acceptance, and service in the local pubs and clubs can also be seen as a sign of God's grace and blessing. If we are to interpret the ministry of Jesus aright, then it is clear that there were no boundaries. Everything was within the orbit of God's blessing.

Alcohol as Curse

The recent news that the legendary soccer star, George Best, had taken to drinking again, less than a year after a lifesaving liver transplant, was greeted with despair by the British public. Regarded by many as one of the greatest players ever seen, George Best captivated the footballing ("soccer" in American English) world in the 1960s and 1970s with his astonishing speed and incredible skill. Only the Brazilian player Péle could be considered greater in skill and achievement. Even so, George Best, the star of Manchester United and the first British sportsman to receive superstar status had retired from the game by the age of 28. Alcohol was to rob Best and the British public of a soccer genius. All that was left was video footage, still regularly played on the television of the remarkable agility and prodigious skill.

The latest revelations about Best's return to drink at the age of 58 were met with anger: Did Best deserve a liver transplant (paid through public funding) only to return to a life of drinking? How could anyone be so foolish as to offer him a drink? Why can't he be protected from the self-destruction brought by drink?

It is a remarkable feature of British public life that it is not the medical profession or the clergy who highlight the perils of alcohol, but rather the world of sport. Sir Alex Ferguson, the most successful manager in British soccer, has achieved a string of successes at national and European levels over the last decade for Manchester United. He has done so by having the fittest players in soccer, insisting on a regime that is teetotal. In his autobiography, he writes:

For longer than anybody cares to remember, boozing has been a blight on the discipline of British footballers. ... Clubs and their managers have frequently shown a weak-kneed reluctance to deal with the menace of boozing.[13]

It is the modern professional sportsman, the healthy living guru, the beauty queen, who is most likely to extol the virtues of abstinence and to offer their lives as examples of an alcohol-free lifestyle. Their self-discipline echoes St. Paul's observation of athletes in the Greco-Roman world: "Everyone who competes in the games goes into strict training."[14] However, what is clearly advocated in the sporting world is scarcely mentioned in contemporary religious circles, namely, that alcohol can be a curse on people's lives.

What Exactly Is Alcohol?

Alcohol is produced by a chemical reaction that through a process of distillation produces the chemical ethanol, which we call alcohol. The amount of alcohol in alcoholic drinks varies. There is now an internationally agreed measure of alcoholic content, with bottles labeled with the percentage of alcohol in their content. Beer, for example, will have an alcoholic content varying from 3% to 5%. Wine between 10% and 13%. Drinks such as Port will contain 20% alcohol, whereas spirits such as whisky will have anything up to 70% alcohol. Strictly speaking, alcohol is the substance within any given drink, not the full drink itself.

Alcohol is a mind-altering drug. It affects the nervous system, and once it enters the bloodstream its impact on the body can affect behavioral patterns, moods, coordination, and judgment. Most important, for some alcohol is an addictive drug and for those who do not have a tolerance for it, it produces a craving that for many is uncontrollable. "Alcohol misuse" and "alcohol dependence" are now medically recognized conditions that can be diagnosed according to clear criteria. Statistical evidence given below will demonstrate the large numbers of people affected by these conditions.

In addition to the well-documented evidence of the damage that alcohol can cause to adults, there is an increasing body of evidence that highlights the dangers to the fetus of women drinking alcohol while pregnant. Fetal Alcohol Syndrome (FAS) is increasing worldwide as the alcoholic beverage industry targets young women as a new market for their products. FAS Web sites offer heartrending stories of children born with mental and physical disabilities. The condition is irreversible. One such site describes the properties of alcohol as being "toxic" (causing damage to body organs), "carcinogenic" (causing cancer), and "teratogenic" (causing birth defects):

> Alcohol is our number one health problem, our leading drug problem, a major cause of economic hardship, and is a leading factor in crime, suicide, domestic violence, unplanned pregnancies, and child abuse and neglect. I am still trying to figure out how to explain to my son why this dangerous chemical is so widely used. He just doesn't understand. My son has Fetal Alcohol Syndrome."[15]

Alcohol is the most powerful legal and lethal drug in western society.

The Effect of Alcohol on Health

Statistical evidence points to the devastating impact that excessive alcohol consumption has on health. The Cambridgeshire-based Institute of Alcohol Studies has undertaken extensive analysis of UK government statistics, drawing together information that highlights the deep-seated impact that alcohol consumption has on British Society. Similar agencies are producing up-to-date data on the United States. The Institute comments that in developed countries, "alcohol is one of the ten leading causes of disease and injury."[16] Furthermore, "beside the direct effects of intoxication and addiction, worldwide alcohol is estimated to cause 20–30% of cancer of the esophagus, liver cancer, cirrhosis of the liver, epilepsy, homicide, and motor vehicle accidents."[17] The Institute further notes that "while alcohol abuse may sometimes be a precursor to alcohol dependence, in most cases they are two separate disorders with varying histories and prognoses."[18]

In the United Kingdom, the National Health Service (NHS) recorded the following number of admissions to hospitals in England in 2000–01 where there was a primary diagnosis of selected alcohol related disease: "Mental and behavioral disorder due to alcohol—27,300; alcoholic liver disease—10,100; and toxic effect of alcohol—1,700."[19] On the following page, figure 10.1 illustrates the number of admissions to NHS hospitals in England where the reason for admission was alcoholic liver failure or toxic liver disease (1995/6–2001/2).[20]

	1995/6	1996/7	1997/8	1998/9	1999/00	2000/1	2001/2
Alcoholic Liver Failure	19,058	22,881	27,083	29,026	33,571	36,923	39,896
Toxic Liver Disease	652	690	757	787	676	749	670

Figure 10.1—National Health Service Admissions Due to Alcohol

Unfortunately, there are no accurate statistical data to indicate how many deaths occur with alcohol being a major contributory factor.[21] Estimates of proportion of death attributable to alcohol from various conditions are found below in figure 10.2:

Cancer of the oesophagus	14 – 75%
Cancer of the liver	15 – 29%
Cancer of the female breast	3 – 4%
Hypertension	5 – 11%
Chronic pancreatitis	60 – 84%
Acute pancreatitis	24 – 42%
Falls	23 – 35%
Drownings	30 – 38%
Fire injuries	38 – 45%
Suicide	27 – 41%
Assault	27 – 47%

Figure 10.2—Estimates of Deaths with Alcohol a Major Factor

What is indicated in these statistics is an alarming increase, particularly of alcoholic liver disease: the 2001 figure of 4,429 mortalities is more than double that of the 1992 figure of 1,777. Moreover, it is reasonable to assume that the number of deaths as a result of alcoholic liver failure is set to soar in the coming years. The statistics, therefore, provide conclusive evidence that the United Kingdom is facing a major escalation in health problems and deaths due to excessive consumption of alcohol. Consumption figures for the period suggest that estimated alcohol consumption per person more than 14 years of age rose from 9.06 liters to 10.52 liters per year. The figure is double that of 45 years ago.[22]

Binge Drinking among the Young

Statistical evidence increasingly points to two areas of concern: Binge drinking particularly among the 16- to 24-year-old age group; and the increase of heavy drinking among women, particularly younger women. These two factors indicate that the figures outlined in the previous tables will increase dramatically in future years.

"Binge drinking" is a loose term for sustained heavy consumption of alcohol in a limited period. It has been a traditional feature of northern European male cultures with the United Kingdom, Ireland, Germany, and Sweden having a high incidence of binge drinking. The emancipation of women has involved a cultural shift so that the pub is no longer a male preserve. The alcoholic beverage industry has adapted to the new potential market by developing drinks particularly attractive to women. A whole new range of "alcopops" and designer drinks are now available as well as low calorie premium bottled beers. Alcohol advertising, moreover, is now targeted specially at women. The advertisements portray alcohol "as fashionable, glamorous, and used by women who are independent, fun-loving and desirable."[23] There are two particular concerns with women and alcohol. One is that women attain a higher blood level concentration than men for the same amount of alcohol— possibly because of having lower levels of alcohol dehydrogenase (ADH). The other major concern is the danger of excessive alcohol consumption when pregnant—particularly in the first twelve weeks of pregnancy—and the possibility of Fetal Alcohol Syndrome. The United Kingdom has one of the highest figures for binge drinking in the 16- to 24-year-old age group. It also has the highest incidence of teenage pregnancy in Europe. It is likely that there is a correlation between the two. Because 16- to 24-year-olds engage in a culture of binge drinking, it is likely that some young women who engage in binge drinking may be unaware of their pregnancy during its early weeks, and consequently their babies may be born with FAS.

The Institute of Alcohol Studies observes that binge drinking among the young has been encouraged by the growth of a "culture of intoxication" in which "young people have adopted a hedonistic approach" that corresponds with a "lack of inhibition and control."[24] The Institute highlights research among young people to try to get them to explain their social and drinking habits. Typical statements by young male binge drinkers include: "You don't have to know the reason for it. You just do it anyway. Everybody does it, it is the way the world is." Similarly, female binge drinkers between 21 and 24 years of age say: "We are a culture that goes out and gets drunk, and we don't go out to drink, we go out to get drunk." Binge drinkers, male or female, report various strategies for accelerating the process such as having a few drinks before leaving home, mixing drinks, and deliberately drinking quickly.[25]

The statistics and the social trends outlined above indicate that, regarding health and well-being, excessive consumption of alcohol is a curse. Changing social trends are actually increasing the devastating impact of excessive consumption, especially among the young.

Alcohol as a Social Curse

An Irish television documentary which aired in January 2002 shocked the nation to such a degree that the Irish government introduced tough new drinking laws. At a time, when the policy makers in England were contemplating the relaxation of licensing laws, the Irish took the opposite approach. Pubs in Ireland must now close at 11:30 p.m., and "happy hours" and other forms of encouragement for excessive drinking are no longer promoted. Drunkenness is now a crime with immediate fines imposed, and pub owners are held responsible if the person gets drunk in their pub. The initial impetus behind this, according to *The Times,* was the primetime slot documentary, which recorded what life on the town is like following a typical Saturday night in Dublin, Cork, and Tullamore. *The Times* records that "the scenes of fighting, vomiting, public urinating, and other antisocial behavior would have shocked even Leopold Bloom in his 1904 all-day odyssey around James Joyce's Dublin."[26] Earlier in the article, the journalist Alan Hamilton notes that "Ireland has a drink problem. Between 1989 and 1999 alcohol consumption rose by 41% to 11.5 liters of pure alcohol per head per year. Roughly, that is 30 standard bottles of whisky per person, assuming the babes-in-arms are drinking at the same rate."[27]

A comprehensive statistical analysis of the impact of excessive alcohol consumption on society would be a major undertaking outside the scope of the present inquiry. It would involve a study of the number of police hours taken up in policing drinking circuits; damage to property; violence to persons; violence within the home; the breakup of marriages due to alcohol; and the number of accidents and fatalities as a result of drunk driving. Economically, it is very difficult to calculate also the number of lost days at work due to alcohol abuse and the wider cost of what the actual price is to society. Suffice it to say that an enormous number of lives are affected and many ruined by the curse of alcohol.

Nowhere is this fact better illustrated than in the haunting poetic autobiography of the Irish-American writer Frank McCourt. Entitled, *Angela's Ashes*, McCourt describes his childhood in New York and then in Limerick. Without remorse, or anger, he simply and movingly states what it was like waiting for his alcoholic father to return home with the week's wages so that the family could buy food to eat:

> Mam says there's no use waiting up any longer. If Dad stays in the pubs till closing time there will be nothing left from his wages and we might as well go to bed. She lies in her bed with Michael in her arms. It's quiet in the lane and I can hear her crying even though she pulls an old coat over her face.[28]

The father's alcohol problem is a constant recurring theme. When he moves to Coventry, England, for work, again the family waits for support in the form of his pay wages sent by telegram. Sadly, the telegram never comes, and eventually there is an explanation: The alcoholic father is "gone pure mad with the drink." Instead of helping himself and his dependent family, he "squanders his wages in pubs ... [and] drinks away his rent money and winds up sleeping in parks when the landlord throws him out."[29] This account of the abject poverty and misery afflicted upon a family by an otherwise loving alcoholic remains a potent symbol of misery due to alcoholism, even in an age when much alcoholic dependence takes place in the context of affluence rather than poverty and is thereby more hidden. Alcoholics Anonymous uses the power of such stories to good effect in the *Big Book*. All these stories are a powerful reminder that alcohol can be a curse that destroys individuals, families, and society.[30]

Theological Response to Alcohol as Blessing and Curse

The Christian Church down through the centuries has oscillated from celebrating alcohol as a blessing to denouncing it as a curse. The blessings of alcohol are readily illustrated in the monastic houses of Europe cultivating the vine, developing new distinctive liqueurs, and consuming large quantities of wine and ale.[31] The Temperance Movement and the emergence of complete abstinence or teetotalism, in contrast, viewed alcohol as a curse, which needed to be eradicated from society.[32] James Munson in his history of *The Nonconformists* records that the movement "insisted on a total abstention from not only spirits but beer, the staple drink of the working man."[33]

The legacy of the two positions is found today on the issue of wine used for Holy Communion. The Methodist Church insists that the wine must be unfermented.[34] The Canons of the Church of England, in contrast, insist that the wine must be "the fermented juice of the grape, good and wholesome."[35] The historical legacy suggests a polarization of Christian views on alcohol. The Temperance Movement was soon overtaken by the greater emphasis on teetotalism. There can be little doubt that the concern for the ravages of alcohol on individuals and families meant that alcohol became progressively demonized, so much so that it was named "the demon drink." One of the unfortunate results of this was the polarization of church and pub. Not only was drink demonized, but also the pubs were considered "dens of iniquity" and hence were cast outside the pale of Christian presence and redemption.

Eventually, with the advent of postwar Britain and the liberalization of life and morals, the church's negative stance on alcohol came to be regarded as that of the killjoy. Christianity became ridiculed as a no fun, straight-laced, otherworldly, out-of-touch religion. Pubs were places where people could enjoy laughter and party, where inhibitions could be released and true joy could be found. The response of the churches in the United Kingdom generally has been one of complete withdrawal. Christians themselves began to enjoy wine at meals and to frequent bars and discover that they were not quite the demonic places that religious rhetoric of the previous century had alleged.

The complete withdrawal from commenting on the evils of alcohol on society, however, is itself an extraordinary failure of the church to act in a prophetic way, for the church's reticence might imply that alcohol was a blessing, and was not posing any problems to individuals or society. For the Church of England there would appear to be complete amnesia that this was one of the major concerns of one of its greatest archbishops, William Temple.[36] In 1901, Temple considered that the Church of England needed clergy of outstanding intellect to provide theological guidance to the Temperance Movement. That same year, at the age of twenty, he wrote:

> The Church has been roused, by Wesley and others, to a new spiritual devotion … and apart from the greatness of such a work in itself, if it can be done, the Housing Problem, the Temperance Question, the differences between employer and employed will solve themselves, and the British Empire will become an instrument of real justice (not legal codes) and real education."[37]

Forty years later, toward the end of his life, his views on the importance of the "Temperance question" remained. His biographer Iremonger writes that later in life, Temple "grew increasingly convinced that strong drink was a grave social danger" resulting in "the inhibition of the faculties of self-criticism and self-control" that the archbishop claimed would occur long before "anything that could rightly be called drunkenness."[38] Temple, who had a passion for social justice, considered alcohol a major issue for the churches to wrestle with throughout his life. The abandonment of that conviction within sixty years on the part of the church would point to a worrying collusion with society. It is therefore imperative for the church to recover a theological perspective on the issue of alcohol.

An important starting point is to identify and name the powers that control and bring about the present social scene. Walter Wink, in his book *Naming the Powers* discusses the nature of evil powers as follows:

> None of these "spiritual" realities has an existence independent of its material counterpart. None persists through time without embodiment in cellulose or in a culture or a regime or a corporation or a megalomaniac. ... As the inner aspect of material reality, the spiritual Powers are everywhere around us. Their presence is real and it is inescapable.[39]

The church's primary task is therefore not to demonize alcohol as intrinsically evil in itself. Rather, alcohol is a potential blessing from God and a potent sign of the joy of the messianic kingdom. It is the use to which alcohol is put by individuals and societies, which needs to be identified and assessed. The present climate of liberalization of drinking hours and tolerance of harmful and excessive alcohol consumption may seem to the church an impossible challenge of Goliath proportions. Even so, the Church is called by Christ to impart a ministry of healing. That ministry of healing and deliverance is to a nation, 25% of whose health problems are directly attributable to the harmful and dependent use of alcohol and smoking. If the Church, therefore, is to be faithful and to heal and deliver individuals and societies in the name of Christ from all that could harm them, then it must speak out and act when the use of alcohol becomes a curse and not a blessing.

In this respect, partnership with the medical authorities and with the police can only be beneficial. The adoption of current medical terminology that focuses on harmful use of alcohol and alcohol dependency fits well with a theological understanding that recognizes that it is the misuse of the created order that brings harm and misery. The drawing on precise statistical evidence may have a significant impact in a society impressed by facts and figures and hence is another important tool. The church is likely to gain a much greater audience by taking a medical approach to the harmful effects of alcohol than simply a moral approach. The emphasis on a ministry of healing makes this a theologically justifiable development.

Engaging with the powers that have created the hedonistic drinking culture, the church has to work with governments, harnessing the medical and statistical evidence to persuade governments that a de-regulated approach to alcohol is not a sensible approach to creating a healthy society. Faith communities do not need to be on a moral "high horse" but, rather, a persuasive voice that can, together with other voluntary agencies, highlight the harm that excessive alcohol consumption brings. The possibility of mitigating the evil effects of alcohol must remain a fundamental hope for the transforming power of Christ to be found in this world.

The call for a more responsible approach to alcohol in any government's strategy could mirror the approach that has been taken toward smoking. Although the reduction in the number of smokers has leveled out in recent years, in the 1990s there were significant reductions in the levels of those smoking. Advertising tobacco products was progressively banned, health warnings were placed on all cigarette packets, and there was a concerted campaign in TV advertising to encourage people to give up their dependency on tobacco.

Similar approaches could be taken toward alcohol: Targets could be set to reduce the spiraling number of alcohol-related diseases; advertising could be banned; and a major campaign launched highlighting the harmful effects of excessive consumption. Just as nicotine and tar levels have been reduced by almost 50% during the 1990s, so too the alcoholic content of drinks could be diluted. Incentives to encourage rapid drinking would be banned as has happened in Ireland. A concerted educational campaign to develop sensible attitudes toward alcohol could feature in schools and on television.

Attention also needs to be given as to why alcohol has to be society's social lubricant: Is society's dependence on the social role of alcohol a sign of its failure to make effective community, and if so, how can such a scenario be reversed? Moreover, the absence of social outlets for the 14- to 18-year-olds apart from the club culture, which is so dependent on alcohol, suggests that a fundamental change in researching and funding new initiatives can be of fundamental importance. Important, too, is the need to provide sufficient detoxification programs for those who have become dependent on alcohol. A recent charity, *Waiting for Change,* highlighted the chronic shortage of detoxification centers in the United Kingdom, warning that "this major shortfall in alcohol services is preventing dependent drinkers from getting the treatment they need."[40]

The church can indeed find theologically appropriate responses to alcohol. The many thousands of people whose lives suffer as a result of alcohol do so primarily because a blessing from God through inappropriate use becomes a curse. This should not surprise us: All precious gifts have the potentiality for good or for evil. Nothing is exploited more horribly than sex, and yet sex is one of the greatest gifts from God. The church must therefore exercise wisdom in proclaiming the blessings of God and teach how they can be fully enjoyed, while speaking out fervently and acting with others effectively in turning what has become a curse back into a blessing. The victims of alcoholism are society's sacrifice for the illusory blessing of alcohol. Christianity looks to Christ as the one, full, sufficient sacrifice, the one who brings in the Kingdom of God. The Church, therefore, needs to enable society to enjoy the blessings of God and eliminate any need for others to sacrifice their lives to the excesses of the age. That can only be achieved by recognizing that alcohol is both a blessing and a curse; that it offers both ecstasy and horror. Ultimately, for God's kingdom to come on earth, the church has to engage in the redemptive task of ensuring that God's blessings are truly and honestly enjoyed by the whole of humanity. That means that the church must actively entertain the hope that humanity does not experience curses, but blessing. For in the heavenly city of which John the Divine writes, there is only blessing.[41]

Notes

1 Daniel W. Hardy, and David F. Ford, *Jubilate* (London: Darton, Longman & Todd, 1984), 73.
2 Ibid., 72, quoted from "The Canal Bank Walk," Patrick Kavanagh, *Collected Poems*, (London: 1972).
3 For example, Mark 2:15–17, Luke 7:36; 14:1.
4 Revelation 19:9, Luke 13:29.
5 *The Times*, August 9, 2003, 41.
6 *The Times*, August 9 2003, 40.

[7] Sergii Bulgakov, *The Unfading Light* in *Towards a Russian Political Theology,* ed. Rowan Williams (Edinburgh: T & T Clark, 1999), 140.

[8] Jonathan Sacks, *Faith in the Future* (London: Darton, Longman & Todd, 1999), 133.

[9] Pete McCarthy, *McCarthy's Bar* (London: Hodder & Stoughton, 2000), 39–40. The references are to television personalities and politicians in Ireland and the United Kingdom.

[10] Galatians 5:22–23.

[11] John 15–1.

[12] Matthew 11:19; Luke 7:34. See James McGrath's essay in chapter 1 of this book.

[13] Alex Ferguson, *Managing My Life* (London: Hodder & Stoughton, 2000), 239–40.

[14] 1 Corinthians 9:25.

[15] Cf. www.addictionnetwork.co.uk.

[16] Institute of Alcohol Studies, *Alcohol and Health Factsheet,* www.ias.org.uk.

[17] Ibid. The Institute also helpfully outlines correct medical terminology currently being used for medical conditions brought about by alcohol, including "acute intoxication," "abuse," and "dependence."

[18] Institute of Alcohol Studies, *What Is Problem Drinking Factsheet, www.ias.org.uk.* See the International Classification of Diseases 10. World Health Organization 1992. *Handbook on Alcohol & Health,* The Medical Council on Alcoholism, 1998. E. Epstein, "Classification of Alcohol-Related Problems and Dependence," in *International Handbook of Alcohol Dependence & Problems,* ed. N. Heather, T. J. Peters, and T. Stockwell (London: Wiley, 2001).

[19] Department of Health, *Hospital Episode Statistics (HES),* Room 430b, Department of Health, 80 London Road, London SE1 6LH, quoted in Institute of Alcohol Studies Factsheet–Alcohol and Health, 4. The codes refer to the International Classification–of Diseases, 10th revision.

[20] Hansard, February 25, 2003: Written answer by Hazel Blears, Minister for Public Health to a question from Tim Loughton, quoted in Institute of Alcohol Studies Factsheet–Alcohol and Health, 5.

[21] The causes of death were defined using the *International Classification of Diseases, Ninth Revision* (ICD-9) codes for the years 1992 to 1999 for Scotland, 1992 to 2000 for England and Wales, and Northern Ireland, and the *International Classification of Diseases, Tenth Revision* (ICD-10) codes for 2000 and 2001 for Scotland, and 2001 for England and Wales, and Northern Ireland.

[22] Institute of Alcohol Studies Factsheet, *Drinking in Great Britain,* 2.

[23] Institute of Alcohol Studies Factsheet, *Women and Alcohol,* 4.

[24] Institute of Alcohol Studies, *Binge Drinking,* 3.

[25] Ibid., 4.

[26] *The Times,* August 19, 2003, 3.

[27] Ibid.

[28] Frank McCourt, *Angela's Ashes* (London: Flamingo, 1997), 121–22.

[29] Ibid., 264.

[30] *The Big Book, The Basic Text of Alcoholics Anonymous,* 3rd ed. (Ayesbury, England: Hazell Watson and Viney Ltd.), 317–561.

[31] See Deborah Vess's review of alcohol in the monastic tradition in chapter 6 in this book.

[32] See Gary Abbott's and C. K. Robertson's essays in chapters 8 and 9, respectively.

[33] James Munson, *The Nonconformists* (London: SPCK, 1991), 195–96.

[34] See Owen Chadwick, *The Victorian Church Part II* (London: A & C Black, 1970), 327: "The use of unfermented wine is first found about 1873 as part of the temperance campaign, the use of separate cups at the Lord's Supper, on medical grounds, not until after the turn of the century."

[35] *The Canons of the Church of England* (London: Church House Publishing, 2000), Canon B17, 36. For a deeper insight into this issue, see B. J. Oropeza's study in chapter 2 of this book.

[36] Archbishop of Canterbury, 1942–44.

[37] F. A. Iremonger, *William Temple: His Life and Letters* (Oxford: Oxford University Press, 1950), 100.

[38] Walter Wink, *Naming the Powers* (Philadelphia: Fortress, 1984), 105–06.

[39] Ibid.

[40] Cf. www.info@turning-point.co.uk.

[41] "Then the angel showed me the river of the water of life, bright as crystal, flowing from the throne of God and of the Lamb through the middle of the street of the city. … Nothing accursed will be found there any more. But the throne of God and of the Lamb will be in it, and his servants will worship him; they will see his face and his name will be on their foreheads. And there will be no more night; they need no light of lamp or sun, for the Lord God will be their light, and they will reign for ever and ever." (Revelation 22:1, 3–5).

Bibliography

The Big Book: The Basic Text of Alcoholics Anonymous. 3rd ed. Ayesbury, England: Hazell Watson and Viney Ltd.

Bulgakov, Sergii. *The Unfading Light* in *Towards a Russian Political Theology*. Edited by Rowan Williams. Edinburgh: T & T Clark, 1999.

The Canons of the Church of England. London: Church House Publishing, 2000.

Chadwick, Owen. *The Victorian Church Part II*. London: A & C Black, 1970.

Epstein, E. "Classification of Alcohol-Related Problems and Dependence." In *International Handbook of Alcohol Dependence & Problems*. Edited by N. Heather, T. J. Peters, and T. Stockwell. London: Wiley, 2001.

Ferguson, Alex. *Managing My Life*. London: Hodder & Stoughton, 2000.

Hardy, Daniel W., and David F. Ford. *Jubilate*. London: Darton, Longman & Todd, 1984.

Heather, N., T. J. Peters, and T. Stockwell, eds. *International Handbook of Alcohol Dependence & Problems*. London: Wiley, 2001.

Iremonger, F. A. *William Temple: His Life and Letters*. Oxford: Oxford University Press, 1950.

Kavanagh, Patrick. *Collected Poems*. New York: W. W. Norton, 1977.

McCarthy, Pete. *McCarthy's Bar*. London: Hodder & Stoughton, 2000.
McCourt, Frank. *Angela's Ashes*. London: Flamingo, 1997.
Munson, James. *The Nonconformists*. London: SPCK, 1991.
Sacks, Jonathan. *Faith in the Future*. London: Darton, Longman & Todd, 1999.
Wink, Walter. *Naming the Powers*. Philadelphia: Fortress, 1984.

✧ Conclusion: Shaken and Stirred

C. K. Robertson

Altogether 1420 in the Shire was a marvellous (sic) year. Not only was there wonderful sunshine and delicious rain, in due times and perfect measure, but there seemed something more: an air of richness and growth, and a gleam of a beauty beyond that of mortal summers. ... The Northfarthling barley was so fine that the beer of 1420 malt was long remembered and became a byword. Indeed a generation later one might hear an old gaffer in an inn, after a good pint of well-earned ale, put down his mug with a sigh: "Ah! That was proper fourteen-twenty, that was!"

J. R. R. Tolkien's *The Return of the King*

The bottle is opened, the cork sniffed, the preliminary sip taken, the declaration made: "A good year, a very good year." With each opening of each new bottle comes the possibility of an experience that is at the same time sublime and ephemeral, timeless and altogether fleeting. It is this paradox that makes each sip something to be savored, as the "fruit of the vine" points the way to a glorious day of consummation and blessing: "For there shall be a sowing of peace, the vine shall yield its fruit ... and I will cause the remnant of this people to possess all these things" (Zechariah 8:12). In a moment of poignant communion with his closest friends, Jesus makes time stand still even as he peers into eternity: "Truly I tell you, I will never again drink of the fruit of the vine until that day when I drink it new in the kingdom of God" (Mark 14:25; Matthew 26:29; Luke 22:18). In each sip, expectation mixes with nostalgia, and the loss of paradise that came with the eating of forbidden fruit is swallowed up in the great invitation: "Come, buy wine and milk without money and without price" (Isaiah 55:1). It is little wonder, then, that from Moses and Mohammed to Tolkien and his fellow Inklings, there has existed that strand of thought which looks ahead to a heavenly feast awaiting the faithful, a feast that boasts at its center a draught of flowing wine of infinite quality. For those struggling through wars and rumors of wars, for all residents of "middle earth," wine can be a sign of hope.

However, it also has long been a red flag of danger for those who are tempted to think they can enjoy the pleasures of paradise before the appropriate time. A little wine might indeed be good "for the sake of your stomach and your frequent ailments" (1 Timothy 5:23), but there are strong warnings in the various religious traditions for those who drink too much too soon, so that there is nothing left but to drink of the fruit of "the winepress of the fury of the wrath of God the Almighty" (Revelation 19:15). Perhaps it is the terror of that winepress of wrath, or an uncertainty about one's own self-control, that has led so many—especially in parts of America—to embrace an all-or-nothing approach to alcohol and stimulants. The teetotaling tendency among several Protestant groups is particularly interesting in light of the fact that Reformation theology was largely born in English pubs and European taverns. This fact notwithstanding, in the minds of many of the devout today, alcohol consumption—not simply drunkenness—is still linked with sin and damnation. Thus, as with human sexuality, alcohol continues today to be a point of disagreement and contention for many devout believers, with some individuals categorizing others based entirely on their approach to drinking.

In the Introduction to this book, it was said that religion has largely approached alcohol with mixed messages. For reasons known and unknown, the issue of alcohol and similar stimulants has stirred up emotions in individuals and shaken the status quo of groups both political and ecclesiastical. I still recall visiting a friend who offered me a beer from his refrigerator, where the bottles were well hidden behind very large jars of other, noncontroversial products. When I asked about the obvious attempt to hide the drink, my friend simply replied, "I like the taste of beer, but not the aftertaste of shame when someone from my church sees me drinking it." To hide or not to hide alcohol if you are a person of faith—it does not appear as if this or any of the debates that accompany alcohol production and consumption will be resolved anytime soon, at least not on this side of paradise. Whether we agree to disagree in this life or unjustly classify one another as drunkards and teetotalers, at least we can take comfort in knowing that one day we will move beyond such arguments and together share in that heavenly feast of food—and wine—that God has prepared for us. I'll drink to that.

✧ Contributors

Gary L. Abbott, Sr. is a graduate of Mercer University, Southwestern Baptist Theological Seminary, and New Orleans Baptist Theological Seminary. He has done additional study at Columbia Theological Seminary and the School of Theology of the University of the South. A Southern Baptist minister for 35 years, Dr. Abbott was ordained an Episcopal priest in 2003. He currently serves as Vicar of St. Luke's Episcopal Church in Hawkinsville, Georgia.

Teresa Blythe is a spiritual director who has written extensively about spirituality and media. She has co-authored the book *Watching What We Watch: Prime-Time Television Through the Lens of Faith*, and has taught a course on religion and media at San Francisco Theological Seminary, where she obtained a Master of Divinity degree in 2000. A Presbyterian who works at Southside Church in Tucson, she knows a number of celibate clergypersons who are not lonely, frustrated, problem drinkers.

John W. Gamble has been a student of religions for the past forty years. He has been involved in meditation for the past three decades, and has served on the board of Southern Dharma Retreat Center, a meditation center near Asheville, North Carolina, since 1989. He holds a PhD from Georgia State University and is a clinical psychologist who has spent his professional career working in both public service and private practice.

James McGrath is an assistant professor of New Testament with a BD from the University of London and a PhD from the University of Durham. He previously taught at the University of Oradea in Romania. The author of a number of articles, Dr. McGrath recently published his first book, *John's Apologetic Christology*. He is married with one son and has a passion for twentieth-century music and science fiction.

B. J. Oropeza holds a PhD in New Testament from Durham University, has taught previously at George Fox University and now at Azusa Pacific University, and has written several books and articles, including *A Time to Laugh: The Holy Laughter Phenomenon Examined.*

Gregory Pepetone is a professor of music and interdisciplinary studies at Georgia College & State University, as well as a concert pianist. Having spent several years living and studying in Britain, Pepetone has spent considerable time studying the life and works of Charles Dickens. He is also the author of *Gothic Perspectives on the American Experience* (Peter Lang, 2002).

Arthur James Powell is a retired university professor of ethics as well as a former missionary and educator in the Middle East. Fluent in Arabic and well versed in Islam, Powell is associated with the Friends of the Episcopal Diocese of Jerusalem and makes presentations to American congregations on the complex realities of the Middle East.

C. K. Robertson is an Episcopal priest and part-time professor of ethics and communications at Georgia College & State University. A Fellow of the Episcopal Church Foundation, he holds a PhD from Durham University and serves on the Advisory Board for Film Clips, Inc. Robertson is seen weekly on the Hallmark Channel Program *Day 1,* and is author of *Conflict in Corinth: Redefining the System* (Peter Lang, 2001), *The Kerygma of Billy Graham,* and *Barnabas: A Model for Holistic Stewardship,* as well as editor of *Religion as Entertainment* (Peter Lang, 2002). He lives with his wife Debbie and three children in Georgia.

Michael Rusk is a convocation dean in the Anglican Diocese of Leicester, England, where he lives with his wife Gill and three children. Prior to this, the Very Rev. Rusk was Vicar of St. John's, Nevilles Cross, Durham, and Lecturer of Classics at the University of Durham, from which he holds a Master of Arts in Theological Research. His theological interests are in systematic theology, particularly in the doctrine of the atonement.

Deborah Vess is a professor of history and interdisciplinary studies at Georgia College & State University. Her area of expertise is monastic spirituality and medieval scholasticism, and she has published articles in *The American Benedictine Review*, *Word and Spirit*, *Mystics Quarterly*, *The Modern Schoolman*, and *The Encyclopedia of Monasticism*. A University System of Georgia Board of Regents Distinguished Professor of Teaching and Learning, Dr. Vess has twice received an Excellence in Teaching Award from the National Institute of Staff and Organizational Development and, in 1999, was named a Pew Scholar with the Carnegie Foundation for the Advancement of Teaching. An oblate of St. Benedict through Mount St. Scholastica monastery in Atchison, Kansas, she struggles to live the principles of the Benedictine Rule within the context of family life as a mother of four and a busy career.

✧ Index